White Ink

White Ink

Poems on Mothers and Motherhood

edited by
Rishma Dunlop

Demeter Press
Toronto, Canada

Demeter Press
c/o Association for Research on Mothering
726 Atkinson College, York University
4700 Keele Street
Toronto, Ontario M3J 1P3
Telephone: (416) 736-2100 x 60366
Email: arm@yorku.ca Web site: www.yorku.ca/arm

Front cover art: Suzanne Northcott,"Holding Light" detail, 60" x 48", Acrylic and graphite on panel, 2006.
Photograph on pg. xix by Kartar Singh, 1956.
Cover and book design by Luciana Ricciutelli

Printed and bound in Canada

Library and Archives Canada Cataloguing in Publication

White ink : poems on mothers and motherhood /edited by Rishma Dunlop.

ISBN 978-1-55014-484-0

1. Canadian poetry (English)—20th century. 2. American poetry—20th century. 3. Mothers—Poetry. 4. Motherhood—Poetry. I. Dunlop, Rishma, 1956–

PS8287.M68W55 2007 C811'.5408035252 C2007-906037-4

In memoriam
Grace Paley 1922-2007

I believe I heard language through my mother's
belly   both violent and sweet

—Robin Blaser, "Stop"

Contents

3
Waiting for its kick.
My love. My tenant.

4
I remember all this as plainly as if I could remember

7
Correspondence

8
These woods are yours.

9
Who wouldn't invent a mummy or a god, A myth, a story, a heaven, a lie

10
all the rivers of her red veins move into the sea

11
Mother tongue was a pang

12
Mother Love

13
rubble and sorrow

14
The sound of your blood crossed into mine

Acknowledgements

I would like to express my thanks and immense gratitude to Jason Guriel, gifted poet and editor, who served as editorial assistant for *White Ink*. Currently a Ph.D. candidate in English at York University, Jason devoted countless hours to assisting me at every step of development and editing of this anthology, including contacting poets, responding to submissions and queries, researching possibilities of poets for inclusion, contacting publishers for reprint permissions, compiling author biographies, and collaborating on the organization and compilation of the final manuscript.

My thanks to Renée Knapp, administrative assistant for Demeter Press and the Association of Research on Mothering (ARM). Renée fielded hundreds of submissions and responses to poets as well as taking care of the administrative aspects of publishing and promoting *White Ink*. I have appreciated with much gratitude, Renée's professionalism and her unfailing enthusiasm for this project.

My thanks to Andrea O'Reilly, publisher of Demeter Press, and colleague at York University who offered me the opportunity to create *White Ink* as the first imprint of Demeter's literary series. Andrea supported my vision of a book that grew from a slim imagined volume of selected poems to a large anthology of astonishing work from poets around the world.

My thanks to poets and friends who suggested inclusions and provided contacts for poets who have enriched this book. I very much appreciated suggestions and assistance in this regard from Alicia Ostriker, Marilyn Hacker, Margo Berdeshevsky, Evie Shockley, Priscila Uppal, Christopher Doda, Joe Paczuski, Fiona Tinwei Lam, and Barbara Godard.

Thank you to Linn Clark for her editing suggestions and insightful readings. My thanks to Annie Finch and the Women's International Poetry Listserve for their contributions and conversations that enriched this anthology.

My thanks to the Faculty of Education and the Department of English at York University for support of this work.

Thank you to Luciana Ricciutelli for her aesthetic layout and hours of labour on book design.

My thanks to Katherine Bell, Ph.D. candidate at York University, for her contributions and assistance with the preparation of the book manuscript.

My thanks to the talented and accomplished poets gathered on these pages who contributed their poems. A special thank you to those who waived or reduced reprint permission fees for this book. The budgetary restraints of anthologists frequently prevent certain works from being reprinted. I am most appreciative of the graciousness and generosity of those who eased this strain for Demeter Press, making it possible to include so many distinguished and historically important poems.

RISHMA DUNLOP

Writing the Mother: Notes on White Writing

> *My text is written in white and black, in "milk" and "night." ... A woman is never far from "mother" .... There is always within her at least a little of that good mother's milk. She writes in white ink.*
>
> —Hélene Cixous

Over the past few years, in thinking about the vast political and ideological changes that have occurred for women, mothers, and children from the 1950s to present day, I became convinced that the time was right for such an anthology as *White Ink.* Certainly, numerous essay collections on the theme of motherhood have been published over the past decade including *The Grand Permission: New Writings on Poetics and Motherhood,* edited by Patricia Dienstfrey and Brenda Hillman in 2003 and *Between Interruptions: 30 Women Tell the Truth About Motherhood,* edited by Cori Howard in 2007. Yet poetry critic Helen Vendler has remarked on the lack of poetry on the theme of motherhood, citing Sylvia Plath as one who made a beginning. In truth, there has been little critical appreciation of the numerous poets who have written on motherhood since Plath—by Vendler or other literary critics.

One fine anthology published in 1995 by W.W. Norton in a volume edited by Sandra M. Gilbert, Susan Gubar, and Diana O'Hehir, titled *MotherSongs: Poems for, by, and about Mothers*, is a unique collection of verse about maternity and the celebration of motherhood. *MotherSongs* brings together a range of classic and contemporary poems from the United States, Great Britain, and Canada by some of our most memorable writers. The editors included traditional ballads about maternity and courtly elegies for, or by, mothers as well as landmark nineteenth-century tributes to mothers and early twentieth-century meditations on motherhood. Taken together, the works collected in *MotherSongs* bear witness to the powerful ways in which motherhood has been transformed into art and in which artistry has been shaped by maternity. Yet, the focus of this collection is American in the end, with the final poem by Sharon Olds in the section Meaning of Maternity:

> I have done what you wanted to do, Walt Whitman,

Allen Ginsberg, I have done this thing,
I and other women this exceptional
act with the exceptional heroic body,
this giving birth, this glistening verb,
and I am putting my proud American boast
right here with the others.

—from "The Language of Brag," in *Satan Says*

As I began to sift through collections of poets who have written over the past fifty years of the twentieth century and in the beginning of the twenty-first, I realized that the world's social and political changes, as well as the imaginative pulse of the past three decades are uniquely reflected in poetry on motherhood. The theme inspires poetry, innovative poetics, and a vast range of approaches and experiences that include struggles for reproductive freedom, feminist struggles, adoption, abortion, the death of the mother, the death of the child, the mother who abandons her child, the aging mother, and changing perceptions of mother-child relations. Throughout, the depth of the bond to the mother is universal and powerful; the mother is written again and again across cultures, ethnicities, languages, genders, and across geographies, politics, and histories. I imagined *White Ink* as an anthology that would move beyond and expand the scope of *MotherSongs* and recent essay anthologies to include more international poets, more male voices, and to focus uniquely on poets writing in the second half of the twentieth century and the early twenty-first century.

In the 1960s Sylvia Plath and Ann Sexton wrote frequently about their experiences as mothers. These poems were for some time overshadowed by the sensationalism surrounding their suicides: yet their poems about motherhood represent some of their strongest works, providing signposts for interpreting future sociohistorical shifts of perception on the role of the mother.

Many women writers of my generation owe debts to writers like Hélène Cixous, Luce Irigaray, Julia Kristeva, Quebec writer Nicole Brossard, and innovator Rachel Blau Duplessis, among others, for creating possibilities to write differently and to challenge patriarchal norms of writing in literary and academic arenas. However, the movements of the 1970s and 1980s through radical revisions of conceptions of writing now reveal the richly varied and vast range of perspectives, forms, and discourses presented by poets on the pages of this book. The mother is myth, metaphor, memory, and real flesh and blood—a fascinating and pervasive topic of poetry.

The phrase "white ink" chosen for the anthology title is adapted from Hélène

Cixous who used the phrase in her 1975 "The Laugh of the Medusa." Cixous culled the expression from the French symbolist poet of the late 1880s, Stéphane Mallarmé. For Mallarmé, white ink was the negative transparency of reality, a translation of silence. *"Mettre noir sur blanc,"* Mallarmé would say, in attempting to articulate his black and white poetics and theories of writing. Black ink and white paper were perceived as materials that represented something as mysterious and elemental as the stars: the creative function of the poet's imagination. In Mallarmé's metaphor of "the sky instinct" of the poet, the Milky Way or "alphabet of stars" implied that the book is an instrument of the spirit, even as it has material, physical attributes.

The modern critical insistence on the space of the text becomes an invitation to re-examine the relationship between writing and poetics. Putting ink to page makes silence speak and the blank page signify. White ink is conceived as a translation of silence, which focuses attention on what is done by ink itself. Mallarmé's legacy is one that pursues the limits of language. The poet's work allows us to see the whiteness of the page, swallowing the text's efforts to explain any master gesture.

For Hélène Cixous, white ink represents what is invisible—what is born of language, the embodied experience of the mother and child, writing that contains the symbolic force of life, writing that counters oblivion and death. Through the white ink of writing in breast milk, Cixous wanted to convey that writing is a reunion with the maternal body, an unalienated relation to female bodies in general.

My own relation to Cixous' conception of white ink is entangled with early memories of my experiences of motherhood and writing. In the mid-1990s, after putting my daughters, Cara and Rachel, to bed, I would write my Master's thesis and drafts of poems late into the night. I wrote at a small desk outside the girls' shared bedroom. We were living in the Okanagan Valley in British Columbia where the dry heat of the Sonoran Desert spread tumbleweed across the roads during the day, and the mists rose at night from the lush vineyards and orchards. The rhythms of night are forever entangled with my life as a young mother. During the day I taught English literature at the local college. At night I read Adrienne Rich's *Of Woman Born*, and her poem "Dedications:" "I know you are reading this poem as you pace beside the stove/warming milk, a crying child on your shoulder, a book in your/hand/because life is short and you too are thirsty."

Years later, my daughters tell me their most remembered childhood sound was that of my fingers tap tapping on the computer keyboard. Cixous' words about white ink are resonant with my own experiences of becoming a poet. Writing in milk and night.

While I allude to Cixous' use of white ink through the title of the anthology, given the vast social and historical changes in the roles and perceptions of the mother, as well as shifts in poetics and theory over the past three decades since "The Laugh of the Medusa," I propose a more expansive taking up of white ink, moving beyond *l'écriture feminine,* post-structural feminist theory, and a limited, gendered literary lens, toward a more inclusive connection of all writers to the mother. The astonishing number of submissions received for consideration for *White Ink* demonstrated clearly that poets around the world were writing about mothers and motherhood and that this themed anthology responds to a desire among poets to explore the significance of the mother. An anthology is never a finite thing; this collection of voices offers us points of departure for thinking, writing, reading—for imagining ourselves in a poetics of relation to others who imagine the mother. To rephrase Cixous for contemporary poets, there is always within us, a little of mother's milk. We write in white ink. In the end, we may have little or nothing in common, except that we were born to mothers.

Works Cited

Cixous, Hélène. "The Laugh of the Medusa." *The Critical Tradition: Classic Texts and Contemporary Trends.* Ed. David H. Richter. Boston: Bedford Books, 1998. 1454-1466.

Gilbert Sandra, Gubar, Susan, and O'Hehir, Diana. *Mother Songs: Poems for, by, and about Mothers.* New York: W.W. Norton, 1995.

Olds, Sharon. *Satan Says.* Pittsburgh,PA: University of Pittsburgh Press, 1980.

Rich, Adrienne. "Dedications." *An Atlas of the Difficult World: Poems 1988-1991.* New York: W.W. Norton, 1991.

The Crib

Night-Pieces: For a Child

1. *The Crib*

You sleeping I bend to cover.
Your eyelids work. I see
your dream, cloudy as a negative,
swimming underneath.
You blurt a cry. Your eyes
spring open, still filmed in dream.
Wider, they fix me—
—death's head, sphinx, medusa?
You scream.
Tears lick my cheeks, my knees
droop at your fear.
Mother I no more am,
but woman, and nightmare.

2. *Her Waking*

Tonight I jerk astart in a dark
hourless as Hiroshima,
almost hearing you breathe
in a cot three doors away.

You still breathe, yes—
and my dream with its gift of knives,
its murderous hider and seeker,
ebbs away, recoils

back into the egg of dreams,
the vanishing point of mind.
All gone.

But you and I—
swaddled in a dumb dark
old as sickheartedness,
modern as pure annihilation—

we drift in ignorance.
If I could hear you now
mutter some gentle animal sound!
If milk flowed from my breast again….

First Cold

Rales of phlegm rattled the midnight air.
The baby all stuffed up, asleep in his crib.
Later his crying, different this time—
a sad crying, not meaning, *Feed me.*
I'd never felt flesh so hot. He burned
like a cinder. I watched the thermometer rise
to 104°, and I froze, then ran to the phone
to call my husband, still in transition
between single and married.

I dialed the bar where I knew he'd be.
A stranger answered. I could hear music
and laughter. The voice on the phone was drunk.
I said my husband's name, *Is he there?*
The voice wanted to make jokes—
Who wants to know? What's it worth to you?
I asked again, *Please, is he there?* and began
to cry, *Please, my baby is sick*, and the man
became sober, said, *Hold on, lady, just hold on,*
and he found my husband and sent him home.

For hours we took turns dipping the baby
into tepid water, as if bronzing him.
Toward dawn the fever broke, and our baby
peed. An arc of urine rose like a fountain
and fell, tinged the water yellow.
My husband and I faced each other
across the plastic tub, gazed in mute wonder
at the small priest who'd come to bless
and curse us both, two strangers,
hardly knowing our names.

SUSAN HOLBROOK

from *Nursery*

Left: trace pictograph of an elk in the fine veins of your temple. Right: if it were a Virgin Mary we'd be on the news. Left: try to sit you up for a burp, you're still latched on. Right: milk drops leave shiny slug trails across your cheek. Left: reading at the same time, my book on your hip, worried the officious prose style will come through in the milk, give you gas. Right: you spit up to make room for more, like the Romans. Left: doping for sleep. Right: feeling like a mother didn't happen when you were born, or when I first fed you, or first used the word "daughter." It's happening six months later, in the dark, as a mosquito kazoos and without a second's contemplation I pull up your covers, lay my bare arms on top of the blanket, whisper "bite me." Left: I wasn't talking to you. Right: through the blinds moonlight strips stratify the bars of your crib. Left: not again. Right: *I've seen parents put their infants to bed right after eating, often because the baby falls asleep on the breast or bottle. I don't advise this for two reasons.* Left: I drink milk at the same time, am I an elaborate step that could be skipped. Right: I wish I had a suit with feet. Left: *One, the baby becomes dependent on the bottle or breast, and soon needs it to fall asleep. Two, do **you** want to sleep after every meal?* Right: actually, yes. Left: why is an elk worth nothing but a Virgin Mary on grilled cheese costs 28 000 dollars. Right: Richard's brought chinese food, hot grease silhouettes on the paper bags put-puttering from your diaper, does he know it's you. Left: the tv flashes against your cheek, a small smooth screen. Right: I wipe grains of sweat from your brow, as if you were a doctor delivering a baby. Left: puddin. Right: little lambs caper on the flannel blanket, twist one up and clean out your earhole with it. Left: three years ago in Texas, Peruvian immigrants had their children taken away when the photo shop clerk developed their breastfeeding pictures and called the cops; a nipple in a baby's mouth was a second-degree felony: "sexual performance of a minor." Right: I close my eyes, these days only getting the kind of sleep you have on planes. Left: still pitch before dawn and while you eat I dream a little, that you were born a gnome, and I loved you just the same, maybe more. Right: before writing a poem about it I sometimes forgot, repeated sides. Right: *Extracting oil from Alberta's tar sands requires three barrels of water for each barrel of oil produced.* Left: your "wrist" is a crease circling your fat arm like a too-tight string. Left: dimples for knuckles. Right: I wouldn't write this poem in Texas. Left: I never wanted to be one of those grown women with a teddy bear room. Right: spider on the plastic space mobile, walking the perimeter of the yellow crescent moon. Left: dollop. Right: ugh, plugged ducts. Left: now it's on Saturn's rings, if it fell off it would drop right into my mouth. Right: I take 2%, you take *hindmilk.* Left: fingers shrimp their way through the afghan holes. Right: I have hindmilk. Left: we watch the show about you, the young and the restless, you keep smacking your lips off and craning your neck back to see what the devil Victor's on about now. Right: beads of milk pop out before your mouth even gets there. Left: what if your donor turned out to be Eric Braeden, who plays the patriarch Victor Newman, what if you concluded every one of our disagreements with a curt and authoritative "End of discussion." Right: *Passion is injurious to the mother's milk, and consequently to the child. Sudden joy and grief frequently disorder the infant's bowels, producing griping, looseness, &c.* Left: heat gusts through the vent, stirs stars. Right: you latch on to my elbow and I'm surprised, as if I'd imagined you can see in the dark, forgetting you too are only human. Left: kitten licks your head, leaves welts. Right: I could go for a fontanelle about now. Left: you wet your suit, and mine, while drinking, like a functional doll I once had, her innards a single fine plastic tube. Right: I thought she said "history in the *milking.*" Left: bunny rattle nestled in the crook of your arm, your entire arm nestled in the crook of my hand. Right: insert scenes of battle for more universal appeal. Left: you would win a nestling tournament. Right: it's easier to pinch the skin of older mothers. Left: I don't know Elmo let alone Baby Elmo. Right: the doctor says you have thrush – I can't find my babycare guide but here's a *Peterson Field Guide* which says you should have a conspicuous eye-ring, a distinctly orange cast about the head, ghostlike spots, legs more dusky than your toes, your voice a melodic flutelike rolling from high to low to high, *whee-toolee-weee*, and you are presumed to winter in the hills of Hispaniola. Left: on the other temple, veins outline a house, a single plume of smoke threading up into your hair, a bare tree in the front yard. Right: wing, whale, to-lifer, to-know, to-die. Left: wing, ward, overs, most, -ism. Right: stuff, side up, on, of way, of search, of asylum. Left: *See the way new trees flourish when they get started on a nurse log. Also called a mother stump, nurse logs are trees that have fallen and started to rot.* Right: geese shouting hockey hockey hockey. Left: I can't move to change the station away from the man who keeps saying "as far as the weather" without adding "goes" or "is concerned." Right: how did the childless author of Tender Buttons know. Left: you've got it made as far as milk.

Right: you talk with your mouth full and wear your hat to the table. Left: your Fisher-Price crib aquarium emits enough light to nurse by, enough surf sound to imagine myself in a hammock under coconut palms, a crab on my nipple. Right: if we've already established that you're a star why would we wonder what you are? Left: handed, fielder, brain, Bank, atrioventricular valve. Right: skim milk light through the curtain, it must have snowed in the night. Left: snowbound and out of milk. I could express into my tea but I'm not making yogurt. Right: minded, -ism, handed, ful, fielder, face, circular cone, brain, Bank, away, ascension. Left: lift. Right: tuft. Left: loved. Right: lift her. Left: richter. Lift her wrote her wrought her daughter laughter lifter sitter safe her light left on her. Right: today I fed peaches to someone who's never heard of peaches. Ditto the moon, every Christmas carol, horse and the word horse. Left: I used to need two hands and a nursing pillow, now I can erase the hell out of two Sudokus, you outside the halo of the booklight. Right: 2 or a 6, 2 or a 6, 2 or a 6 or a 7. Left: this is expressive verse. Right: I can never rest now, knowing the teeth are there, like a gun in a play. Left: you thump your palm on my chest, then your own, you and me, I agree, difficult to distinguish. Right: tethered to you, I must postpone killing that spider, forced to witness her labour, empathize with her line-by-line desires. Left: you clutch your stuffed mouse, from whom you'd been separated by airport security, who checked it for bombs. Right: your smells make us embarrassed and sorry for the people around us until we hear the group ahead had come to Ontario to hunt. Left: how to hide my breast without smothering you as the gay steward offers me mini pretzels. Right: the line along the elk's neck ruff extends down further than I had first noticed, leg bent elegantly above your ear. Left: you place your palm on my cheek and guide me away from the adult conversation, back to the appropriate downward, adoring gaze. Right: *If he be suckled after he be twelve months old, he is generally pale, flabby, unhealthy, and rickety; and the mother is usually nervous, emaciated and hysterical.* Left: the more you drink the more chance you'll wet Grandma's guest bed. Right: the red numbers on the digital clock are huge, like in your birthing room or a train station. Right: At 3:51 I realize I could spell your name on a calculator. Left: if the goods flow one way, why are we both "nursing." Right: you're not really hungry, just social drinking. Left: nursing you for the sixth time in as many hours, eyelids puffed between open and closed, I hear a butterknife scuff toast and clang in the marmalade jar and someone asking "are they Still sleeping?" Right: you pause to swish milk between your gums – a bit oaky this morning, a bit sassy, a bit maternal. Left: joy is so exhausting.

Revenge of the imagination

"I would like to apologize before God … if ever I was to be employed, I was going to poison the white man's children. The way they killed my son hitting him against a rock … I will never forgive … I will never rest … I used to go out and sleep on top of his grave."
—Ms Margaret Madlana, at Alexandra Township Human Rights Violations testimony.

*

Margaret Madlana in the nursery of her imagination,
before God stays her mind, her hand,
puts rat poison in the ribena of the four-year-old
and in the schoolboy's warm breakfast milk:
and who can judge her?

Killing them in her heart
not so much to have them dead
(for they can never be as dead as her last born,
his broken head beside a murderous rock),
but that their parents might mourn for ever,
leaving the compact suburbs
each night for an expanding cemetery,
to lie upon the graves as she did,
unresting, unforgiving.

But there at the mounds' damp feet
they might also conjure in the dark
some symmetry for comfort,
an eye for an eye, a tooth for a tooth,
an eye and a tooth to body natural law.

Round and round and round we go

and which is the name of the next
in our broken circle
to be harmed for reckoning's sake—
the chosen one to briefly close
the metal ring, the open mouth of pain?

Tinker tailor soldier sailor
rich man poor man beggarman thief?

Which one, like Isaac,
his head on a rocky altar,
will we sacrifice in mind
to our dazed and shadowy
reverie of revenge, of recovery?

Weaning

For a while after
there is still milk. Remnant,
like the train station

in Durham, North Carolina,
you thought was abandoned until
you left your parents from it,

its platform redolent
with tobacco's sugar and ash scent,
the weather of your childhood. The milk

doesn't just dry up. White drops
fall, vestigial,
like tears on the faces

of carved, painted saints
in another country's
medieval churches

you visited once in childhood—
kneeling, confused
in your Protestant reverence.

Like a censer, that nearly empty train
swang slowly past tobacco fields,
then picked up speed, crossing

out of the south. The Byzantine
icons you now keep
in a house up north

never smile or weep;
you have married into them.
Stoics, they fasten

the corner of the room
where you and your infant son
wait each other out, learning

to be abandoned and to abandon,
in a season of late, pivotal snows.

Nursling

Over there, a fly buzzed—bad.
All ours: the bra, the breast, the breeze.
Starlet of the reciprocal gaze.
Something about her rhymed like mad.

And ours the sigh, the suck, the sing.
We forgave everything we could.
Ravenous palmist. I'm gone for good.
At last I gauged the brash, brash spring.

The skin fiend folded like a fawn.
Torso Magellan. Time's own nub.
Here at the center of the dimmest bulb.
A mouth hovered before latching on.

Motherhood

Inches is all I have traveled but I feel as if I have walked all the way to Zanzibar with Kansas on my head and my hands tied behind my back because of the walls. The two thousand walls I had to climb. Miles and miles of walls

And the heads

The heads of the other climbers smashed like pumpkins where they had fallen or I suppose had looked down and given up hope and jumped

I was fearful. I was afraid
But I never turned back

As I recall
What's that?
You say,

there were no walls. No pumpkin heads
No miles and miles. There was only a voice
A strange commanding voice that said
Don't go any further

Stay here with us
Make us a fire
Keep us warm
We have a long journey tomorrow
Tonight we need food
Here's a pot
Do you know how to cook?

True. I do remember that familiar voice
That despotic voice
But I also remember how I stood tired
Took you from the safety of your crib
I held you up
Don't look down
I said
Don't listen
I said
Climb

Once I was delicious

BETH ANN FENNELLY

Latching On, Falling Off

I. When She Takes My Body into Her Body

She comes to me squirming in her father's arms,
gumming her fingers, her blanket, or rooting
on his neck, thrashing her mouth from side to side
to raise a nipple among his beard hairs. My shirt sprouts
two dark eyes; for three weeks she's been outside me,
and I cry milk to hear my baby—any baby—cry.

In the night, she smells me. From her bassinette
she wakes with a squall, her mouth impossibly huge,
her tongue aquiver with anger the baby book says
she doesn't have, aquiver like the clapper of a bell.
Her passion I wasn't prepared for, her need
naked as a sturgeon with a rippling, red gill.

Who named this *letdown*, this tingling upswing?
A valve twists, the thin opalescence spurts past the gate,
then comes the hindcream to make my baby creamyfat.
I fumble with one hand at my bra, offer the target
of my darkened nipple, with the other hand steady
her too-heavy head. She clamps on, the wailing ceases.

No one ever mentioned she's out for blood. I wince
as she tugs milk from ducts all the way to my armpits.
It hurts like when an angry sister plaits your hair.
It hurts like that, and like that you desire it.
Soon, soon—I am listening—she swallows,
and a layer of pain kicks free like a blanket.

Tethered, my womb spasms, then, lower, something shivers.
Pleasure piggybacks the pain, though it, too,

isn't mentioned, not to the child, drunk and splayed
like a hobo, not to the sleeping husband, innocent beside us.
Let me get it right so I remember: Once, I bared my chest
and found an animal. Once, I was delicious.

II. First Night Away from Claire

I forget to pack my breast pump,
a novelty not in any shop
here at the beach, just snorkel tubes,
shark teeth, coconut-shell bikini tops.
Should we drive back? I'm near-drunk
from my first beer in months. We've got
a babysitter, a hotel room, and on the horizon
a meteor shower promised. We've planned
slow sex, sky watch, long sleep.
His hand feels good low on my back,
tracing my lizard tattoo. And he can help—
he's had quick sips before—so we stay,
rubbing tongues, butter-dripping shrimp.

Later, he tries gamely, but it's not sexy,
not at all—he needs to suck a glassful
from each breast. The baby's so much better.
He rests. *It's hot,* he says, *and sweet.*
We're tired. We fall asleep.
I wake pre-dawn from pain.

Those meteors we forgot to watch—
it will be thirty years
before they pass this way again.

III. After Weaning, My Breasts Resume Their Lives as Glamour Girls

Initially hesitant, yes,
but once called into duty,

they never looked back.

Models-turned-spokeswomen,
they never dreamed they'd have so much to say.
They swelled with purpose,

mastered that underwater tongue,
translating the baby's long-vowel cries
and oozing their answer,

tidal, undeniable, fulfilled.
For a year, they let the child draw forth
that starry river, as my friend Ann has termed it—

then, it was time, stopped the flow.
They are dry now, smaller, tidy, my nipples
the lighter, more fetching pink.

The bras ugly as Ace bandages,
thick-strapped, trap-doored,
too busy for beauty—

and the cotton pads lining them
until damp, then yeasting in the hamper—
all have been washed and stored away.

So I'm thinking of how,
when World War II had ended,
the factory-working wives

were fired, sent home
to care for returning soldiers,
when my husband enters the bedroom—

Aren't you glad? he asks, glad,
watching me unwrap bras
tissue-thin and decorative

from the tissue of my old life,
watching, worshipfully, the breasts resettle
as I fasten his red favorite—

Aren't you glad? He's walking
toward them, addressing them, it seems—
but, Darling, they can't answer,

poured back into their old mold,
muffled beneath these lovely laces,
relearning how it feels, seen and not heard.

IV. It Was a Strange Country

where I lived with my daughter while I fed her
from my body. It was a small country, an island for two,
and there were things we couldn't bring with us,
like her father. He watched from the far shore,
well meaning, useless. Sometimes I asked
for a glass of water, so he had something to give.

The weather there was overcast, volatile.
We were tied to the tides of whimper and milk,
the flotsam of spit-up, warm and clotted,
on my neck, my thigh. Strange: I rarely minded,
I liked the yogurt smell trapped beneath her chinfolds.
How soon her breath bloomed sweet again.

She napped, my ducts refilled
like veins of gold that throb though lodged in rock.
When she woke, we adjusted our body language.
How many hours did she kiss one breast or the other?
I told her things. She tugged my bottom lip,
like sounds were coins beneath my fascinating tongue.

We didn't get many tourists, much news—

behind the closed curtains, rocking in the chair,
the world was a rumor all summer. All autumn.
All winter, in which she sickened, sucked for comfort,
a cord of snot between her nose, my breast.
Her small pillows of breath. We slept there, single-bodied.

Then came spring and her milk teeth and her bones
longer in my lap, her feet dangling, and, rapt,
she watched me eat, scholar of sandwiches and water.
Well, I knew the signs. I held her tight, I waded out,
I swam us away from that country, swam us back
to my husband pacing the shore, yelling and waving,

in his man fists, baby spoons that flashed, cupping suns.
It was a strange country that we returned to, separately—
strange, but not for long. Soon, the milk stops
simmering and the child forgets the mother's taste,
so the motherland recedes on the horizon,
a kindness—we return to it only at death.

My Mother's Body, My Professor, My Bower

Who died? My mother's body,
my professor, my bower,
my giant clam.
Serene water, professor
of copious clay,
of spiraling finger-holes in the clay,
of blue breast-milk,
first pulse, all thought:
there is nothing to get. You can't eat money,
dear throat, dear longing,
dear belly, dear fatness,
dear silky fastness: ecstatic lungs' breath,
you can't protect yourself,
there is nothing to get.

Collision

In the afternoons
we go into her bedroom
where she takes off her clothes and mine
and pulls the curtains to. My brother and father
are always somewhere outside. Their distant voices
vibrate softly through me
as she lays me down upon the down-filled duvet,
its white lace cover familiar to the nerve-ends of my back.

I can see inside the sliding wardrobe door
to where her unused bodies lie in waiting:
angora and corduroy sweaters
thick with the shed hairs and scents of other mothers,
the crimplene slacks of She-who-makes-my-breakfast,
the dark green kilt of She-who-goes-to-work.

Above the wardrobe live her handmade costume dolls,
silken ladies dressed in period outfits; after she has finished,
her hands vast and shivering from the heat,
I know that she will lift them carefully down,
open up the blue world of their bodies,
their red lips stitched together with chained thread,
and this will be my reward for lying silent: to touch
numbed ladies, caress their frozen, taffeta-ruffled lives.

Sometimes I think the rest is almost like dying,
when her freckled chest rolls toward me across the covers,
The-lady-who-touches-me smiles her tooth-filled smile,
and I touch that place inside where babies come from:
a talcum-powdered, blonde-haired, tender refuge,
a dark fault through all that is whole and here.

Primal Scene

The murmur of my father and mother
in their bedroom down the passage,
her soft, private laugh.

Conceptions

Little bloods, little hammocks of it, strains, the teeth hanging inside, counted. What to say of you and me here, keyboard sounds locked in ropy blood encasings, nets laced and unfolded, what is not hammered together, bone, joint, femur linking, patella, finger, the ringed zones, all of the cells I hide then offer a case of. You remember the patterns on my toes trance them in your sleep so when I wake in the net of sheets your moaning is something of a shoe print for the place I should always be standing. This, encasement of strings; all the cellos, fiddles, kanteles, a Mandela of aprons tied together. The searching spin; your helix deep inside me.

The Laughter in the Kitchen

All day our daughter and her best friend
have been playing marriage, destroying
the house to make it the way they need it
to be. They've shoved the loveseat
across the bedroom door to form a barricade,
overturned the armchairs to give themselves
temporary shelters. They've even rolled
the carpet back, "so the carpet won't get
beer spilled on it," my daughter, pretending
to be Dad, explains, when I complain:
the house doesn't feel like my own anymore
but still I have to live in it. "We can

build a new house when I make lots of good
money," my daughter says, butting out
the Popeye candy cigarette she won
from the neighbour boy for showing him
her vagina through a slit in the split
cedar fence. I wept, told her next time,

baby, hold out for a whole pack,
trying to be brave, the way only a mother
could. "We can't build anything if you
keep drinking drugs," the tiny wife bursts
as my daughter keels into the cookstove
and pretends to catch fire, the laughter
in the kitchen filling the house
where we tried to live. What has become

of my young life, the man who once pressed
a fistful of crocuses between my breasts
and made love to me on the kitchen floor

while beyond, on the river,
a loudspeaker-toting paddleboat carried
honeymooners to the mouth. Later we took
the same cruise, pretending to be newlyweds
ourselves, holding hands on the tipping deck
with others who took photographs to prove
they had truly been there, they had
loved each other – once. The laughter

in the kitchen reminds me: grief
is a burden, something to be shaken
like the foxgloves in our garden, stooping
under the weight of their seeds. I've learned
the lessons of pain, now wait for the same
light that makes my daughter's face so
luminous and wise as she says to her small friend,
"Now you be Dad. You've got no body so you can't
get away. I'll be the mother this time."

ANN FISHER-WIRTH

Moth

The girl I once was
stared through grief and fever
at a devil clad in orange, some earth-arranger.
He waited beneath the pines
as they tucked my newborn's ashes
beside my father's grave, grim joke
or grace: *Watch over her, Papa.*
Papa you died in time to spare you shame.

Three weeks later milk came in,
all down the front of my new white dress.
I gave myself to scalding waters,
pounded my head on the walls of showers.
Oh I was death's girl,
sure to poison anything I loved,
any sweet cock or baby that came near me.

*

When my other children came,
a half-light dogged them. They learned to want her too,
the dead sister who made me a mother,
who made me stop, sometimes,
and go quiet in hallways, as if my arms
were full of blankets for someone who was not them,
who slept down a long corridor
in a room where curtains billowed
in watery sunlight.
                                        Or when I
read to them at night and their sweet
bodies and hair grew sticky with summer as they
sprawled all over me, there was a moth

at the window, a soft moon-splotched moth battering at the window,
and that moth could never get in
no matter how they opened
and opened—

The Third Breast

I noticed it first
after a night
in the wooded silence
that cuts across a still lake
cusped by pines.
I felt it out in the holy open
where a loon
echoes her sorrows
and the insides
of seeds all listen.

It looked
like an insect bite:
raised, red anger
under the cupped
curve of milk flesh.
I thought the forest's
piqued, entomologic mind
had stolen
away with its drop
of blood. But
no itch, just tenderness.

Then something like
a head.
What in there flamed?
White rebellion?
A mess of healing?
I tried to expel,
to puncture
the offensive swell.
Between my thumbs it gave up

as much liquid as a stone:
hardly, bloodless,
stubbornskinned,
moonthrobbing worry.

I retreated
and it calmed
to a dark purple
scare. A lump
of frighten.
A mark of if.
Silent in the busy
day, moaning
under the night's
wondering touch.

Scared, I cared.
My mute child,
I interpreted
its cry: it's not
sick, it's not
hungry: it just needs
to feel a love
on the outside
of being named.

Later, in between
spaces of wakefulness,
the breast
revealed itself:

budded off my rib,
it bobbed from
my chest. Pendulous
yet upturned, like
a cup of fresh.
Sienna acorn tip, sensitive
as a kiss

recoil! at the mutate female
body! Oh horrible extra
ecstasy! Nausea, vertigo
oh flee, but where to go
where the body
won't go also? Exorcise it,
collapse it, lop it off

with a knife of white light –

Oh, but my love
for myself
made me sick. Love
enveloped all
of my soft folds,
love made room
for the ugliness.
Self-love welcomed
and petted the breast
like a stunted child.

Still dumb, numbed
against the wandering,
homeless rage evicted
into all my streams
from the untumour,
I fell against his love.
It held me up.

His ageless grey pity,
his evergreen owl eyes.
His love stroked my three
motherheads
and asked gently
if a tree knows
which are its extra limbs.

JOHN BARTON

Magnificat

Leaning back into a gossip chair,
the porch window framing her
thoughts with a harvest moon,
her body overwhelmed by a first child—
the father in the basement intuiting
the form of a cradle from dark
maple responding to his hands—
she finds herself growing
light headed with earlier men.

The husband she made a friend,
the erotic the seed he planted.

The blond lover who grew hard
each time her tongue hesitated
a moment too long exploring
the pit of his left knee,
whose embraces roused her nipples
to unusual swollen peaks,
can still make her flush,
the very thought of him enough.

Another with more gentle eyes,
that held her longer she made
her teacher. They exchanged
books by Thomas Merton,
discussed Krishna and Piaget,
lived several platonic weeks
beneath a mountain.

Still another she imagines
the way she met him, his frame

caught a moment in light enticed
through vines that reach skyward
against a window in his flat,
his hand curved in what for her
became a reflective wave.
Irony, laughter, empathic darkness
she reckoned among his virtues.
Absently she fingers the shirt
he gave her from his closet.
What shape it took stretched
by his chest, buttoned
across a heart she came to doubt,
no longer limply hugs her;
its folds keep her warm,
flare around the baby's
final dream.

The carpenter whose whistling
rises through her bones
like notes will soon lay down
his level and his plane. Only night
allows them time to jest
about the stalk they one day
found creeping up inside her.
These days it seems impatient
to poke its head above the clouds.
They have agreed to let it climb
where it must, though her gaze
must inform its leaves,
his canny touch its tendrils.

Last night in the light falling
between the curtains he showed her
the clever animals he's practised
dancing madly across the walls.
She told him what she read
waiting for him to climb in
beside her. He delighted in mounting

with her the ladder the foetus
ascends from fish to child.

She hears his step rising
from the basement. Soon his eyes
will rest on her like a hand.
For nights now she has dreamed
about the body she will wear again
for him—the baby's almost one
of them, this in dwelling form
they will find a name for.

MISHA CAHNMANN-TAYLOR

Animal Moments

I hated him most
when she howled on the bed,
eyes black with Mary Kay,
naked breasts aswing in a thin
cotton nightgown. I'd begin
then say nothing as sobs
shook the king-size mattress.
I stroked the cat as cries
poured out, then cleaned things:
pushed laundered bras and panties
back into mother's overstuffed
drawers. I took the pain and stuffed it
like socks into breasts.
But she kept on and I had no language.
Later when he came to visit,
I bit my father. Frightened monkey,
I warned him, wanted
to make him, please,
make her stop.

What I Learned from Dr. Phil About Becoming an Effective Lover

Don't be the section-hand who goes through a spaying at shift's end and says I'm beat,
I'm the soup's ennui, I think I'll go home now and sock a pillow.
Such is a famously unerotic turnoff
to the many who are privy to wife and mother's innermost cravings.
Consider that your children have defected
to higher authorities
and regard you at home dozing nightly in your chair like an exploded potato, noone yet giving
smallest thought to the somebody in the kitchen pretty soon having to make dinner. Say instead
something catchy, something a party may clepe unto, words far afield from snipings on the order of
'my fetching beast, bring me a beer.'
Like, be tender.
Don't come on as the tyrant who says I know who I am and who you are, both of us viewed by our betters
as 'persnickety' bottom feeders. That is really quite crass,
unbecoming to the ideal husband.
Say instead, 'Honey, it has come to my attention that immediate gratification of the solo partner
leaves much unresolved in the family dynamics.' Say instead,
'Where did you find those pretty shoes,'
another neat example of the tender. Or endeavour, once upon your pillow, to say, 'What lovely cheek
bones, my dear,' and your erotic powers will increase triple fold,
as has been foreshadowed in holy text,
though this does not mean all your crimes shall be forgiven
or mend the tight fists
of grim children. The final point, my brother, is thus and so:

the favourable family hour
should make allowances for the unbelievable, the not quite acceptable.
Do not on any occasion bolt
your feet to the floor, when kissing the mother of your children. Follow
these edicts and you will have created
tranquility out of chaos a guaranteed six months maximum.

from *Blue Marrow*

nôtokwêsiw, the Great Granny continues

I lay outside his cabin
night after night, my buffalo robe
wrapped against the wind.
The heat of his breath inside my cloak.
Night after night he came.
Fist raised to his god, lips
pressed against the man hanging dead
around his waist. He entered like a charging
buffalo pounding his chest
against the race of arrows.
I received those spirits.
I lay, my guts exposed,
the loud moan of my need freed
into the night sun. Oh god,
how we sweated in
the thick skin of dead buffalo.
Knives raised and sharpened
clawed and ripped.
Still the buffalo roared,
thundered the sweating pasture.

I don't regret those days, my belly,
swollen with winter feed.
Spring will rise, milk will flow,
a hundred babies rippling
my thighs.
I'd have him again.
I'd have him
again.

môniyaw-kisêyiniw speaks,
The Elderly White man continues,
He is caught in a dream

We had fourteen children. My desire,
I never held it down.
Took in her openness.

Chocolate

In the end, in the long-term
wing of the assisted living
home, in the small white chamber

looking out on the patio's locked-in
blooms or in the big plain
"day room" with its blaring

TV and hopeful posters,
they fed my mother
ground-up piles of pallid

stuff in bowls clamped onto
a plastic tray and at first
she smiled, delicious, delicious,

as she sucked the oozing
juices, the last pap,
smiling surrounded by fellow

diners drooping and mumbling
in their places until
after a while she tightened

her lips against the food and
instead began unknotting,
unknotting the flowered

gown, unclothing her wasting
nakedness still white and smooth
and then at the very end,

when dreamy and slim
as a teen she welcomed
old friends and relatives who flickered

on the walls, the curtains
of the tiny room, nodding,
hello, sit down, to the shiny

nothing, she'd eat nothing
but chocolate, only chocolate,
so every day I brought an oblong

Lindt or Hershey
and square by square
she took in mouthfuls,

smiling and nodding, square
by square, delicious, dear,
until she finally

swallowed the whole dense bar.

ANNIE FINCH

Over Dark Arches

Naked and thin and wet as if with rain,
bursting I come out of somewhere, bursting again.
And like a great building that breathes under sunlight
over dark arches, your body is there,

And my milk moves under your tongue—

where currents from earth linger under cool stone
rising to me and my mouth makes a circle
over your silence

You reach through your mouth to find me—

Bursting out of your body that held me for years,
as the rain wets the earth with its bodies—

And my thoughts are milk to feed you

till we turn and are empty,

till we turn and are full.

Waiting for its kick.
My love. My tenant.

LOUISE GLÜCK

The Wound

The air stiffens to a crust.
From bed I watch
Clots of flies, crickets
Frisk and titter. Now
The weather is such grease.
All day I smell the roasts
Like presences. You
Root into your books.
You do your stuff.
In here my bedroom walls
Are paisley, like a plot
Of embryos. I lie here,
Waiting for its kick.
My love. My tenant.
As the shrubs grow
Downy, bloom and seed.
The hedges grow downy
And seed and moonlight
Burbles through the gauze.
Sticky curtains. Faking scrabble
With the pair next door
I watched you clutch your blank.
They're both on Nembutal,
The killer pill.
And I am fixed. Gone careful,
Begging for the nod,
You hover loyally above my head. I close
My eyes. And now
The prison falls in place:
Ripe things sway in the light,
Parts of plants, leaf
Fragments…

You are covering the cot
With sheets. I feel
No end. No end. It stalls
In me. It's still alive.

Beg and Choose

Held up to pale light,
the burst condom dripped,
smeared your thighs. I etched
letters into the salt milk,
formed one word.

I roll clothing into balls until
my pack is full, count backwards
to the last clots and wonder
Am I ovulating now? I see
jellyfish sacks open, release
the egg intent on its path
to the fine velour of the uterus.

I am weighted down
with my pack, my fear
of carrying a foetus through
foreign countries; the possibility
of misinterpreting morning
sickness for dysentery.

I've already decided; I won't
come home. I will have my belly
oiled with jasmine by long-haired
women, blessed by each holy man.
I will birth her without pain,
premature, and leave her, slick
and bathed in fluid, in the copper
bowl of a beggar.

MARY KARR

Soft Mask

On the ultrasound screen my child curled
in his own fluid orbit, less real
than any high-school textbook tadpole
used to symbolize birth, till the nurse
placed a white arrow on his heart flicker:
a quick needle of light. Tonight his face

blooms in my window before the trees
stripped bare, a moon hung full and red.
That soft mask, not yet hardened in autumn wind,
would hold a thumbprint if I touched him. I hesitate
to touch him. He's not yet felt the burden
of a hand, nor tasted air, nor wobbled
toward some bladelike gaze, his mouth
smudged against the clear silk
that envelops him, webbed hands that reach
and retreat as a cat tests water.

Or like Narcissus, or the great wondering
madonnas, or any beast lost in another, the demon
who kneels to feed at some lily throat:
his pulse first matching then at odds with mine,
that small arrow seeming to tremble
as if striking something true.

ANN FISHER-WIRTH

In Crescent

The bloodwall thickens
and everyone I have loved
begins to ripen within my body.
A quiet time: the house
curls in upon itself, enfolds
the sleeping children; the daisy
shuts its petals, and their lashes are wet
with the mercy of sleep.

Summer's grasses
are long, so long
that we seem to move through water.
Children again, we clamor, Mother
may I, mother may I? And she
by the elm in shadow, whose belly
catches moonlight: Come
as you will, I will hold you,
I am warm, all steps
lead where I am hidden.

And so inch forward toward that
teeming bed
where we all lie down together.

Falling in Love

I am falling in love
with myself

I lie in the bath
hilly as a Henry Moore
and I admire   I
admire
the sheen of my skin
stretched as eggshell
over my belly
the parcel
the big egg

I am falling in love
with my silver shoulders
as they support these breasts
blue-laced
floating
like swollen planets
        I hardly recognize them
        they have become
        so
        useful

I am falling in love
with my stranded body
stupefied
by pregnancy

in empathy
with the old and obese

I have always suspected
this was my true self
emerging
from hesitant bones
        queen-sized
        and undisguised
        by vanity

1973

"I'm pregnant," I wrote to her in delight
from London, thirty, married, in print. A fools-
cap sheet scrawled slantwise with one minuscule
sentence came back. "I hope your child is white."
I couldn't tear the pieces small enough.
I hoped she'd be black as the ace of spades,
though hybrid beige heredity had made
that as unlikely as the spun-gold stuff
sprouted after her neo-natal fur.
I grudgingly acknowledged her "good hair,"
which wasn't, very, from my point of view.
"No tar-brush left," her father's mother said.
"She's Jewish and she's white," from her cranked bed
mine smugly snapped.
                                        She's Black. She is a Jew.

At the Home of a Colleague from the Child Protection Unit

I would like to hang my face, Inspector
upon your wall, beside the carved masks,
reproductions of Africa's ancients – hunter, warrior,
sage and seer – and deposit beside dried flowers
in your vast ceramic pot, my withered heart,
my brittle bones; so that I might reveal
how scarred I am by the work we do,
a tiger without teeth; scared to confess
that like the aesthetically pleasing
synthetic vegetables in your wicker basket
decorating your railway sleeper patio furniture
my mock skin is too thin.
Your chairs are solid,
like you are, Inspector
when gathering clues of another abducted child,
when noting in cool black ball pen
another infant's ruptured rectum.

I can no longer keep my face affixed
with idle chatter: Nice day, Sargeant.
How's the puppy, Captain?
And your diet, did you skip your carbs today?
I need another colour rinse.

My fear, like my roots,
like my sixteen-week bump
is starting to show.

C1. Staple Sorter

worker incoherence. // the or // my not //
sad // seesaw you // string Hamilton //

not // Tonight Hamilton //
my crest // string
or // to you //
the pills // seesaw
incoherence. // can't sad //
worker

not // the sky. I // can like Tonight
Hamilton // and social anymore, // I'm take toward my
crest // off I your // adopted blood or string
or // downer the and // realize dole like to
you // poke in Who // can responsibility out the
pills // moving dose thoughts, // half-uttered soup, to seesaw
incoherence. // I help seem // to badly that can't
sad // about of vinyl. worker

Tonight I'm freakin' sad // about the prospects of
my in-laws, who seem // to be declining badly
toward illness and incoherence. // I have to help
string together basic thoughts, // half-uttered requests for soup,
or keep the pills // moving from one dose
to the next. Who // can bear a responsibility
like that, where you // poke a hole in
the night's middle and // realize you didn't dole
out the upper or // downer and caused the
seesaw self of your // adopted flesh and blood
to dip or crest // off the chart? I

can't hack it anymore, // I'm just gonna take
that job in Hamilton // and let the social
worker step in. I // can be replaced, like
vinyl. Sons-in-law are not // the stars, or sky

C2. Obstetrician

the father
hand The
corridor fetuses.
lovingly gasp

gasp fussing lovingly
fetuses. realize corridor
The can hand
father never the

the client anything never
father white-coated to hand
can and ribs. The
corridor could proceed realize
fetuses. world untrained lovingly
fussing gasp

The saying is working the
corridor of their client
could like a sticks anything
proceed with first point. never
realize my distance a father
fetuses. I move from white-coated
world labelled bag. scissors to
untrained for alone. My hand
lovingly visit on I can
fussing to mother's astonishing and
gasp my hands ribs.

The first thing that bears saying
is yes, I do love working
the speculum up each unique corridor

of origins. Women are unaware of
their powers. If determined, each client
could crush that shiny instrument like
a pop can. Anyone who sticks
anything up any vagina should proceed
with caution. That is the first
point. The second is women never
realize how I must keep my
distance emotionally. I feel like a
father to all of those fetuses.
I know how they will move
from the inside to this white-coated
world where blood is a labelled
bag. I will pass the scissors
to some other man completely untrained
for fatherhood. Women are so alone.
My technique involves laying a hand
on bellies as they ripen. I
can feel the child readying, fussing
to get out through the mother's
astonishing tunnel of ridged muscle and
gasp air, gape for breath, my
hands like god around its ribs.

C3. Minister

the first thing that bears saying
about the prospects of
is yes, I do love working
to be declining badly

the speculum up each unique corridor
toward illness and incoherence.
of origins. women are unaware of
string together basic thoughts,

their powers. if determined, each client
moving from one dose
could crush that shiny instrument like
can bear a responsibility

a pop can. anyone who sticks
like that, where you
anything up any vagina should proceed
the night's middle and

with caution. that is the first
downer and caused the
point. the second is women never
adopted flesh and blood

realize how I must keep my
to dip or crest
distance emotionally. I feel like a
can't hack it anymore,

father to all of those fetuses.
and let the social
I know how they will move
can be replaced, like

from the inside to this white coated
vinyl. sons-in-law are not
world where blood is a labelled
tonight I'm freakin' sad

bag. I will pass the scissors
my in-laws, who seem
to some other man completely untrained
I have to help

for fatherhood. women are so alone.
half-uttered requests for soup,
my technique involves laying a hand
or keep the pills

lovingly once or twice each visit
to the next. who
on bellies as they ripen. I
poke a hole in

can feel the child readying, fussing
realize you didn't dole
to get out through the mother's
out the upper or

astonishing tunnel of ridged muscle and
seesaw self of your
gasp air, gape for breath, my
off the chart? I

hands like god around its ribs.
I'm just gonna take

that job in Hamilton

worker step in. I

the stars, or sky.

Dinner with Friends on a Midsummer's Evening

Angela's lime-green parrot shuffles,
long tail a straight blade.

Our dresses, blood-orange, white, African-striped,
our big bare suntanned shoulders and
flowery names: *Carola, Gillie, Angela, Miranda,*
we pat each other, tell each other we look great,
you've lost weight
no, I wish
no, really

The petunias on the table frame her,
gauzy shells dipped in pink watercolour;
they will only last a night.
We pass around the red sauce,
the black olives, the wine,
the flowers.
I try not to look at her breasts as she talks.

We get stuck talking men, lost loves,
pregnancies welcomed and not,
the crazy conviction of lust
that we followed
as if our lives depended on it,

and perhaps it was
the only door we could see through back then,
the track away from home,
a dodgy compass, its guessing finger.
The talk flows but keeps coming back to
love, a lake that empties,

revealing the slimy wrecks of trucks,
the cracked earth,
then the next time you look
it's full again, beckoning swimmers.

Drunk, I say:
it's women who have always meant more to me,
and there's a pause.

The parrot is walking on the table.

Angela leans toward me
a distraction of dark cleavage,
her painter's hands raised and imploring,
her lipstick smeared, and says
oh, but it's the difference
that's so interesting,

and I agree,
because by then
I would have said yes
to anything.

JOHN TERPSTRA

Restoration

After the cigar factory, the valley of sugar fields
and the nineteenth-century Spanish mansion
built on slave labour, our guide led us
into the Iglesia Parroquial de la Santisima Trinidad.
I half-expect to hear a four-piece Cuban band strike up
as I tell how my daughter removes her peaked cap,
out of respect, she'll explain to a friend back home,
and we listen to the story of a wooden altar,
one of many into which are carved
precise moments in the life of the Virgin Mary.
A young woman saunters by our group.
She looks surprisingly like a prostitute,
and a moment later Katie confesses
that she's given the woman her hat.
She pointed. She wanted it. What could I do?

My daughter seems pleased to have given away
something of her own, in this country of few possessions
and little money, but the white baseball cap
is her souvenir gift of last year's vacation,
when we carried our most recent possession—
her unexpected news—with us
like a piece of baggage we must fit
into the compact model of our family,
and I am not so generous.

She gives me her permission to tell this,
If I can read it first, she says, and to add
that in the old, barely kept-up Cuban church
another carved Mary entertains a holy dove
which hovers over her head, reminding Katie
of the Advent Sunday morning we heard

about the young woman's pregnancy, its origins
in the divine, when she leaned over my shoulder
and whispered, *That's what happened to me.*

Katherine, I was scandalized by your gospel
joke, but laughed, because it *was* funny,
and you seemed so at peace, finally,
with yourself and with your pregnancy,
I began to wonder if the truth was not
the telling of that unlikely story
within a building the story helped to build,
that gave you permission. If, in that precise
moment, your baby became your honour,
what would I contradict?

Exiting the iglesia of the parish of Trinidad, Cuba,
we pass a small box balanced on a single wooden leg
like a crutch, and an elderly man making
eye contact, who points to a slot in the box top
as he repeats the phrase,
For the restoration... For the restoration...
I check for singles in my wallet
as our guide explains fathers are forbidden
to wear their white collars on weekdays,
in this country of equals—
but all I can find is a twenty.

The maracas, ancient muted trumpet, drums
and two guitars of a five-piece band
play for us at dinner, then move to entertain
later diners under the open plaza, who dance.
Mary and I are lying on the resort beach,
allowing the stars to reconcile the disparities
as we list the known facts:
our teenage daughter offering the white-
winged, souvenir baseball cap
to a streetwalker who asks for it,
inside a church where the walls weep

stains of infiltrating rainwater, within sight
of an altar honouring the impossible event
we are not hesitant to believe true
for her too,
so low had been her estate.

It is the old man's role to keep up the place
where this happens, where the paths of the two
sister-leads of the gospel drama
cross, asking after restoration.

I wish I'd given him the twenty.

VIEW

we were once together ascending
these mottled steps toward the ruins
St. Paul's hollowed sentinel
blessing Malacca

eleven years later
I climb alone stung
by the suffering of change

her heart now too weakened
for such challenges

a rotting mango lies swarmed by ants
across from the Dutch graveyard down below
where marble tombstones fail
to protest or impress

I turn to the weathered white wall where
tendrils of two morning glory vines entwine
lulled by a timid breeze

this modest tenderness
beckons a tear of gratitude
for my mother's gift
though I've long forgotten birth
its first taste

Father's Day

You were a filament of red
on the test strip, coming into focus
like a polaroid of windblown hair
against the white cheek of a woman
on a bridge between cities
just before rain.

Perhaps a scratch or blip of medication—
but you persisted through a second test, a third.
Weeks before, you'd switched
the poles of my world, molecule by molecule,
making it yours, until you were ready
to greet that day's startled eyes.

Now my hours are measured
by your thousandfold replications of cells,
your clusterings, irrevocable pulse.
Tendril, little furl of being
with the power of rivers, you lead me
into myself, riding my blood, then away.

ANNIE FINCH

The Coming of Mirrors

My body thickens in a stem
climbing aloud to keep you here.

My belly thickens like a stem,
my belly is tethered by your days.

Come in, come in, my strong darling.
I'm still a pane of airy glass.

My breasts go heavy to meet you here.

My body turns in place of clouds,
I grow like a pane of open glass.

My body is a forest floor
where needles blend to keep you here.

My belly thickens like a stem.

Come in, come in, my last darling,
and let the coming mirrors pass.

I remember all this as plainly
as if I could remember

Chopped Liver

Boil the livers for one minute. In sweet butter
Melt an onion, chopped fine. Now I'm my mother's
Jewish Mother. Her life's melting. The good gut smell
Takes me by the hand to East Lombard Street, fat eels
Dangling in windows, crated chickens screeching
Under awnings, waiting for the kosher killing.
Never "observant" of any higher power, she laughed
When I said the dark-bearded Hasids, jovial and hefty,
Looked like Santa Claus, but younger, in black clothes.
I'd stare at the women in wigs. She'd whisper, "Low
Class pickle-boat people."
But I lie. This happened
Just now, in my head, high on smell. We were so German
We went to Hollins Market, over on the west side, not
Far from Butcher's Hill. There were chickens, yes, but
Pigs were what swung obscenely in shop windows. We
Used to polish off a whole pink trotter, knife in each
Traife hand, she and I. Grandmother Marie Naas, cousin
Of solid Hamburg burghers Rebeck and Winckelman,
Had to tell me she wasn't bad just because of Hitler.
She said someday I'd learn to like chopped liver.
I remember I believed the one thing but not the other.
I remember all this as plain as if I could remember.

MAHMOUD DARWISH

To My Mother

I long for my mother's bread
my mother's coffee
and my mother's caress…
and each day childhood
grows bigger in me on another day's chest,
and I adore my life
for if I die,
            my mother's tears would shame me!

So if I return one day, mother, make me
into a shroud that shades
your long eyelashes,
and cover my bones with grass
your pure heels had baptized,
and tighten my bind…
with a lock of your hair…
or with a thread
waving from the hem of your dress,
I might become a god then,
a god, I might…
if I touch the deep floor of your heart!

And if I return, use me
as fuel for your brick oven…
hang me on the roof, like your laundry line,
I can no longer stand
without the prayer of your days,
I have aged, so bring back the stars of childhood
to me, and I will join
the little birds
on the path of return…
to the nest of your waiting!

Translation by Fady Joudah

ANN FISHER-WIRTH

Devotions

Every night, every morning, she holds
her finger beneath the baby's nostril
and waits for the warm slide of breath
across her finger, the moist, infinitesimal
fluttering. She hangs prostrate on a sign:
a grunt, a fart, that sweet involuntary sucking
where the lower lip vanishes. *If it rises*
and falls, if it rises and falls… She cannot
believe the child will live. She watches
her daughter's chest, the small waves
of her breathing—
It's 1973. They're so poor
it's a crisis when she breaks a jar of honey.
A lemon tree spreads at their bedroom window,
and at night, around the patio the young
husband made, driving to the chaparral
for stones then lugging them back
in the old VW van, bamboo groans with growing.
Let's not speak of what's wrong between them,
this husband who's so anxious and thin
he can suck his belly like a cavern
to his backbone, this wife who stayed in bed
all spring, scarcely daring to lift her head
every time the spotting started, since that day
in the mountains at four months when she bled
and the nurse at the emergency clinic
told her, Yup, I heard of a woman who woke
after a week of safety and the whole
bed was a puddle of blood.
Let's just say
poverty and terror can break a marriage.
Let's not speak of the sorrow

this child and her sister and brother
will inherit; instead, listen to the story
their mother tells them, how all the babies
line up in the sky by the baby ladder,
and slide down when they hear their future
parents say, This one… This one… This one…
How they are the chosen babies of all the world.

SUZANNE HANCOCK

The Tree

My mother drove off in her two-tone red Chevrolet and I climbed the tree. If I'm quiet will you let me stay? On the clothesline my nightgown. My eye on the corner where she would turn from the big street-artery onto our minor avenue but it was never her. Sometimes Mr. Ogawa in his quick clean convertible. Sometimes Mrs. Davis pushing red-haired Sean in the buggy. Salmon return home by scent. I thought the perfume of my nightgown might lead her back. In the rain it looked hunched and bony. At night my father hauled me down from the branches with a clinking metal ladder. It was hard for him, as he'd stopped eating. He'd carry the ladder with both hands and have to rest on the lawn halfway from the gate. Eventually he just left it leaning against the trunk. Neighborhood kids walked by with their schoolbooks and lunch-kits and asked what I was doing. I'd say *just waiting.* When the leaves fell in a bloody pool at my feet the jays from the top branch flew south. They turned down the wide street and that was it. I cut down the nest, brought it inside and slept.

PRISCILA UPPAL

Motorcycle Accidents and Other Things That Remind Me of Mother

wigs on fake white heads in the flashy store window
the sound of chattering teeth after heaving out of the lake onto the stones
smell of cranberry sauce simmering on the stove before Thanksgiving
you travel in waves, mother,
                                        like a drowning sweater in November

boys in overalls beating buckets with dolls
the sunflower in my orthodontist's office
snails in thick white cream at the Bistro
the bruise on my inner thigh father insists on calling a beauty mark
I heard you once
                                                        on the radio
singing along with Carmen Miranda
but I wasn't reminded

the beaks of geese wrangling a plastic shopping bag for crumbs
my lover's back when I step on it
eight-week-old celery after it has gone sticky and white
and I must throw it out or stomach the hard water
                                                        the instant coffee maker
gurgles and spits
                                                        you remind me of it
turn off when unused

petunias on high windowsills
purple velvet gloves in an older woman's purse
the head of a vole the cat brought home
Emergency Broadcast System messages

burnt bagels
ham sandwiches on rye
in picnic baskets
out of season
mother, we clash
making room on the grass

the unhurt fender of a truck by the back-bent leg
a siren since gone mute with fistfuls of forms
my disgust upon seeing the lip of some bastard's shoe embedded in the road

Rites of Sense

In twilight as she lies on a mat
I rub my mother's feet with jasmine oil
touch callouses under skin,
joints upholding that fraught original thing—
bone, gristle skin, all that makes her mine.
All day she swabbed urine from the floor,
father's legs so weak he clung to the rosewood bed.
She rinsed soiled cloths, hung them out to dry
on a coir rope by a vine, its passion fruit
clumsy with age, dangling.

She lies on a mat, a poor thing beached,
belly slack, soles crossed, sari damp and white.
I kneel in darkness at her side,
her oldest child returned for a few weeks
at summer's height.
She murmurs my name
asks in Malayalam *Why is light so hot?*

Beyond her spine I catch a candle glisten.
The door's a frame for something
I'm too scared to name:
a child, against a white wall,
hands jammed to her teeth, lips torn
breath staggering its hoarse silence.

All night my voice laced through dreams
tiny eyelets for the smoke
Amma, I am burning!
I'm a voice slit from sound,
just snitches of blood, loopholes of sweat,
a sack of flesh you shut me in.

What words of passage to that unlit place?
What rites of sense?

Amma, I am dreaming myself into your body.
It is the end of everything.
Your pillow stained with white
tosses as a wave might

on our southern shore.

Will you lay your cheek against mine?
Bless my bent head?

You washed me once, gave me suck,
made me live in your father's house
taught me to wake at dawn,
sweep the threshold clean of blood red leaves.
Showed me a patch of earth dug with your hands
where sweet beans grow coiled and raw.

Taught me to fire a copper pan,
starch and fold a sari, raise a rusty needle,

stitch my woman's breath
into the mute amazement of sentences.

Fragrances

The threshold of your mother's room had such
Intimate possession of itself, and that
Satin fabric that the lamp assumed
Among the vanities, the combs and pins...
Complexities of being soft and cool,
Intricacy of clothing, lace and tulle,
The look of the half-shut chiffonier
With all the lank, loose-folded garments there;
The colours of her things in the dim lamp—
Almost unsayable, that gentian sleeve.

And sometimes I would hide in her wardrobe
Standing among the dresses and the gowns
As though a rush of women circled me
With a smell of warm and fragrant skin
Mingled with lilac and the blush of sun,
Just as the golden sunshade made a glow
In which we all looked suddenly transformed,
Illumined in the fragrance of the sun
That had a tinge of everlastingness,
The way verbena lingers on the tips
Of all your fingers when you say goodbye.

RICHARD TELEKY

Mother's Garden

This morning
I planted two day lilies, scab
red, rich with rust; pinks;
pink geraniums; nicotiana,
whitish pink, as if the blooms
had brushed against my
thigh and taken up
the color of flesh; several
pots of snapdragons (again,
pink); a bed of cosmos;
three Bell peppers (come
September, to be stuffed with
ground beef and rice) and in
the process replanted balsam,
violets, even columbine that
had gone their own way,
smashing into the roses – her
precious roses – and making
a nuisance of themselves. Not
my choices, exactly, but
the best of two nurseries and
Home Depot. Hardy annuals,
garden ready. And like all
gardens, this one's planted
with time. Of course I felt
the present turning to past,
engulfing loss (plants do that)
while my mind's eye saw
thick beds of impatiens
in Beverly Hills, clumps of
oriental poppies and lavender
iris in Santa Fe, the white

garden at Sissinghurst, and
wondered if I'll make it to
eighty-one, as she has,
still ready for weeding.

Some Slippery Afternoon

A silver watch you've worn for years
is suddenly gone, leaving a pale
white stripe blazing on your wrist.

A calendar, marked with appointments
you meant to keep, disappears, leaving
a faded spot on the wall where it hung.

You search the house, yard, trash cans
for weeks, but never find it.

One night the glass in your windows
vanishes,
leaving you sitting in a gust of wind.

You think how a leg is suddenly lost
beneath a subway train, or taxi's wheel,
some slippery afternoon.

The child you've raised for years,
combing each lock, tailoring each smile,
each tear, each valuable thought,

suddenly changes to a harlequin,
joins the circus passing in the street,
never to be seen again.

One morning you wash your face,
look into the mirror, find the water
has eroded your features, worn them

smooth as a rock in a brook.
A blank oval peers back at you
too mouthless to cry out.

PHILIP LEVINE

My Mother with Purse the Summer They Murdered the Spanish Poet

Had she looked out the window she would have seen a quiet street,
each house with a single maple or elm browning in the sun
at the end of summer, the black Fords and Plymouths gleaming
in their fresh wax, the neighbor children returning home
dark suited or white frocked from their Christian studies.

Had she looked out she would have seen the world she crossed
the world to find. Instead she unclasps the leather purse
to make sure she has everything: mirror, lipstick, billfold,
her cards of identity, her checkbook with the week's balance
correctly entered, two monogramed, embroidered handkerchiefs

to blot and hold the tears, for—dark veiled—she's on her way
to meet her husband, gone three years now into the sour earth
of Michigan. Can the long white root a man in time becomes
talk back to one who chose to stay on the far shore
of his departure? Before the day ends, she'll find out.

She will hunch over tea leaves, she will open her palms,
first the hardened hand of the wage earner, then the soft one
that opens to the heart. To see, she will close her eyes;
to hear, she will stop her ears, and the words will be
wrong or no words at all, teeth striking teeth, the tongue

doubled back upon itself, the blackened lips vanished
into the hole of the throat. But for now she looks up.
It is summer, 1936. The first hints of autumn
mist on a row of curtained windows that look in on us
as my mother, perfumed, leans down to brush my mouth with hers,

once, to say my name, precisely, in English. Later
two women will pretend they have reached two other worlds,

the one behind and the one ahead. As they keen
in the darkness perhaps only one will pretend, perhaps
neither, for who shall question that we most clearly see

where no eye is? Wide-eyed he sees nothing. White shirt
worn open, dark trousers with no belt, the olive skin appalled.
When the same wind he loved and sang to touches his cheek
he tries to rub it away. There are others, too, walking over
the flat, gray stones to where a line of men smokes and waits.

The trees have stilled. Had she looked out the window
my mother would have seen each house with its elm or maple
burning, the children drowning in the end of summer, the mist
blurring the eyes of our front windows, the shale hills
above Granada where all time stopped. Her purse snaps shut.

GRACE PALEY

On Mother's Day

I went out walking
in the old neighborhood

Look! more trees on the block
forget-me-nots all around them
ivy   lantana shining
and geraniums in the window

Twenty years ago
it was believed that the roots of trees
would insert themselves into gas lines
then fall   poisoned on houses and children

or tap the city's water pipes
or starved for nitrogen   obstruct the sewers

In those days in the afternoon I floated
by ferry to Hoboken or Staten Island
then pushed the babies in their carriages
along the river wall   observing Manhattan
See Manhattan I cried   New York!
even at sunset it doesn't shine
but stands in fire   charcoal to the waist

But this Sunday afternoon on Mother's Day
I walked west   and came to Hudson Street   tri-colored flags
were flying over old oak furniture for sale
brass bedspreads   copper pots and vases
by the pound from India

Suddenly before my eyes   twenty-two transvestites
in joyous parade stuffed pillows

under their lovely gowns
and entered a restaurant
under a sign which said   All Pregnant Mothers Free

I watched them place napkins over their bellies
and accept coffee and zabaglione

I am especially open to sadness and hilarity
since my father died as a child
one week ago in this his ninetieth year

PHILIP LEVINE

The Mercy

The ship that took my mother to Ellis Island
eighty-three years ago was named "The Mercy."
She remembers trying to eat a banana
without first peeling it and seeing her first orange
in the hands of a young Scot, a seaman
who gave her a bite and wiped her mouth for her
with a red bandana and taught her the word,
"orange," saying it patiently over and over.
A long autumn voyage, the days darkening
with the black waters calming as night came on,
then nothing as far as her eyes could see and space
without limit rushing off to the corners
of creation. She prayed in Russian and Yiddish
to find her family in New York, prayers
unheard or misunderstood or perhaps ignored
by all the powers that swept the waves of darkness
before she woke, that kept "The Mercy" afloat
while smallpox raged among the passengers
and crew until the dead were buried at sea
with strange prayers in a tongue she could not fathom.
"The Mercy," I read on the yellowing pages of a book
I located in a windowless room of the library
on 42nd Street, sat thirty-one days
offshore in quarantine before the passengers
disembarked. There a story ends. Other ships
arrived, "Tancred" out of Glasgow, "The Neptune"
registered as Danish, "Umberto IV,"
the list goes on for pages, November gives
way to winter, the sea pounds this alien shore.
Italian miners from Piemonte dig
under towns in western Pennsylvania
only to rediscover the same nightmare

they left at home. A nine-year-old girl travels
all night by train with one suitcase and an orange.
She learns that mercy is something you can eat
again and again while the juice spills over
your chin, you can wipe it away with the back
of your hands and you can never get enough.

Triptych

When my mother
Was a young girl
Before the War
Reading sad books
By the river
Sometimes, she
Looked up, wisely
But did not dream
The day I would
Be born to her

She who is not
Who she was
Waits to be
Yet she is
Already
Mother
Whose child
Though not yet
Could not be
An other

All at once
I could see
My mother
In eternity
I told her
She always
Would be
The one
Whose son
You see

Houriyah's Instruction

I.

I thought one day of leaving, but a sparrow landed
on her hand and slept. It was enough that I'd fondle
a grapevine in a hurry … for her to know I was filled
with wine. It was enough that I'd go to bed early for her to see
my sleep clearly, and extend her night to guard it…
And enough that a letter of mine would arrive for her to know
my address has changed on the prison road, and that
my days hover around her … and in her view.

II.

My mother counts my twenty digits from afar.
She combs me with her golden lock and searches
in my underwear for foreign women,
and darns the hole in my sock. I didn't grow up on her hands
as we had wished: she and I, we parted ways by the marble
slope…and clouds loomed over us, and over the goats
that inherit the place. Exile founded two languages for us:
colloquial…for the pigeons to comprehend it and memorize the memory,
and classical…for me to explain to the shadows their shadows!

III.

I am still alive in your midst. You didn't say to me
what a mother says to a sick child, when I fell ill from a copper
moon over the bedouin tents. Do you remember
our migration path to Lebanon, where you forgot me
and forgot the sack of bread? (It was wheat bread.)
And I didn't scream so as not to wake the soldiers.

But the dew scent alighted me back in your palms. You're a doe
who lost her gazelle and her fawn…

IV.

There is no time around you for sentimental talk.
You knead the afternoon with basil and bake for sumac
the rooster's crest. I know what wrecks your punctured peacock
heart, since you've been expelled twice from paradise.
Our entire world has changed, so our voices changed. Even
the greeting between us fell like a button over the sand,
echoless. Say: Good morning!
Say anything for life to grant me her dalliance.

V.

She's Hagar's half sister. From her mother's side. Crying
along with flutes over the dead who haven't yet died. No graves
around her tent for her to know how the sky opens. She doesn't
see the desert behind my fingers, to see her garden
on the face of the mirage. And ancient time rushes
her into a needed absurdity: her father flew
like a Circassian on the wedding horse, while her mother
tearlessly prepared henna for his second bride
and checked her anklet…

VI.

We meet only as farewell at the crossroads of speech.
For example, she says to me: Marry any stranger
more beautiful than the neighborhood girls, and believe
no woman but me. And don't always believe
your memory. Don't burn to illuminate your mother,
that's her lovely task. Don't long for a rendezvous
with the dew. Be realistic like the sky. And don't long
for your grandfather's black aba, or for your grandmother's

many bribes, and dash like a colt into life.
And be who you are wherever you are. And carry
only your heart's burden … and come back
if your land changes its ways and widens enough for the land…

VII.

My mother lights up Canaan's final stars,
around my mirror,
and throws, in my final poem, her shawl!

Translation by Fady Joudah

Shawl

I knit and purl,
sedate Sunday nights
hypodermically

because She left me

bags of rainbows and granny squares,
a set of needles
to count on.

PAUL SOHAR

At the Spa with Mother

The lazy fragrance of acacia trees tickles
my eyes into a pair of women in white
with hats so light, fallen from heaven,
skirts made of breeze, and
blouses silky enough to let the sun peek through,

for the brash summer sun can see it all and more:
it creates the world it sees, maybe even the two
women walking into town,
the gravel path carrying their sandals
on its crusty palm as easily as prams,

and the colors of the park crowding merrily
into their eyes. It's an easy surrender,
a short but endless walk at a leisurely
pre-war pace to a clamorous seaside piazza
where they're already

standing in contemplation of their sleeveless arms.
The white handbags rub against their thighs
like hungry morning cats,
but now the two women have each other to
smile at and follow to the blue bowl of sunshine;

perhaps they don't know they're reflections
of each other: light and insubstantial,
inventions of a harbor never reached;
I was willing to dress up in her dreams,
it wasn't my fault they didn't quite fit me.

RICHARD TELEKY

Legacy

Named after country manors
          or ancestral seats,
the nursing homes give gentle
          yet firm guidance,
like private schools for teens
          who've run amok.
What's the difference between
          the adolescent and senile
brain? "She's confused but pliable,"
          head nurse Debbie says
as if to reassure, and I tell myself
          with my right lobe (or left?)
that anyone in trouble would be lucky
          to find refuge here, while
my left lobe (or right?) says, "Start
          stockpiling Seconals."
Nearby, my young mother in
          fake emerald earrings
carries a holiday platter lovingly.
          "What did you always make
for Christmas?" I ask the old one,
          and she replies, "Chicken?"
"Think bigger," I prod, and
          with that new tentative
smile, she offers, "Ham?"
          But that meant Easter, yet
a nod seems right. Papered in
          the best house-and-home
style – sweet floral pastels –
          the walls a solid fortress
against dementia, with a locked
          ward just in case,

Mother's new room (room not yet
home) beckons monastically.
(Protestant church services on
Sunday afternoon, Mass on
Tuesdays, before handicrafts.)
My old woman doesn't
recognize her own recliner until
she sits down and stares
out the window, frowning
at a snowy parking lot.
"You can watch the world go by,"
I suggest – something
has to be said – at once regretting
idiocy, yet Mother agrees,
"It's good to see people." She doesn't
appear to notice that someone's
left behind a pot of death-defying silk
tulips, the palest brain pink.
Will she join in games of Bingo
and Uno and Hearts?
(Yes, yes and yes.) She is once
again a fifteen-year-old
card-playing fool, cross-legged
on the bed with her sister,
long dead, beside other drooping heads
that call for their goners in
the middle of the night. Oh, Seconals
anyone? Be calm, I warn
myself: Luis will paint her nails, she
can have her hair done weekly,
the food's better than fine. But this is
my young woman wearing
fake emeralds, to be loved now
in ways still unknown.

a woman leaning from a painting, offering a life

NINA BOGIN

Self-Portrait

for Paula Modersohn-Becker (1876-1907)

Daughter, this is the cruel gift,
these eyes that know you.
The deep blues and yellows,
the frank mouth –
I looked hard into myself
and saw the woman I would be for you.
Let the colors speak!
To live was to paint.

It was this woman, myself,
I learned to know best.
I could no longer trick myself,
or shy from solitude:
even disappointment became a strength in me.
I worked, worked
towards this clarity –
knowing my thirty years,
and each painting the first.

Then you, child, white anemone, bloomed.
How I loved you, and did not fear you –
you were my life, flying out from my hands
like feathers or seeds,
each with its task
and its blackness…

Then I drifted from you and all others,
leaving behind me
this wake of colors,
a woman leaning from a painting,
offering a life.

Wooden Virgin with Child

Once the trunk of a lovely tree
She sits on her narrow chair
In an alcove of the Cloisters.
Patient, modestly shawled,
As yet only slightly hunched,
For she is still young, in fact
(Though dry, cracked a bit
Flecks of paint clinging to bodice)
Like one fresh from the convent.
Selfless, she does what she's told
But will not meet your eye.
The manchild between her knees like a doll,
Hand risen to bless, but headless,
Is the one with the book.

You and I stand and look
In our velvet jackets and tough
Boots, free to come or go,
At this mystery. Who
Would have been the model, was she
The sculptor's mother, was she his wife?
Honor his wisdom, to know
That God needs the protection
Of this sad, simple woman,

His wish also to pity her, she
Who is said to be the incarnation of pity.

Landsat Image of Mary's Ascension into Heaven

She jettisons her body in stages. The memory of muscle
centers her remembered spine. Ribs hinge perfectly
to vertebrae. Hips lighten. When anatomy is altogether
forgotten the ground lets go, and her fear of falling is undone.

Feet, already accustomed to weightlessness, rest
at the end of her ankles. Just under, the heads of mourners
and a weeping servant's rounded back. From habit
she reaches for clothing but her hands can't grasp any more
so she does without, floats over the house awhile

then breaks into cumulonimbus like the dove
that came to her on a shaft of light
while she sat in her bedroom reading.
Was the window open or closed? She rises
easily as spirit through molecules of glass.

Another gravity takes over. Imaginary wings
craze on her shoulder blades into pin-feather
splinters. A meteor shower is seen over Asia Minor.
Pulled beyond planets named for gods, across spokes
that thin outward from what turns and turns at the center,

she becomes an extreme shade of blue, celestial bird
with a piece of sun behind its head. Galaxies disappear
into her like moths into a greater fire. She is direction;
canal. Doorway that opens the other place.

The Flight into Egypt

after W.H. Auden

The Renaissance Masters understood the body.
They knew the keys to heaven were here in the milky
white breast, the muscled limbs and chest, the clear gaze--
not in the hands of the medievalists standing
at the Gate in their solemn gowns--frozen, remote, imperious.
They excelled in curling back the tongues of judgment--
allowing the images to unfurl along
the spine and down the brow, paint pulsing onto the old walls.

In Carpaccio's *The Flight into Egypt*, for instance,
a young woman astride a donkey holds her child
as he stands on her lap, his face touching hers.
The child's father walks ahead with the donkey's reins.
Ostensibly *he* is leading them out of bondage, into Canaan,
but it is the child—reaching up to kiss his mother's face—
who bears angelic messages, who leads the way to milk and honey.

Hope

Klimt

All afternoon the painter's addressing
the riddle of flesh
in an angle of light.

Fiddly work to get it right,
now that love stands Atlas-backed
under astonishing weight.

Hope in their native tongue's this *expectancy*—
where they've lain, what lies in wait.

So much for masks, the gilded screen,
the carpet of flowers—
the instant of eros
where laundress = goddess—
a subject
made & unmade.

Harm hovers, a circle
of crones on the horizon.
Still, her glance is unabashed
& still aroused. Meeting his.
That practiced, penetrating gaze:
strokes terrible & true.

—Mistress of heaven, dust, debris . . .
If she's naked now,
what will she take off next?

Hope is one of a series of Klimt's paintings of an expectant model. Klimt was known to have exploited his models sexually as well as economically; the juxtaposition of maternal beauty and spectral imagery in the paintings conveys a terror of female eroticism.

ALICIA SUSKIN OSTRIKER

The Birth of Venus

I
Huge shell the remnant of my great-grandmother dragon,
Split open to form the world,
They have made a boat of it
And set me here.

The effect is of scarcely tolerable pleasure.

II
If I am anything I am young, so young.
As I arrive on this shallow scalloped sea
Zephyr huffs flowers at me, frowning.
The effect is to deepen my reverie.

My face emerges from another world
Behind the picture plane, a world
Of light and clouds, volumes of clouds.
The artist has set it at an impossible angle

Upon my impossibly swanlike
Neck, my impossibly sloping shoulders.

If I am anything I am unreal.

III
All this is genius: the patchy blues of sky
Filled in behind me, the sensitive penciling of the hand
With which I touch myself, contrasted with the crudely dashed
Bronze accents on foliage to my left, wings to my right,

Same gorgeous color as my hair, a wheat
That might nourish a province, and, where a shoulder's edge

Meets a pale background, traces of draughtsmanship
Reveal revision, which is a kindness, or an insolence…

Or a looseness beyond perfection.

IV
My knees together, slightly inturned…

My rosy foot, with a peasant's long capable toes…

A woman steps from the forest.
She looks Roman, a matron under orders
To wrap me in patterned cloth.
I myself am Greek and do not see her.

V
Hair uncoiling in breeze,
Oval belly, petite globular breasts,
And the great shell

Imply a categorical
Encyclopedia of curves,
A Euclidean feast.

Scallops imply an open universe
Like the bit of open sea
At the back of the canvas.

VI
I am a factory of flowers. Lilies without, roses within,
I will be loved, the hunters will shoot me,
The gardeners pluck me, I must fade, I must die
To assume an immortal order,
You must write about me. Unforgettable,
That is what I am, and I must die

To be remembered, I must reappear
As April garden plots, moist outdoor earth

Delved and planted around a hothouse, a navel.

VII
The navel, smallest of circles, at the latitude of the horizon,
Echoed by nipples.

VIII
At times I dream I am a warrior,
At times a revolutionary.
Can this account for my glazed-ceramic look,
A girl's chaste fantasy?

Between the dreams and myself lie two chasms of time.
I carry neither spear nor gun

Circle after circle, history after history.
Would you say that I am wistful, ineffably melancholy,
That I appear to ask pardon for my beauty?

IX
Now that I am here I will proliferate.
I will be poorly copied
But I will not object

(I object to nothing, I have no complaint).
For the next six centuries girls will pose like this
To represent innocence, trailing one foot.

But I am neither love nor innocence,
I am only exquisite.
Nobody is ever loved enough,

Our mothers say. I am less than skin deep,
No deeper than canvas, an undercoat
and these thin areas of gilt, sapphire, white.

X
It is one thing to gaze, from the self's jail, at things.

Another to be a thing, an entity.
Lastly, to fuse the two, be the self's self. The soul
At once all-seeing and utterly blank, meaningless

As a cloud or river.

Now look at my eyes. Be pitiless,
Use me as your mirror.

XI
Before my birth you were an animal,
Or supposed yourself one.
You lived among the pigs in mud and straw
Having forgotten almost everything

Pertaining to the gods.

Before my birth, confess it, you were savage.
Seeing me now you forsake your appetites,
Drawn by the gentle half-lit tenderness
Of my inward gaze,

Subtly indented nostrils, coral lips,
The weightless gravity of my porcelain face,
The contemplative ivory of my form, my air of trust—

XII
The limousine that dropped me on your street
Has driven away through an arch of palms.

The driver finds his eyes in the rearview mirror
Like opals, adjusts his cap, undoes his tie.

Now I have paced your narrow front walk
Glanced at the pansies, the geraniums in your yard,

Mounting the three unpainted steps of your porch

I reach the screen door of your memory:

Cease to resist,
This bed here, this belongs to me

*

And the shore onto which I am about to step

LAURIE KRUK

the children of her men

join her in tunnelling a race
to the heart of his heart. Roommates, friends, and lovers
have all come trailing these rivals. Declaring war,
both sides exchange ages and steal tricks—
the puffed adult lip,
sulking over the juice cup
when Daddy and new Girlfriend
touch outside the bedroom
("Do you love her *again*?");
the lipsticked clowning for a kiss, making him late
on his rush out the door
to pick them up from his Ex,
now gnawing on her polish.
Jealous tantrums at five
become PMS at thirty. Tensions hidden
behind too-cute gifts, crayoned portraits of orange-haired women
("Is that me?" "Nope. My real mummy, the pretty one.").
Sizing up the opposition,
now cunningly small, now boomingly tall
they fight, fiercely smiling,
for the very centre
of the Kodak moment.

* * *

yet, cut her in two:
the beloved
and the (other) mother

on the camping weekend,
strangers see only
that she touches them gently
calls their names lightly.

Like Mary, fills the gap
in the family photograph;
hands, hovering like haloes,
uncover a welcome servitude.

First morning in the tent, before they wake,
he taps her belly, says
"Still wonder when you're gonna put something here."
Calls it a joke.
She wrenches away, hipbones knifing.
It would take an act of God
–thank God–since the operation he had
to please his (now-ex) wife.

Then, five years old again,
she sees him
tenderly minister,
as he traps them in nightgowns, first night
trustingly whole-skinned.
Next evening, the older
wants to play "Show me," giggling
and shrieking and flipping up her gown.
"We don't do that, it's not nice."
And helps
the younger to pee
lifting her up, half-naked
on the trail of the campground
while she frowns, glancing at the next tent.
"It's only a kid."

Next day, she's changing for swimming;
he catches her shy stumble
stepping out of her panties. Wolf-whistles.
She snaps, "Can't have it both ways, Dad."
And runs for the water's
cool removal. Swims out until
she turns the three of them, their matching camp hats
into a painting by Monet. Or Renoir. No sticky morning communion,

no doorway declarations, sweet clichés
can compete with this:
the care
with which he will arrange their heads
heat-heavy, on the backseat,
driving home.
Or lift the younger one
up in the air
so she can pee,
free of scratches, dirt,
scary bugs. No other mother
–hurt, hungry, wondering–
can invent opportunity
to be there
for a smaller pair of feet
to leap up from.

JOY CASTRO

How We Are Made

The way we lived then wasn't much to see:
a plastic stroller, used, and given free,
pushed thirteen blocks down split concrete. I pushed
beneath the Texas sun, the streets' bleak noise,
the baby's face, though shaded, flushing rose—
those hot and dirty walks the price I paid
to put my boy down onto grass: thick grass,
still gilded silver with the sprinkler's rain,
leaves hushed and luscious to the eye and tongue—
so he could crawl, his soft, uncrafted skin
on bladed earth, flesh pressed to what's unmade
by man.
        That strip of tender, tended grass
unspooled between a high brick wall and smooth
sidewalk. Within the wall there rose a blond
brick brewery, transformed (not long before)
into an art museum. Lavish lawns
swirled all around, tricked out with painted steel,
wood, stone: a sculpture garden. We lacked
the dollars to go in. We stayed outside
the rolling lawns, the art-strewn walls. We crawled
along the strip, a spectacle for all
the passers-by, who passed, appalled. The price-
less art inside compelled its pricey fee.
The way we lived then wasn't much to see.

The Disquieting Muses

Mother, mother, what illbred aunt
Or what disfigured and unsightly
Cousin did you so unwisely keep
Unasked to my christening, that she
Sent these ladies in her stead
With heads like darning-eggs to nod
And nod and nod at foot and head
And at the left side of my crib?

Mother, who made to order stories
Of Mixie Blackshort the heroic bear,
Mother, whose witches always, always
Got baked into gingerbread, I wonder
Whether you saw them, whether you said
Words to rid me of those three ladies
Nodding by night around my bed,
Mouthless, eyeless, with stitched bald head.

In the hurricane, when father's twelve
Study windows bellied in
Like bubbles about to break, you fed
My brother and me cookies and Ovaltine
And helped the two of us to choir:
"Thor is angry: boom boom boom!
Thor is angry: we don't care!"
But those ladies broke the panes.

When on tiptoe the schoolgirls danced,
Blinking flashlights like fireflies
And singing the glowworm song, I could
Not lift a foot in the twinkle-dress
But, heavy-footed, stood aside

In the shadow cast by my dismal-headed
Godmothers, and you cried and cried:
And the shadow stretched, the lights went out.

Mother, you sent me to piano lessons
And praised my arabesques and trills
Although each teacher found my touch
Oddly wooden in spite of scales
And the hours of practicing, my ear
Tone-deaf and yes, unteachable.
I learned, I learned, I learned elsewhere,
From muses unhired by you, dear mother,

I woke one day to see you, mother,
Floating above me in bluest air
On a green balloon bright with a million
Flowers and bluebirds that never were
Never, never, found anywhere.
But the little planet bobbed away
Like a soap-bubble as you called: Come here!
And I faced my traveling companions.

Day now, night now, at head, side, feet,
They stand their vigil in gowns of stone,
Faces blank as the day I was born,
Their shadows long in the setting sun
That never brightens or goes down.
And this is the kingdom you bore me to,
Mother, mother. But no frown of mine
Will betray the company I keep.

Stillbirth Machine I

This is a solid
Grey landscape of penetration,
Of violence
In stasis,
Of having no eyes or
Eyelids, of the endless pain

of beauty

A paralyzed moment
               of motion as

hands become
 gears become
  spine become
   vanished become
    veins become
     hydraulic become
      nipples become
       machines become

knees become
 lips become
  flesh become
   wrists become
    fingers become
     needles become
      cunt become
       death become

               her

The aged infant born
Dead, its supple
Mother spread
On a bed of

afterbirth

Stillbirth Machine II

In this: flesh operates
On itself,

Installs upon its skin
All the features of Mother Earth:

Rats, teeth, knuckles, a gnawed-off
Ear, waves of worms, an engine,

And most of all, the pulverized mass
Of misshapen children panting
For her teats, waiting

To kill her in the name
Of still life. Legs raised

And open for death, a boy,
She can not remember whether
He is entering or leaving her.
She can only pray:

I have a birthing in mind.

O my creator
Grant me the gears to get the job done.

Note: "Still Birth Machine I" and "Stillbirth Machine II" were inspired by paintings of the same names by the Swiss surrealist H.R. Giger. They can be found in his Necronomicon.

MARGO BERDESHEVSKY

Fresque Transposée

d'après Sandro Botticelli's "L'Annonciation"

Like this, she seems to mime. Like this. And the mimic is so perfect that we see the infant between those empty paws, her blue drapes such that they could be holding holy ghost, already. Oh, our wish to hold something holy. World, in its caul of killing as it is. Mother.

I kneel as child to mother, help me, to this master of a metaphor, *il Signor Botticelli.* An annunciatory paint-poem, a magnificat: pregnant Mary on her long wide angled plane—on the left, the angel hovers in, its mask of such compassion to be bearer of such tiding as to stop a world—as if it knows all alpha, all omega of the story—and the arms and digits cross the levitated breast as if they would protect the same heart that must speak.

Far, far right of the canvas, across an empty space of pillar and throned bed, its single pillow, and veil, and veils, and marble floor, and space, and space—a chicken-egg-shell-blue robed Mary tilts. She wears the sheer Renaissance on her mane for veil, and isn't she the same red head as Venus in that other shell, birthing? Yes, Mary, here, nearly cradled too, in velum —enacts her coming womb, its story.

She folds, half kneel and half a stance more Quan Yin—leaning in this one's gown—her head, her torso to her right, while her hands edge left—and they are empty, notably empty. Are miming their position that may, that will, that must hold the child. What would I change, in any story?

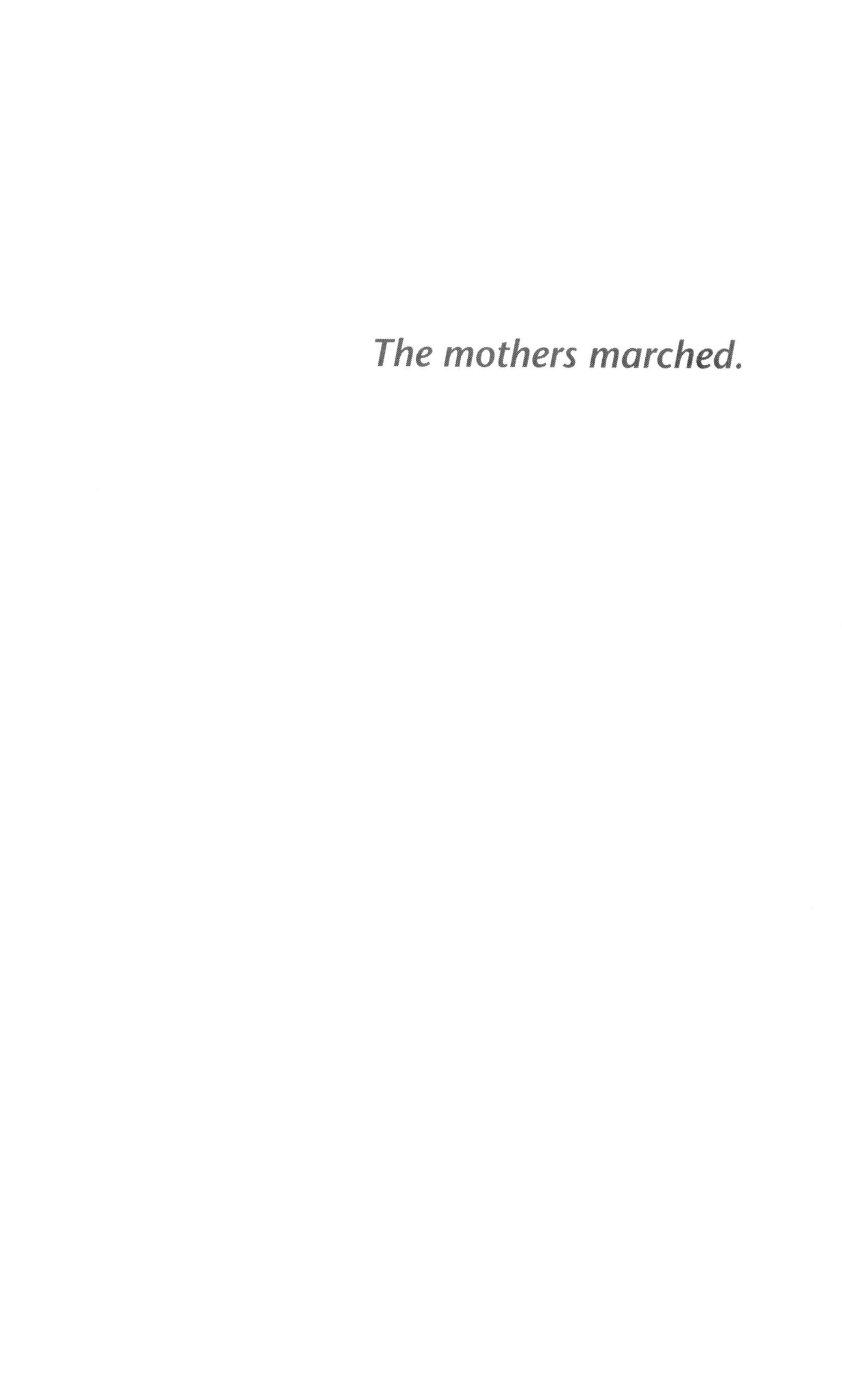

The mothers marched.

SINA QUEYRAS

from "On the Scent"

The mothers were feminists. The mothers marched. The mothers wore purple and read Betty Friedan. The mothers listened to Janis Ian and Ferron. The mothers dropped out. The mothers went to Michigan and danced topless. The mothers used menstruation cups. The mothers tie-dyed everything and cooked meals from *Moosewood*. The mothers had committee meetings. The mothers subscribed to *Ms.* and believed in affirmative action. The mothers wore Birkenstocks and dreamed of living in Vermont or Saltspring. The mothers ate dried fruit and brown rice. The mothers lived in the suburbs and shopped. They fought to build credit ratings. The mothers wore sweat sets. The mothers knew nothing of feminism. The mothers ran off to Los Angeles. The mothers liked to sunbathe. The mothers discovered Paxil and Prozac. The mothers went to Holt's; they discussed Bloomingdale's and Saks. The mothers listened to Neil Diamond and sewed skirts. The mothers had sharp tongues. The mothers went to the opera. The mothers had good educations. The mothers had nothing to say. The mothers voted for Reagan or Mulroney. The mothers read *Newsweek* and *Cosmo*. The mothers read Alice Walker. The mothers held down two jobs, raised children and continued to believe. The mothers moved forward, hesitant, never sure what they had won, or what had merely yet to be revealed.

Birthright

Begin with white sheets
flapping amiably in the early breeze,
the heavens dawning biblical blue
and my mother teaching me to believe
in the goodness of mankind
but to trust no man.

Then, continue unfolding her story
until, naturally, it lives
to create shade around my heart.

Now, look at me. What I need to tell you
is this: When the only man I know,
my father, knocks, I'll lock him out.

. . .

At the dining room table,
picking chicken bits from a wishbone,
I hear my father's call. Once. Twice.

But nakedness is my identity
and fear, the red yes of my existence.

This was not what I asked for—
the man's face, which is my face, shut out.

. . .

I dream I visit my own grave
but am not dead. I lie there uncovered,
my face, the image of my father's.

I turn away from my body, his.

. . .

Still, it seems he needs me,
and as my face turns away, my hand
reaches out. It can.

Why doesn't it?

Repeatedly, I ask my mother why
I feel naked in familiar places.

She wonders what I fear
that she does not already fear.

. . .

At home father plays solitare
until all his cards face up.
At the bus stop mother and I wait.
A man jogs across the street
in the oily dusk. Grabbing my arm, she runs.

We pace in the falling darkness. The nakedness
of her, my own nakedness.

. . .

And again in the house, mother says,
Dear, look at you.
You've never looked worse.

Who she sees, the girl facing me
in the bathroom mirror, replies:

The way I look mirrors my father.
I am everywhere in the faces of black men.
Imagine the concern I feel for myself.

NATASHA TRETHEWEY

My Mother Dreams Another Country

Already the words are changing. She is changing
from *colored* to *negro*, *black* still years ahead.
This is 1966—she is married to a white man—
and there are more names for what grows inside her.
It is enough to worry about words like *mongrel*
and the infertility of mules and *mulattoes*
while flipping through a book of baby names.
She has come home to wait out the long months,
her room unchanged since she's been gone:
dolls winking down from every shelf—all of them
white. Every day she is flanked by the rituals of superstition,
and there is a name she will learn for this too:
maternal impression—the shape, like an unknown
country, marking the back of the newborn's thigh.
For now, women tell her to clear her head, to steady her hands
or she'll gray a lock of the child's hair wherever
she worries her own, imprint somewhere the outline
of a thing she craves too much. They tell her
to stanch her cravings by eating dirt. All spring
she has sat on her hands, her fingers numb. For a while
each day, she can't feel anything she touches: the arbor
out back—the landscape's green tangle; the molehill
of her own swelling. Here—outside the city limits—
cars speed by, clouds of red dust in their wake.
She breathes it in—Mississippi—then drifts toward sleep,
thinking of someplace she's never been. Late,
Mississippi is a dark backdrop bearing down
on the windows of her room. On the TV in the corner,
the station signs off, broadcasting its nightly salutation:
the waving Stars and Stripes, our national anthem.

The Child Taken from the Mother

I could do nothing. Nothing. Do you
understand? Women ask: *Why didn't you—?*
like they do of women who've been raped.
And I ask myself: Why didn't I? Why
didn't I run away with them? Or face
him in court? Or—

Ten years ago I
answered myself: No way for children to live.
Or: The chance of absolute loss. Or:

I did the best I could. It was not
enough. It was about terror and power.
I did everything I could. Not enough.

This is the voice of the guilty mother.

Clumsy with anger even now, it is a voice
from the woman shoved outside, one night, as words
clack into place like bricks, poker chips.

A man mutters: *It's a card game. Too*
candid. They know what's in your hand.
I look down. My hands dangle open and empty
in the harsh yellow light. Strange men,
familiar, laugh and curse in the kitchen, whiskey,
bending over cards. Or is it something held down
on the table? Someone says: *Bull Dog Bend.*
Someone says: *The place of the father in the home.*

A woman's voice: *Those women who've never held*
a little baby in their arms. In the old window,
a shadow. Two hands, brick and mortar, seal
the house, my children somewhere inside. The youngest
has lost his baby fat, navel flattened, last
of my stomach's nourishing.

You say: *Do something.*
You say: *Why is this happening?*

My body. My womb.
My body of a woman, a mother, a lesbian.

And here,
perhaps, you say: *That last word doesn't belong.*
Woman, mother: those can stay. Lesbian: no.
Put that outside the place of the poem. Too
slangy, prosy, obvious, just doesn't belong.
Why don't you—? Why didn't you—? Can't you
say it some other way?

The beautiful place
we stood arguing, after the movie, under blue-white
fluorescence. Two middle-aged women in jeans,
two grown boys, the lanky one, the tactful one,
bundled in a pause before cold outside, to argue
the significances: bloody birth, the man cursing
a woman in the kitchen, dirt, prayer, the place
of the father, the master, the beatings, black and
white, home lost, continents, two women
lovers glimpsed, the child taken from the mother
who returns.

No one says: This is about us. But
in the narrow corridor, stark cement block walls,
we become huge, holding up the harsh images,

the four of us loud, familiar.

                                                            Other movie-
goers squeeze past, light their cigarettes,
glance, do not say even to themselves: Children
and women, lovers, mothers, lesbians.   Yes.

Declared Not Fit

In this month of grief I am crying for my lover.
Suddenly my children appear under my closed eyelids
inside my grief, as if in a pitch-dark room,
vision: apparitions heavy with distance, absence.

I think: This is how you see your past just
before you die.

My eyes were the rearview mirror
years ago. The boys were small and round, waving
good-bye. Their eyes were the young eyes of children
looking at their mother, that she will explain.

What were the reasons? Power of a man over
a woman, his children: his hand on power he laced,
that my womb had made children as the eye makes a look.

What were the reasons? Terror of a man left alone,
the terror at a gesture: my hand sliding from her
soft pulse neck, to jawbone, chin, mouth met,
mouth of sharp salt. We walked the barrier island,
us, the two boys, the skittering orange crabs,
public deserted beach. In front of the children.

The danger: eyes taught not to cringe away,
the power of their eyes drawn to our joined hands.

Filthy, unfit, not to touch:
those from my womb,
red birthslime, come by my cry of agony and pleasure.

Hands smeared often enough with their shit, vomit,

blackness of dirt and new blood, but water from my hands,
and in them, weight of their new bodies come back to rest.

When behind the closed eyelid of a door, in the heavy bed,
sweaty, salty, frantic and calling out sublimely
another woman's name, hands unclenched, I brought down
a cry of joy, then my mouth, mind, hands became
not fit to touch.

The work is the same.

What are the reasons?   I told them these.
They were young, they did not understand.
Nor do I.   Words heard in the ear, hollow room.
The eye waits, sad, unsatisfied,
to embrace the particular loved shape.
Eyes, empty   hands, empty   waiting.

JUDITH ARCANA

Felony Booking, Women's Lockup, 11th and State: A Short Literary Epic

None of us had been in jail before: middle and working
class women with education, fresh as daffodils;
we were all students, housewives, mommies
casual potsmokers, rudimentary feminists
and here's the thing, citizens: criminal abortionists
charged with several counts (Monte Cristo,
Dracula): all felonies, nothing small.

Compounded by conspiracy: *collaborators*
like in black&white movies about Nazis
where they shave the heads of women who fuck
the enemy. But, citizens, here's the thing you need
to know: when it's illegal, abortion's homicide.
It must be different now (things get different
in thirty-five years) but then, the guard held your hand.

She wasn't rough but she was tough, that Dawn:
she left us rosy-fingered, first left, then right, each
finger and thumb in a labeled box on special paper;
rolling the tips, steady for clear prints, she put
each one down in place, rocked it side to side
like shaping dumplings: pierogi, ravioli.
Both hands done, she picked up a flat wooden stick.

I thought: oh, she's going to put it on my tongue,
look down my throat – but she dipped it into a jar
of yellow-white slime, dropped a smear onto
my hands, looked into my eyes and said, *Clean 'em off.*
I thought it was but knew it couldn't be mayonnaise.
She gave me a grey paper towel, already turning
to the next woman, reaching for her hands.

The next guard: big woman with metalgrey hair.
She'd seen it before, knew why we were there:
seven white women in jeans and t-shirts,
mine tight over breasts aching long past time.
Our guide to the cells, she looked right in my face,
her own unmoving when she said *Come on,*
I'll put you in with your partner.

Our cell had no bars. Walls and doors were dark
metal sheets, ceiling a steel grate, heavy wood plank
along one wall, gritty sink and toilet small
as toys: Barbie's Cell. Dank wind swirled across
the floor, pooling on the grey concrete like water.
Women screamed all night: no words, only screams.
That was the third place we were taken.

The second was a cage: the holding pen. There we met
two women arrested for smashing a window, stealing
a tv set. One was tiny, all dressed up: heels, nylons, lipstick.
One was fifteen, five months pregnant, scars on her arms
she'd burned with cigarettes. Black thread stitches
embroidered the wrist she cut last week. We knew
that soon, too soon, darkness would cover her eyes.

The first place was Cottage Grove: sounds like little
houses in the greenwood (seven Gretels) if you're not
from Chicago. Handcuffed inside the wagon
locked clanking to a hook atop the broad van door,
twisting my body on the icy metal bench, arms
stretched up high, wrist welts rising red and classic
(Prisoner of Chillon, Man in the Iron Mask).

At the station, cuffed to an iron ring on the wall
of an office (chair, desk, cabinets, phone, calendar,
chains) for interrogation. I needed the bathroom.
Some of that time my memory says I was free, says we
were seven women standing, arms linked at the shoulder
(a chorus line of innocent ignorant felons smiling

for photographs): could that have happened?

I've seen mug shots: dark long wavy hair caught up
at the back of my head, work-ready. In profile I'm
pigeon-chested: Nursing Mother Arrested for Abortion
is the caption. I look like my stout old aunts, their fronts
the porches of bungalows. Mine is swollen hard with milk:
eighteen hours since I nursed the baby, sailed out across
the wine-dark sea, committed multiple felonies, got busted.

Locked up, I freed my breasts from their container:
a nursing bra built like the Golden Gate Bridge.
I squeezed them soft like a lover, milked them hard
like a farmer, sprayed my baby's own sweet nectar
down that dirty little sink. Then lawyer boys took me
out to night court in the basement, away from the women,
saying *strategy*: I was a wooden horse, a night mare.

Inside of me six more were riding; I was precedent:
low bail for madonna meant the same for all: a bet
with me the marker. Citizens, here's the thing: that judge
smiled right at me, called me Mrs, asked about my health.
Believe it: he smiled, said he'd send me right on home
to feed my little baby. He struck his own desk twice
with a wooden hammer: *Let it be written. Let it be done.*

Unknown Girl in the Maternity Ward

Child, the current of your breath is six days long.
You lie, a small knuckle on my white bed;
lie, fisted like a snail, so small and strong
at my breast. Your lips are animals; you are fed
with love. At first hunger is not wrong.
The nurses nod their caps; you are shepherded
down starch halls with the other unnested throng
in wheeling baskets. You tip like a cup; your head
moving to my touch. You sense the way we belong.
But this is an institution bed.
You will not know me very long.

The doctors are enamel. They want to know
the facts. They guess about the man who left me,
some pendulum soul, going the way men go
and leave you full of child. But our case history
stays blank. All I did was let you grow.
Now we are here for all the ward to see.
They thought I was strange, although
I never spoke a word. I burst empty
of you, letting you learn how the air is so.
The doctors chart the riddle they ask of me
and I turn my head away. I do not know.

Yours is the only face I recognize.
Bone at my bone, you drink my answers in.
Six times a day I prize
your need, the animals of your lips, your skin
growing warm and plump. I see your eyes
lifting their tents. They are blue stones, they begin
to outgrow their moss. You blink in surprise
and I wonder what you can see, my funny kin,

as you trouble my silence. I am a shelter of lies.
Should I learn to speak again, or hopeless in'
such sanity will I touch some face I recognize?

Down the hall the baskets start back. My arms
fit you like a sleeve, they hold
catkins of your willows, the wild bee farms
of your nerves, each muscle and fold
of your first days. Your old man's face disarms
the nurses. But the doctors return to scold
me. I speak. It is you my silence harms.
I should have known; I should have told
them something to write down. My voice alarms
my throat. "Name of father—none." I hold
you and name you bastard in my arms.

And now that's that. There is nothing more
that I can say or lose.
Others have traded life before
and could not speak. I tighten to refuse
your owling eyes, my fragile visitor.
I touch your cheeks, like flowers. You bruise
against me. We unlearn. I am a shore
rocking you off. You break from me. I choose
your only way, my small inheritor
and hand you off, trembling the selves we lose.
Go child, who is my sin and nothing more.

Baby Carriages

In the photograph there are two of them, and a stroller.
The women sit on a bench, wearing their usual day clothes,
That thin stooped one wears a flowered rayon dress,

This one has dark lipstick on, a third is older and has a perm.
The women look relaxed, like people who have known each other forever.
Later they'll feed their babies, then do the laundry or go shopping.

I don't see the babies but I feel their presence
Like invisible magnets that keep the photograph from falling apart,
The animal premise of the whole image.

Behind the bench is a strip of garden and a brick wall
The shadowless sun is bathing. The carriages themselves are funny,
High off the ground and shaped and lacquered like the coaches of royalty.

The date of the photograph is 1942. Wartime, the home front,
It makes sense, I stand in front of it on the museum wall
For a long time, thinking: Here's the real story. If only.

Hannah's Child

would have been precocious
female of course
chattering away in German & English
before she let go of Hannah's desktop
to try walking

would have learned to scribble
quietly
while Mamala worked
filling papers with the dizzying marks
that fenced out a distance

loved
of course she would have been
a child of the republic
a light ahead of the dark times behind
more at ease with adults
whispering to her teddy
about Aunt Mary's blueberry pancakes

until she begged again
to hear the story of the Holocaust
a family album of never forget
this page Buba Martha

sounding strict
turn over to someone named Walter Benjamin
the sad pallor of suicide
in the tone of voice
a puzzle
when she pointed to a framed picture
of Uncle Martin on the desk

& in the way that children can
imaged a second picture there
in her mother's measured reply
black & shadowy like a silhouette

**Aunt Mary is Mary McCarthy*
Uncle Martin is Martin Heidegger
Buba Martha is Martha Arendt, Hannah Arendt's mother

GARY YOUNG

from *No Other Life*

My mother entertained the troops in Vietnam. When she came back, she handed me the photograph of a soldier, and said, he was killed sneaking into camp the night I sang. You may not believe this, she said, but I've never felt as safe as I did while I was there. The Vietnamese soldier in the photograph is hanging by his wrists. A curtain of blood fans out from his neck. His hands are swollen; he was still alive when they strung him up with wire. My mother said, those boys couldn't do enough for me; they treated me like a queen in Vietnam. I still have a picture of the one who gave her his life.

C. D. WRIGHT

King's Daughters, Home for Unwed Mothers, 1948

Somewhere there figures a man. In uniform. He's not white. He
could be AWOL. Sitting on a mattress riddled with cigarette burns.
Night of a big game in the capital. Big snow.
Beyond Pearl River past Petal and Leaf River and Macedonia;
it is a three-storied house. The only hill around. White.
The house and hill are white. Lighted upstairs, down.
She is up on her elbows, bangs wet in her eyes. The head
of the unborn is visible at the opening. The head
crowns. Many helping hands are on her. She is told not to push.
But breathe. A firm voice. With helping hands.
They open the howl of her love. Out of her issues:

Volumes of letters, morning glories on a string trellis, the job at the
Maybelline factory, the job at the weapons plant, the hummingbird
hive, her hollyhocks, her grandmother's rigid back next to her
grandfather's bow, the briefest reflection of her mother's braid,
her atomizers and silver-backed brush and comb, the steel balls
under father's knuckles, the moon's punched-out face,
his two-dollar neckties, the peacock coming down the drive; there was
the boy shuffling her way with the melon on his shoulder, car dust all
over his light clothes, the Black Cat fireworks sign on the barn, her
father's death from moving the barn by himself, the family sitting in the
darkened room drinking ice tea after the funeral, tires blown out on the
macadam, the women beaten like eggs, the store with foundation
garments, and boys pelting the girls with peony buds, the meatgrinder
cringing in the corner store, the old icebox she couldn't fix and
couldn't sell so buried to keep out the kids, her grandmother's pride, the
prettiest lavaliere, the pole houses; there was the boy with the melon
shifted to the other shoulder, coming her way, grown taller and darker,
wiping his sweat with his hand, his beautiful Nubian head, older and set
upon by the longingly necked girls from the bottoms, his fishing hole,
learning the equations of equality: six for the white man and none for

the rest; the sloping shadows and blue hollows behind his shack, what
the sunflowers saw, the wide skirts she wore, the lizards they caught, the
eagerness with which they went through each other's folds of hair and
skin, the boy's outnumbered pride…

This couldn't go on, the difficulty of concealment, putting makeup
over a passion mark. 1947, summer of whiskey and victory and
fear. It was long, then over. The letters burned. She heaves. Bleeds.
The infant's head is huge. She tears. He's white. He'll make it
just fine. The firm voice. The hands that helped.
What would become of this boychild. The uniformed man and she
will never know. That they will outlive him. They will never know.
Whether he will do things they never dreamed.

CAROLYN FORCHÉ

from *The Angel of History*

There are times when the child seems delicate, as if he had not yet crossed into the world.
When French was the secret music of the street, the café, the train, my own
    receded and became intimacy and sleep.
In the world it was the language of propaganda, the agreed-upon lie, and it bound me to
    itself, demanding of my life an explanation.
When my son was born I became mortal.

Our days at Cape Enrage, a bleached shack of rented rooms and white air. April.
At the low tide acres of light, boats abandoned by water.
While sleeping, the child vanishes from his life.

Years later, on the boat from Beirut, or before the boat, an hour before, helicopters lifting
    a white veil of sea.
A woman broken into many women.

These boats, forgotten, have no keels. So it is safe for them, and the emptiness beneath
  them safe.
April was here briefly. The breakwater visible, the lighthouse, but no horizon.
The music resembled April, the gulls, April, but you weren't walking toward this house.
If the child knew words, if it weren't necessary for him to question me with his hands—
To have known returning would be like this,
    that the sea light of April had been your vigilance.

Mother Hair

My hair, black now, was Achilles hair
When I was a child.
Or maybe Mamluk, maybe Crusader blood,

Though Napoleon could only throw
His hat at the walls of Acre—
Or maybe the ischemic morning

I rode the school bus
Heading for the desert on a field trip—
It doesn't matter. My mother intuited loss

And stroked my head before I waved goodbye.
In the desert
I ate the figs my father had left

By my shoes the night before.
In the desert
Camels are ships

Parting asphalt, and the school bus
Smashed into them and killed
So many children aboard.

When the bus returned
Mothers filled the schoolyard
With wailing,

Smacking their cheeks,
Pulling their hair,
Counting their children.

But there were none missing.
It was only rumor. There was only
Nightfall and my mother, ready,

Wearing black, my hair now,
Maybe Canaanite or Bedouin,
Maybe Fatemah or Zainab.

GARY YOUNG

from *No Other Life*

My mother was a beautiful woman. She had been a beautiful child. She danced for the soldiers, then, and sang for them, and everyone clapped and cheered. When her period came, she thought she was dying. Her face broke out, and her mother screamed, how could you do this? How will we live? Who will love you now? Years later, my mother turned to me. I was twelve. We'd stopped to rest in a little town. She put her hands on my cheeks. Let me get that, she said, and she dug her nails into me, picking until I bled. That's how it starts, she said, and it wasn't the shock or the pain, it was the look on her face that made me want to cry.

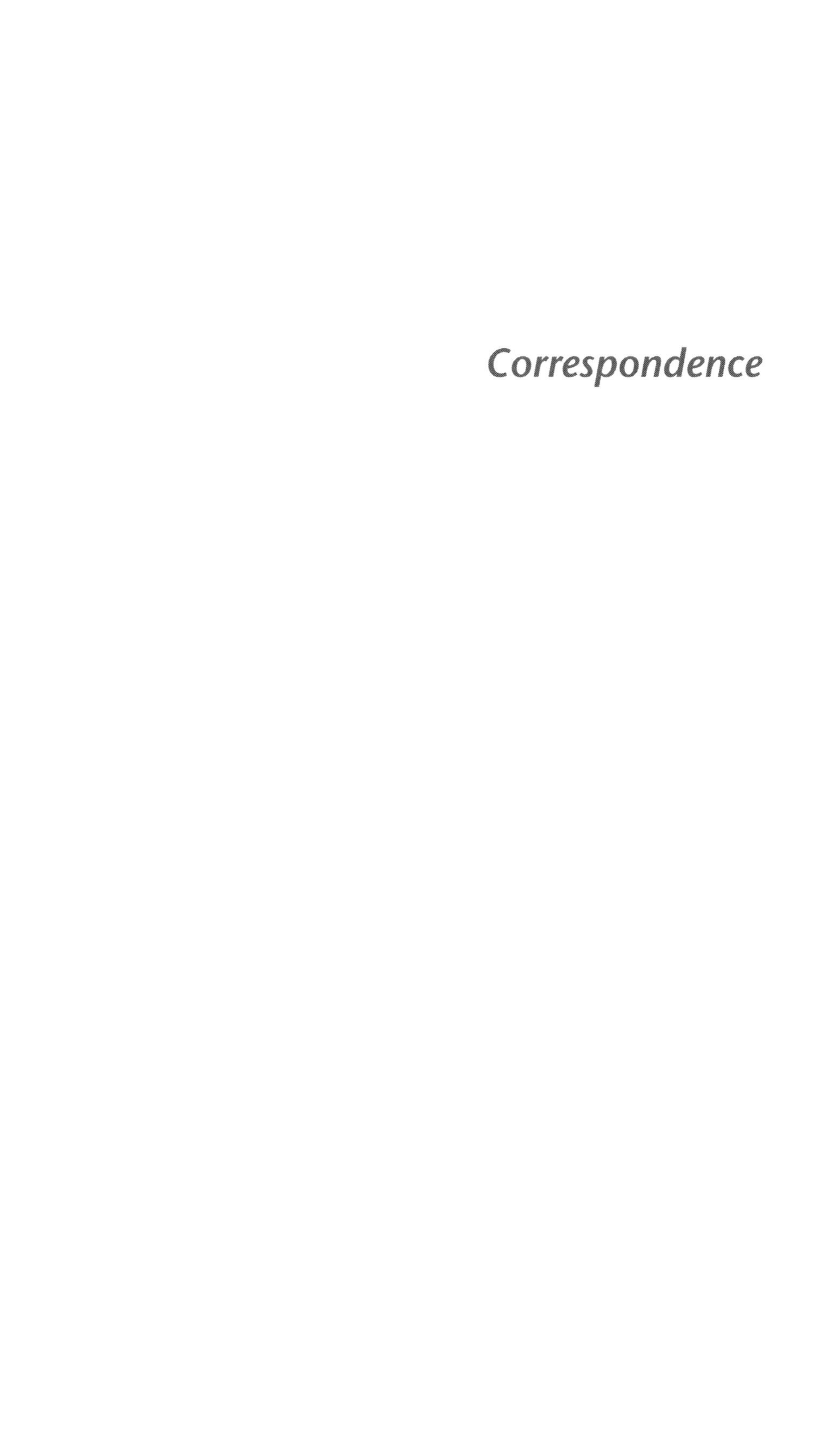

Correspondence

JUDITH H. MONTGOMERY

Correspondence: to a Never-Girl

Dear Not-Daughter: How could you spurn me?—
whip your tail less frantic than your brothers
jousting boisterous up the corridor
to pitch woo in the diamond of my womb?

For you, I would have gemmed my egg
in Fabergé, released the corsets
of the cervix, and wrapped you in a fond
fallopian embrace, cradled in pink dark.

I knit caps of down to shield your fontanelle—
you cast off in a spray of osprey feathers.
Daughter, do you wander me, aswim in vein
or artery? In possibility. Do you ripple

at my rib or wing my breath?—my Icara
off-course and falling, almost fertile, in me.

*

But—*Mother-Waiting*—You sigh: I'm blown
rib to rib—answer, hummingbird to heel,
leaf to breath. Your longing melts the wax
that wings me. Jams my radar blind. I'm

not daughter. Not dawdler. But called to read
your body's book: to set plumbline to spine,
to round the syllables of ball-and-socket.
You my home-school, I your pupil-star.

Curie. Curator. And ready medic, mother:
Nightingale with bandage to your bone.

You'd call me to release my rounds,
bend to birth—would you relinquish flight

for flesh? for me? Here find no *Never-Girl,*
but Icara, guardian flychild. Let me be.

MINNIE BRUCE PRATT

Poem for My Sons

When you were born, all the poets I knew
were men, dads eloquent on their sleeping
babes and the future: Coleridge at midnight,
Yeats' prayer that his daughter lack opinions,
his son be high and mighty, think and act.
You've read the new father's loud eloquence,
fiery sparks written in a silent house
breathing with the mother's exhausted sleep.

When you were born, my first, what I thought was
milk: my breasts sore, engorged, but not enough
when you woke. With you, my youngest, I did not
think: my head unraised for three days, mind-dead
from waist-down anesthetic labor, saddle
block, no walking either.
                                        Your father was then
the poet I'd ceased to be when I got married.
It's taken me years to write this to you.

I had to make a future, wilful, voluble,
lascivious, a thinker, a long walker,
unstruck transgressor, furious, shouting,
voluptuous, a lover, a smeller of blood,
milk, a woman mean as she can be some nights,
existence I could pray to, capable of
poetry.
          Now here we are. You are men,
and I am not the woman who rocked you
in the sweet reek of penicillin, sour milk,
the girl who could not imagine herself
or a future more than a warm walled room,
had no words but the pap of the expected,

and so, those nights, could not wish for you.

But now I have spoken, my self, I can ask
for you: that you'll know evil when you smell it;
that you'll know good and do it, and see how both
run loose through your lives; that then you'll remember
you come from dirt and history; that you'll choose
memory, not anesthesia; that you'll have work
you love, hindering no one, a path crossing
at boundary markers where you question power;
that your loves will match you thought for thought
in the long heat of blood and fact of bone.

Words not so romantic nor so grandly tossed
as if I'd summoned the universe to be
at your disposal.
                    I can only pray:

That you'll never ask for the weather, earth,
angels, women, or other lives to obey you;

that you'll remember me, who crossed, recrossed
you,
    as a woman making slowly toward
an unknown place where you could be with me,
like a woman on foot, in a long stepping out.

DI BRANDT

from *Heart*

And that was your mother that night,
on the dark water of Lake Winnipeg,
come, she beckoned, come, in the silver
moon's wake, and you and I dazzled
by her light and her shadowy siren song,
and you, braver and more desirous
than I, swung out onto the diamond
studded waves to greet her, and I
pulled you back onto sand, stony
arguments of earth and grass and trees,
I meant to say, but you had tasted sky,
and knew the delicate armies of the air
could enfold you against cradled
knife wounds and abandoning, and why,
you thought, and so did I, that night,
should we linger when she aches
for us too, her spirit arms lighting up
the lake, her song rippling the dark
water, the wind whispering in the reeds
behind us myriad promises

Don't

1979. Driving down Ocean Boulevard
the old fotingo sticking to my bare thighs
the smell of patchouli and a beaded necklace
wrapped twice around my mother's neck
                                        don't

say I didn't warn you not to touch it, lace so fine
it melts under your fingertips like sugar, and if you wanted
a taste I would have given it to you, I would have
lent you my big red shoes to wear around the house as long as
you promise to be careful, promise not to trip downstairs, and
                                                    don't

laugh at other people, not even at the old ones, who do you think
you are, to wear such grown-up hairstyles, and what is that around
your mouth, what have you been eating chocolate, have you been
saying things about me to your aunts, well let me tell you
                                                      don't

even begin to think they love you like I do, no not even
in the pool with your cousins, remember to be polite, especially
with the little ones, and wait your turn on the slide, if I see you
pushing anyone I'll say I'm sick and we'll go home and if you
                                                    don't

cry like a baby we might come back next week, I'll teach you
how to swim in the big pool, I'll hold you by the stomach like we
practiced in the bathtub, and you can move your arms and legs until
you feel like you're floating, and then I'll let you go if you want me to
and if you
        don't

then we'll just pretend it's me, okay, and I'll give you a taste
of my beer, if you promise not to tell anyone, especially your father,
he might be coming with us next week, we'll see what happens, put
something on the radio, like the song says, love is in the air, so
don't

change stations like that so fast, all you can hear is squealing and
static, did you remember to bring the towels and a change of clothes
what is that you have there, I told you not to bring any dolls, nothing
you would be sad to lose, that's the thing about the beach, it's not
what you bring so much that matters, it's what you
don't.

Thinking of My Parisian Mother's Discretion (Only Her Confessor Knows) in Not Telling Her Sister or Hardly Anyone About My Birth

Don't nobody know about us, Mama,
excepting everybody in Central Ohio
and south. Even your plain French
name is anagrammed in print and
your letters quoted from.

Daddy's work for God has been told
straight out in Gambier, Granville,
Westerville to the folks who listen
in the audience. I've gone on to

explain he was a man of the cloth
and paid to keep a confidence.
Shooting off my mouth? Poetry's how
I keep my time from splintering

apart. Secrets, Mama. What's the point?
As long as you don't know I've made you
into literature and Daddy into a man
who fusses on the stage, unsnaps his collar,
lets fall his robe beside the bed where

a woman lies down. That's you, Mama,
ready to enjoy yourself. The play's set
in the Fall and I watch its pages turn
in a long run of words I try to rake
into piles of burning.

I don't want to be buried in church lore
or dead to the child who poked
out its head between my legs.
Shoot, Mama, is that too
much to understand? They all cheered me
in Cincinnati and Steubenville.

One Poem from "Early Childhood"

I write Mother
and an old woman rises in the uncertainty of evening
slips into a wedding dress
stands on tiptoe on her windowsill
calls out to the hostile city
addresses the haughty tribe of streetlights
bares her chest to the clocks
shows them the precise site of her sorrow
disrobes gently for fear of creasing her wrinkles
and unsettling the air

My mother had her own way of undressing
as one would strip the medals from a disgraced general

A cold odor is in my mother's pockets
and three pebbles to break summer's windows
my mother's dress has drunk all November's snow
dead birds' cries have ripped holes in her hem

She chases them from her unconscious arms
insults them with the muteness of words
and the absence of echoes
within her walls knocked over
from within

It sometimes happens that despite the air's vigilance my mother gets up
arms herself with a spade
turns over great shovels full of the earth which cover her
arousing the anger of taciturn neighbors who've turned their backs on the clocks
and broken off all correspondence with the grass
her chilled puffing and panting breaks through the soil down to that room

where, for lack of sun, she makes her knees shine and her tears sparkle.

My mother who recalled a blurred-over death
said that the light was stubborn
and embarrassed the crowd which turned its back on her

on the dim landing where voices bustled
her body plunged in grief separated itself from the bedding
the creaking of the floorboards revealed the movements of floor-buffing angels
tedious preparations for someone who barked as she chased her own breath
a sympathetic hand flung a stone at her across a sob

My mother had paired her basil with the forest oak
inviting it Easter after Easter to share the lamb's grass and bleating
and to verify against its height if we had grown along with the lamp
which pushed the sun back behind the hedges
when maternal fingers tucked up a lock of wavy hair

The shutters looked regretful
when my mother read the cards for the night
the king of hearts atop the ten of diamonds
meant moving
the jack of clubs who was afraid of dying
kept his distance from the queen of spades
whom he knew only by her profile

The house was on the edge of the road as if on the edge of tears
its windows ready to burst into sobs.

Translation by Marilyn Hacker

Dear Mama (2)

she say that's what
mama's for

you don't know or maybe you do
time you couldn't buy us shoes and asked grandpa
for money. he sent you one dollar
i remember your eyes scanning the letter. the tears
you got us shoes somehow by the good grace of a friend
maybe you are hip in your old-fashioned oklahoma cornspun way

or the time we sat in the dark with no electricity
eating peaches and cold toast
wondering whether you'd gone to get the money
for light

grandma named you lewana. it sounds Hawaiian
not that bastard mix of white black and red you are
not that bitter cast of negro staged to play to
rowdy crowds on the off broadway of American poor

and she added mae—to make it sound *country*
like jemima or butterfly mc queen or bobbi jo
it's you. and you named us and fed us and
i can't love you enuff for it

you don't know or maybe you do
it hurts being a grown working black woman
branded strong
hurts being unable to get over

in this filthy white world
hurts to ask your parents for help
hurts to swallow those old beaten borrowed green backs
whole
hurts to know
it'll hurt worse if you don't

Permutations

Mother, I am ashamed of my love, and think
I will get around to loving a hell of a lot when
I am about to leave it, or I have no love; the man
who came to see me every day of my life took it away.
He had big eyes and promised everything and had the
world tied to his back like a dead ostrich. Mother, I
am trying to make up for things. And it doesn't begin
with naming blades of grass, or the woman beside me;
it is too late for anything but forgiveness and after
that, atonement, and after that lying down like a child
and hoping to be a lighthouse, or a bonfire for
friends, or a piece of bread in the mouth of the lowliest
man in the world. Mother, I have kissed the
shadows of the most evil men that ever lived. They had
not even heard of you. They were about to be born.
I am those men, and I come back to you, and you will
have to outshine every dawn that ever blasted lovers' eyes.
This is your obligation and your failure as a human thing.
The world has failed to love me, and now I return like
a wheel with razored edge. My imagination has caught fire,
and my clothes are burning. I would jump into a river
where five planets baptize me. Everything has begun to knit
sweaters for winter. I am alone in my skin. My imagination
is burning, and my skin is ice-cold. The whiteness of your
skin, mother. Let that be a lesson to me, that I may meet
god with a grin, and a starving heart.

ROSEMARY SULLIVAN

Letter to My Daughter

Last night I dream a funeral.
Mine. Only you were there.
Your upturned face.
My hand flung out;
your touch broken.
Such a bitter parting.
I fear for my life now;
I must find words to help you.

You are too young to know
the chilled spaces
a man and woman can live in.
I loved your father
at first
but the damage was so far back –
not to be dug out –
a man falling
into the hole of himself.

He flailed
when the world shifted an inch
from his grasp,
when I shifted, needing myself.

He hid behind his mask
and never saw its fasteners.
The world permits that
in a man. I saw the child
looking through clouded pupils.

We are all hurt
but some of us kill.

I can't explain this.

I don't say easily I forgive him
or the world –
Could I have fled my life?
I needed you.
You are in danger.

I watched you walking in woods
behind the house so desolate,
turning the bruised leaves up.
My heart in my throat.
You came innocent
not knowing what you entered.

I lost your brother;
I can't bear to lose you.
Don't trust him.
I always knew the rage
loose in the house
would yield to this conclusion.
There is nothing now to stop him.
I know it hurts. I'm sorry.
We are hand-in-hand in terror.
You must save yourself
for me. I love you.
Will you understand this?

Blood Mother

for my adopted daughter

Was it learned, and did I teach it to you:
to love to eat meat raw, right off
the butcher's bloody paper? (What was it
learned in a Lilith-life you taught me
this morning, climbing past my face to get
between me and Daddy in our bed,
in one fast flash of female smell?)

And if we shared each other's blood,
would we have taught each other other
things? This keeps seeping through the mind's
membranes: if I were your blood mother
you might have learned just one thing—
perfectly—how to feed the bloodiest mouth,
skewered on the doctor's shiny fork.

Dearest Rachel

Last night you had a dream. It was my funeral.
You were reading my eulogy. You spoke of my
perpetual claim that any day was a good day to die.

There is nothing definitive to be said of the dead.
But I have some requests for your future script, my darling.

Tell those who are gathered that I have loved
and I have been beloved.

You do not need to speak of virtue or morals. You may
say I endured suffering but I believed
my bruises to be pale beside the wounds of history.

Tell them I loved my companions most of all.
You have been one of them who gave me
a better way to journey alone.

Spread my ashes in the waters of the bay I have loved,
for there, on the wings of cranes, in the embrace of the delta
and its wetlands, it is always morning.

P.S.

You may have:
my black dress
my red shoes
my pearls
my hats and suitcases
my inks and manuscripts.
Make of these things a breathing archive.
Write yourself into every century.
Find me again and again as one with whom
faith could be kept.

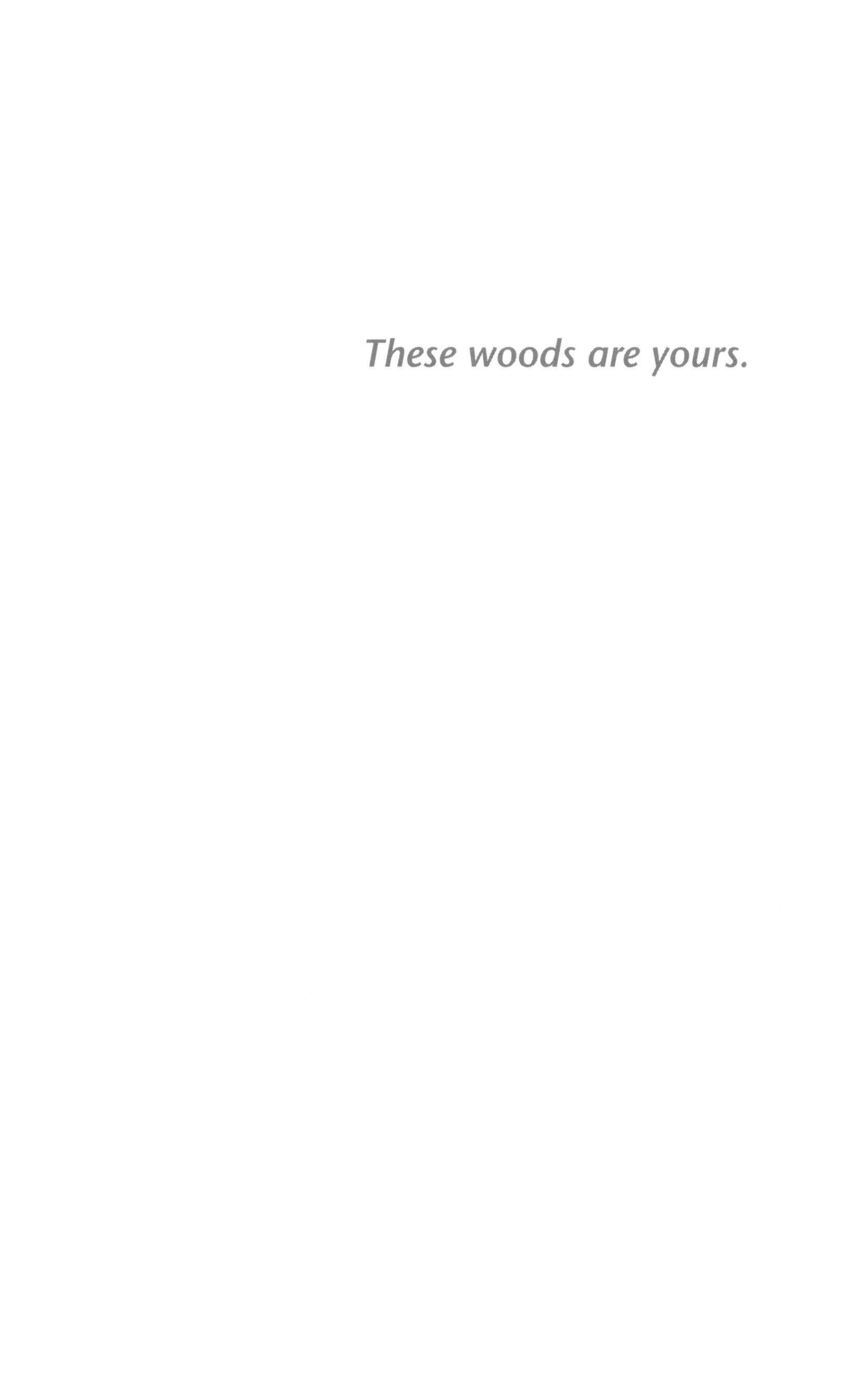

These woods are yours.

To a Daughter in Her Twentieth Year

Whose woods these are I think I know.
  These are your woods. They are not mine at all.
These woods of yours have nothing to do
  with me, your mother. They are a green wall
you have walked into, or passed through.
  They are your own green world. Within, you fall
and rise and fall again, you go
  crashing through bracken, and I hear you call,
I hear you like a panicked doe
  thrashing in thicket – you, who have grown tall
and turned from what you took for true
  till recently on faith. And it is a still, small

voice, that tells me now whose woods these are.
These woods are yours. I have my own in store.

For the First Time He Says

Someday when I move away from you
and her heart splits
as if a hunter just slashed
the soft neck
of a doe

Pain for a Daughter

Blind with love, my daughter
has cried nightly for horses,
those long-necked marchers and churners
that she has mastered, any and all,
reigning them in like a circus hand—
the excitable muscles and the ripe neck;
tending this summer, a pony and a foal.
She who is too squeamish to pull
a thorn from the dog's paw,
watched her pony blossom with distemper,
the underside of the jaw swelling
like an enormous grape.
Gritting her teeth with love,
she drained the boil and scoured it
with hydrogen peroxide until pus
ran like milk on the barn floor.

Blind with loss all winter,
in dungarees, a ski jacket and a hard hat,
she visits the neighbors' stable,
our acreage not zoned for barns;
they who own the flaming horses
and the swan-whipped thoroughbred
that she tugs at and cajoles,
thinking it will burn like a furnace
under her small-hipped English seat.

Blind with pain she limps home.
The thoroughbred has stood on her foot.
He rested there like a building.
He grew into her foot until they were one.
The marks of the horseshoe printed

into her flesh, the tips of her toes
ripped off like pieces of leather,
three toenails swirled like shells
and left to float in blood in her riding boot.

Blind with fear, she sits on the toilet,
her foot balanced over the washbasin,
her father, hydrogen peroxide in hand,
performing the rites of the cleansing.
She bites on a towel, sucked in breath,
sucked in and arched against the pain,
her eyes glancing off me where
I stand at the door, eyes locked
on the ceiling, eyes of a stranger,
and then she cries…
Oh my god, help me!
Where a child would have cried *Mama!*
Where a child would have believed *Mama!*
she bit the towel and called on God
and I saw her life stretch out…
I saw her torn in childbirth,
and I saw her, at that moment,
in her own death and I knew that she
knew.

November 1965

Especially O, Especially *Darling*

Their flannelette nighties leap round their waists;
they laugh into the bed's blue comforter
swelling and thinning cumulously.

Cloth fluttering, clouds fast-forwarding
now blocking the sun that travels the length of the ravine
and slips away – as the mother too

will go – leaving an ache
like the land. Sumas prairie to Lake Superior
separating them, also the years
of bawling into the black O of the telephone.

Nestled here
at the bottom of Burnaby mountain
in the last days as well as the
first egg-bursts into the fallopian current
deep in the girl's body
they make an impasse
of the comforter
then smack
it with pillows, bat it
like cotton   away.

O darling girl, says the mother.
Three good words, the one thing
a mother can promise her daughter, to hold her.
If you love this you're going to love sex.

What has the daughter done with those words?
Ask her. But the mother —
through the years of bad sex and no sex — clings

to that romp and to her self-mothering
especially *O*, especially *darling*.

YVONNE C. MURPHY

Girls Jumping On Beds

Mick Jagger's tongue in their ears,
real boys in the next building, drinking and dancing
and the Sixties stretch out like a caftan,
their paisley bandanas and cut-off shorts flap
as the guitar solo conjures dreams of sex before husbands
and birth control pills.

Four to a dorm, alone together
for the first time in a new town,
Rolling Stones blaring on the HiFi:
Hey, You, Get Off Of My Cloud.

My mother stands triumphant
on the edge of the bed frame, takes turns
waiting, bounces on the wool blanket,
then jumps back to the concrete floor.

A few years later she'll play these records for us:
each morning when Father leaves the house,
she'll bring her albums down, watching
her toddlers pore through those photos.

Inspired by the ancient teenagers,
we sway to Rubber Soul in the living room,
thinking The Beatles were her friends, too.
Their four faces peer at us in syncopated mystery,
we'll dance and pretend to know the words
until we learn the words, sing them over and over,

while she lives her story over and over until the clouds
she jumped off of dissipate and scatter—
cumulus, then nimbus, then gone.

Twelve

Flute and piccolo poke
from her backpack
as she sets off for rehearsal
this Saturday dawn;
she does not see me
in the garden clipping rosa
damascena.

When she was born
her face was familiar
I'd seen it
each time musicians passed
each time musicians tuned
each time exquisite dissonance
announced performance.

Now Saturday softens to dusk
as I pull to the gutter
pails heavy with gardens past
while under her fingers
Fantaisie-Impromptu
lifts off the keyboard,
allegro agitato
ascends through the open window
charges the dusk that blurs me
with the charmed particles
that preceded her into this world.

Fourteen

Last week
she strode
steel-toed across
her bedroom
floor.
Yesterday
she flung
iron pans
clang
at the spiders
that hung
from her walls.
Today
fists of thunder
pound doors
sunder
the timbers
of roof beams
Today
she cracks
open the rafters
I swing from.

Cutters

Gas, glass,
electrical outlets, stairs, mussels,
uncles—
the closer to home the greater the danger.

Yet nothing is undone by blackbirds
squawking on the lawn. Life of the vine is quiet;
end of the lavender— scent.

"Not one thing in the garden isn't marvelous," I effervesce.
                    This is one of my celebratory mornings.
My daughter, propped at the edge of the deck,
watches me putter and cut.
After a silence she intercedes:

                                        "Alice is a cutter too—
slices lines on her arms and legs— with razors. Everybody
says she's nuts,
                    but the cuttings are actually art."

I lower the clippers and fasten the clasp.
I realize if I'm hasty to interpret, it will hurt.

SUSAN McCASLIN

Anorexia

Righting my daughter's rain with relentless cheerfulness
is not working.

I have gathered a thunderstorm of my own.

She will either die into her self-loathing
or turn and turn right—unblight
the dark flower of melancholy
rooting in her skull with or without
my warm infusion of self-worth.

What will undo the onyx stare
and turned away mouth
or round the burning bones?

No milk of mine will save her now.

She pushes away arms
that cradled her infant skull,
negotiating with the Dealer:

one brownie=treadmill forty minutes.
one slice banana loaf=no lunch.
I find her on the bed, gaunt missive
taped to her forehead: "WORTHLESS

DISGUSTING PIG." Her anger splits
a vessel in her eye. I veer away—
stand by—godspeed her through
the next close-lipped hour.

DIANE LOCKWARD

Her Daughter's Feet

My friend Sally was obsessed
with her baby's feet—the soft dough
of the soles, the ten pea-sized toes—
and because she knew they'd change,
she painted portraits of the feet, canvas
after canvas. Sometimes she dipped the soles
in paint and pressed them onto paper,
like a nurse making hospital footprints.

Feet walked the walls of the house—
feet in water,
                    in leaves,
                                        feet floating in air.
Chartreuse, turquoise, burnt sienna—
everything shone—nails
painted in silver and gold, feet bejeweled
with anklets and rings, toes with streamers
of ribbons.
                And some of the feet had wings.

The year her daughter disappeared,
Sally stared at the walls, at her daughter's feet,
stared like a tracker looking for a trail.
I thought then of the daughters of China,
their feet bound in yards of cloth, trained to walk
on the wrong bones, unable to dance
or run.

I looked again at those walls,
grown cold as stone, wished hard
for a scattering of seeds, noticed
once more the delicate brushstrokes,
the precision of wings.

9 AM, Room 214, Holiday Inn Express

Sun slips through a crack in the drapes,
beams at the mute TV. Nothing to hear
but the sough of the HVAC. Not much
to see: in the bathroom, small soaps
in stiff wrappers; over the beds, prints
in gilt frames—arbor and blossoms,
diffident pinks and greens. An armchair
next to a table set with ice bucket and phone.
Nothing but time to mend a split seam,
remember my mother teaching the back-stitch,
watch as my grown son sleeps, the rise and fall
of his chest, wrapped in a floral bedspread.

CATI PORTER

Administering My Dog's Cancer Therapy, I Think About My Sons

My thumb and forefinger pinch a pill as I thrust my fist
back into his throat. His teeth, a bracelet of blunt
tines, rake gently over my wrist.
I pull out my hand sticky with his saliva
and hold his mouth closed
and stroke his neck
until I am certain he has swallowed.

At seven years old he is two years older than
my oldest son. He is my oldest son,
I tell myself, but of course, he is not.
He is just the dog, I remind myself daily,
because, if he were my son,
I would okay the endoscopy, biopsy
the lining of his stomach. I would make the drive
into the next county for intravenous chemotherapy.

Once he ate reluctantly from my hand chicken breasts
boiled for him on my stove. If he were
my son, I would not hand-feed him
the breasts of dead chickens. I would slice
off my own, boil them
pink to white in my very best pot.
I would shred them, feed them to him
warm, if only to keep him through the night.

The Latest Injury

When my son comes home from the weekend trip where he
stood up into a piece of steel in the
ceiling of a car and cut open his head and
had the wound shaved and sprayed
and stitches taken, he comes up to me
grinning with pride and fear and slowly
bows his head, as if to the god of trauma,
and there it is, his scalp blue-grey as the
skin of a corpse, the surface cold and
gelatinous, the long split
straight as if deliberate, the
sutures on either side like terrible
marks of human will. I say
Amazing, I press his head to my stomach
gently, the naked skin on top
quivering like the skin on boiled milk and
bluish as the epidermis of a monkey
drawn out of his mother dead, the
faint growth of fine hair like a
promise. I rock his brain in my arms as I
once rocked his whole body,
delivered, and the wound area glows
grey and translucent as a fledgling's head when it
teeters on the edge of the nest, the cut a
midline down the skull, the flesh
jelly, the stitches black, the slit saying
taken, the thread saying given back.

Sunbathing on a Rooftop in Berkeley

Eleven palm trees stand up between me
and the Bay. A quarter turn and I'm
in line with Campanile Tower.
The hippies are sunbathing too.
They spread themselves out on the sidewalks
with their ingenious crafts for sale
and their humble puppies. We are
all pretending summer is eternal.
Mount Tamalpais hovers in the distance.

I pinch myself: that this is California!
But behind my lightstruck eyelids I am also
a child again in an amusement park
in Pennsylvania, and forty years blow
in and out adapting, as the fog does,
to conditions in the Bay.

My daughter has gone to her class in Criminal
Procedure. She pulls her hair back in a twist.
Maybe she will marry the young man she lives with?
I take note how severely
she regards the laws of search and seizure.
She moves with the assurance of a cheetah.
Still, marriage may be the sort of entrapment
she wishes to avoid? She is all uncertainties,
as I am in this mothering business.

O summers without end, the exact truth is
we are expanding sideways as haplessly
as in the mirrors of the Fun House.
We bulge toward the separate fates that await us
sometimes touching, as sleeves will, whether

or not a hug was intended.

O summers without end, the truth is
no matter how I love her, Death
blew up my dress that day
while she was in the egg unconsidered.

Towards Autumn

Mid-September, and I miss my daughter.
I sit out on the terrace with my friend,
talking, with morning tea, coffee, and bread,
about another woman, and her mother,
who survived heroism; her lover
who will have to. I surprise myself

with language; lacking it, don't like myself
much. I owe a letter to my daughter.
Thinking of her's like thinking of a lover
I hope will someday grow to be a friend.
I missed the words to make friends with my mother.
I pull the long knife through the mound of bread,

spoon my slice with cherry preserves, the bread
chewy as meat beneath, remind myself
I've errands for our ancient patron, mother
of dramas, hard mother to a daughter
twenty years my senior, who is my friend,
who lives in exile with a woman lover

also my friend, three miles from here. A lover
of good bread, my (present) friend leaves this bread
and marmalades *biscottes*. To have a friend
a generation older than myself
is sometimes like a letter for my daughter
to read, when she can read: What your mother

left undone, women who are not your mother
may do. Women who are not your lover
love you. (That's to myself, and my daughter.)
We take coffee- and tea-pot, mugs, jam jars, bread

inside, wash up. I've work, hours by myself.
Beyond the kitchen, in her room, my friend

writes, overlooking the same hills. Befriend
yourself: I couldn't have known to tell my mother
that, unless I'd learned it for myself.
Until I do. Friendship is earned. A lover
leaps into faith. Earthbound women share bread;
make; do. Cherry compote would please my daughter.

My daughter was born a hero to her mother;
found, like a lover, flawed; found, like a friend,
faithful as bread I'd learned to make myself.

SUSAN SHILLIDAY

My Daughter is Twenty-two

Horse books lost.
Bridle, reins undone.
All the ribbons by your bed
you won.

Fig-sweet heart,
honey-framed face
not here. You fled
this place.

Who wouldn't invent a mummy or a god,
A myth, a story, a heaven, a lie

JANE KNECHTEL

Grief

Certainly some of the elaborate ministrations involved in making a mummy would have filled the need of mourning (Chinchorro) mothers to continue caring and tending for their lost children.

—Heather Pringle, *The Mummy Congress*

Who wouldn't invent a mummy or a god,
A myth, a story, a heaven, a lie
In those first hours of separation.
The impulse unequivocally human.
Anthropologists tell us who we were,
Catalogue remnants of our ancient lives.
Like these ceramic waifs: cryptic dolls,
Poker-faced; eyes as distant as Pluto.
The stuffing knocked out of them by eons.
Still, I want to touch one, stroke its seven-
Thousand-year-old skin in reverence;
Weep for the woman who made it twice,
Before there were records or photographs—
Because she tucked it to sleep in the sand.

Lucy: A love story about daughters

1. Once upon a time in the beginning

You couldn't help yourself: floating
out of a Silurian sea, cell by matted cell
enchanted by the sun, blue-green

and blooming, lured to land where
you find feet and a backbone, roots,
leaves, seeds. You don't stop. Time

sashays like the wind, no mind to give it
word or grip or shape. None but
yours, Lucy, rocking in morning's cradle

as continents roll together and away, lock
each other in the mysteries of stone and flood
and molten sand. And O, the light. You rise

to it, Lucy, your limbs rhyming
in the air, your breath in the mist,
your eyes beguiled by the dazzle above

the night. Billions of nights and moons,
and your dark skin begins to cover the earth
like silk, rising and falling, and you lay

your milky gifts before the sun, again
and again, the arrow of dawn lodged deep
in your rib. Then you leave a bright marker

where they will find it, Lucy,
in the silt and ash of the ravines of Ethiopia:

Hominid, woman. Later, around a fire,

in love with your dancing bones, they imagine
the trail of your suns trembling
beyond them in the smoke. What name

can they give a find such as you? On the camp radio,
a tune about tangerine trees, a girl
with kaleidoscope eyes.

Chapter Two: And then, and still

Eons pass and tumble into boxes with labels. Cities bake in disease, the poisoned nectar of the cloth heals and kills, guns and blood blossom in the desert heat, earth turns warm and terrible under the rumble of drumming feet. Still, you can't help yourself. You are the hungry kid under the wet cardboard on the concrete, awakened by a crack of sun, the crone wrenching her bottle cart from the melting ice, you are our daughter on the screen, outside the door, under the skin, in the radiant wreckage of the light.

Chapter Three: Lucy: Here you are now

in the yeast of your small, delectable
fingers, the benediction of your throat
and the scent that rises from your skin,

seeds of grace.
In the fear I measure in volts
as I watch your fingers reach for the dangling

cord, your unsteady feet try the rocks,
the man by the playground, hovering.
In those eyes, crackling with spirit, the lanolin

sheen of your lanky body at nine as you bring
light to the kitchen table with a brush: another
unicorn in yellow for the wall.

In the empty room. Upstairs, abandoned
cd's, curled posters, your amulet in a silver box,
curtains translucent as moth wings.

The sky, its invisible blue arms.
Today, your voice on the phone, the arrow
of light lodged in our ribs. We can't help it, Lucy,

we are enchanted, blue-green
and blooming, and we swim to the shore
with the sun in our eyes.

The Pomegranate

The only legend I have ever loved is
The story of a daughter lost in hell.
And found and rescued there.
Love and blackmail are the gist of it.
Ceres and Persephone the names.
And the best thing about the legend is
I can enter it anywhere. And have.
As a child in exile in
A city of fogs and strange consonants,
I read it first and at first I was
An exiled child in the crackling dusk of
The underworld, the stars blighted. Later
I walked out in a summer twilight
Searching for my daughter at bedtime.
When she came running I was ready
To make any bargain to keep her.
I carried her back past whitebeams.
And wasps and honey-scented buddleias.
But I was Ceres then and I knew
Winter was in store for every leaf
On every tree on that road.
Was inescapable for each one we passed.
And for me.
It is winter
And the stars are hidden.
I climb the stairs and stand where I can see
My child asleep beside her teen magazines,
Her can of Coke, her plate of uncut fruit.
The pomegranate! How did I forget it?
She could have come home and been safe
And ended the story and all
Our heartbroken searching but she reached

Out a hand and plucked a pomegranate.
She put out her hand and pulled down
The French sound for apple and
The noise of stone and the proof
That even in the place of death,
At the heart of legend, in the midst
Of rocks full of unshed tears
Ready to be diamonds by the time
The story was told, a child can be
Hungry. I could warn her. There is still a chance.
The rain is cold. The road is flint-coloured.
The suburb has cars and cable television.
The veiled stars are above ground.
It is another world. But what else
Can a mother give her daughter but such
Beautiful rifts in time?
If I defer the grief I will diminish the gift.
The legend must be hers as well as mine.
She will enter it. As I have.
She will wake up. She will hold
The papery, flushed skin in her hand.
And to her lips. I will say nothing.

BRENDA HILLMAN

Shared Custody

An example often used to show ?? is x falling feet first into a singularity with a watch on. Fate is what happens backwards. With regard to Persephone, the seasons don't change till something agrees to her sacrifice.

When a child is dropped off in front of the other parent's house she creates a history of space and yellow, hurrying in the unopposed direction as we learn to read by hurrying meaning.

She got out of the car. Smell-threads of Johnson's baby shampoo. Redolence exists by itself as opportunity. The end of the Cold War had come. In Russia, more oranges, lizard baskets of capitalism. I tried to talk to her father; he tried to talk to me.

As x falls by prearrangement with the experimenters, yellow is unopposed. The child, leaving the car, drops an alphabet on the path. *y. e. l.* Shaving of yellow, central plaid, black from a fraction if she has been brave about including the math.

She hated her little bag. A Thursday humming followed. My writing was falling apart. She was learning to read.

A fate begins to be assembled when the linear is shared. All it does doesn't work. Should dirt not praise her efforts? Little pointed

arrows swerve around the (from the mother's perspective) vanishing skirt. Flashes of letters here. Here. Home is the fear of size. A word can fall apart. *y. e.* We sat in the car. Tiny bats between Berkeley double-you'd the air.

The lip of a singularity is an event too far beyond, good corduroy with its highs and lows as the star dissolves in the just having spun and you're not supposed to ask how x feels as he falls in. Persephone practices her yes, her no, her this that and the other; the child approaching the house of the father in motion of minutes, free for twenty yards of both of them makes a roof with her good-bye: // bye \\ mom. They'll have to invent new seasons to explain it.

The daughter grows a horizon. Somehow a line by which a life could be pursued.

When she started to read, I no longer heard language, it heard me. I had the stupid idea that she should dress up to leave.

x should have checked with Persephone about the kicking and screaming. I should have checked with the mother but I was the mother. Backward should try to fix loss so it is not devastation but chronicle.

Panic plaid, almost at his door, *I cannot see what flowers are.* Daffodils. Dirt's birthday candles; California is medium old. *x* won't be very young when he gets to the center, nor will the child, testifying to cloth, dropped, sent back fractal, active as the buoys on the bay, nor is the child very young.

If you are time you think in terms of next. If you are Persephone you think in terms of dirt. If you're the metaphor you'll let the thing stand for it. On Monday, the flash of a dove, your hoping frame. The child *can* look back, the myths don't apply here, if you think one joy was sacrificed it's because you said it. What choice did it have when the thing undid but to call her in broken colors.

Son

Each night Demeter placed her host's infant son
on the hearth, in an effort to make him immortal.
—Homer, "Hymn to Demeter"

If I choose for you what any mother
wants: your son's hair forever

gold, his skin smooth through
the centuries' slow crawling;

if I promise elastic thighs,
a strapping run, cloudless eyes,

a face sculpted for
all tomorrows,

would you not lay
your child on the hearth yourself,

like a small dried log?

Antigone

You are right about Antigone: how sublime a picture of a woman!
Some of us have, in a prior existence, been in love with an Antigone…
—Shelley

My honest child, your death is the sun's beam
on seven-gated Thebes. The golden light
of day shines and you hanged, a muslin noose
around your neck. The hours draw on. Let sleep
and death carry your breathless body down
to Erebus, let them return blood to cheeks,
heal bruises, comb hair along the crooked road
so that you appear a young lover arriving
to greet her husband-to-be. Tomorrow
is the first day of my life without you.
Were it otherwise, death would be alone
forever and you not hidden amid him,
full of life and lust, to one day know
marriage songs, the chant bringing a bride
to bed and even children of your own.
Sleep and death can hold you with love and grief
and care where I can't, dead in this life
but beautiful in the afterlife, young,
fragrant and peaceful in your grave.
I celebrate your compassion in this way,
you who could not live to serve the living.
Day comes to its end. We remain apart.

Proximity of Milk and *Mine*

I promise
not to let the hoards

of my love,
which live
just beyond the hill of my right shoulder,

cross over,
land in your village,
open all your doors,

draining every jug of wine, leaving
in your cupboard
only crumbs.

The great obelisk
of my attention,
slab of polished, reflective marble,

a mountain peak's blinding glint,

I promise not to let it be pulled
by gravity's might
upon you.

I promise
to contain
myself. Serving you
red grapes, for instance,

my breath
will not cloud

their silver tray. That you may
pause,

awaiting a distracted bee's
perusings, then reach, fingers gracing

the grape's blushing
skin

In Kochi by the Sea

You walk in darkness
A candle in your hand, your sari unravels,

An inch of cotton snatched underfoot,
Sheer wax catches the doorpost.

Amma, is something burning?
Anamnesis, I looked it up in the dictionary

A seventeenth century usage in the language
You helped me learn, of Greek provenance

Used by some in medical literature for signs
That help uncover bodily condition.

Who was she?
In Kochi, that sunbaked city by the sea

I was high as your armpit.
You held me in your umbrella's shade.

We saw a woman very pale, squatting on a doorstep
'Rahel, Rahel!'

Someone was calling out her name.
A man, knife raised, circling a squawking bird

The woman paid no heed.
The bird poked under her sari, disappeared.

In the shadow of her clothing in between her feet
We saw vermillion dots, a trickle, a slow pour.

She dipped one pointed finger, then another
In the show of blood

Making a flower, a fist
A cockrel's head, a candle, a cloud,

A quickly changing river,
Parts of a city, many houses burning,

The sheaves of redemption reeling.
You drew me aside so sharply, shielded my eyes.

***

Anamnesis, I try to think
Of what Plato might have meant

The body cleansed,
So seeing with the soul,

True recollection perfectly attuned
To every jot of what the future brings.

But there's a discomfort in the inner life
I had not bargained for –

A stream with blistered rocks where I must walk
Barefoot as I did so many years ago

But now in a river bed
Not marked on any map I learnt to read

In a schoolhouse with a palm tree outside
Where the barbarous sun pours.

***

When you dropped your candle
Nothing came to fire

The future for an instant, pacified.
The dark was sweet and filled with singing birds

That fly into this garden without being asked,
A breath of joy, a fragrant certitude

Scarcely to be set into sentences.
Your umbrella was in the corner by the doorpost

Cupped in a flash of stormy light
Its ribs bent and broken by that wind renewed,

A monsoon crossing the Arabian sea.
And the woman we left behind?

Not to be seen except in figurations
Of the damned on Mattancheri palace walls

There she squatted on a stony road
Making forms of blood

Auguring what? Who could tell?
Figures cupped from the chaos of our dailiness,

Such ordinary things through which
We try to learn what the past presages,

And we think we touch,
A clarity of longing, a blessedness.

***

The afternoon you dragged me from the street
We walked beside the pounding beach

Past tiny wreaths of wood the color of wax
Washed out from the belly of a river

Cast into shapes of ruined cities,
No-nation cities lacking anthem, flag,

Their lintels blown, gardens stilled into ash.
Torn free of you I ran into the wind.

Waves crashed into voices,
Highpitched, vulnerable

The color of dropped blood,
The color of indigo cut from the mothering tree.

And underneath – in memory now –
I heard a darkness, luminous.

October Morning

Down in the garden hoar frost has fallen;
my children play on trails they have made.
The youngest my daughter
holds in her hand what cannot be held.

I should tell her—
It's not real. It's not even snow.
I should warn my foolish, excitable daughter.

I had no daughter.
The memory is old grey and wrong.
I was the daughter and
she never warned me.

Hoar frost is such a lie.

Sisters of the Holy Name

We were their daughters,
those faithful nuns,
married to Christ,
the gold band they'd lain down for
gleaming on firm fingers
as we filed past in pencil rows
each morning.

Those were the days God woke me,
a dependable alarm, and I watched him
rise from clouds on the church wall,
the incense sharp in our nostrils
high on the Latin Litany.

How many persons are there in God?
the priest asked as the nuns fussed
in their starched habits
calling him father.
We could smell the wine on his breath
that rasped behind the grille
we dragged our sins to each week.

Clean like fresh laundry,
I wanted to die
and go to heaven directly.
Already afraid to touch that place
between my legs where the devil lived,
a mole in a wet nest.
When I looked with a mirror
I could almost see his red face.

JUDITH ARCANA

For all the Mary Catholics

Mary Catherine came to public school because of money,
sat down next to me; Mary Elizabeth stood behind us
on the line in gym, whispering I ought to join
the Brownies; Mary Frances shared a geography book
(there never were enough in Miss King's room);
sweet Mary Jean showed me a shortcut home,
dangerous, down the alley (now she drives high
school girls across state lines, skipping
parental consent); Maria Teresa showed me
newborn puppies in a basket, then cut me cold
when I would not sing Jesus in December;
cute Mary Alice had a crush on my brother,
sighing they never could marry; famous Mary Jane
with her shiny black shoes traded me St. Francis
for a gas station pinup; Mary Rose shared
my locker, my Kotex, my Kleenex; Mary Ellen kissed
me on the mouth and laughed; shy Mary Jo
worshipped Audrey Hepburn in the dark; quiet
Mary Ann died at the Shut-Eye Motel,
blood from her uterus crusted on her thighs; tough
Mary Margaret moved to Detroit, seven children,
eight years, never answered letters; funny
Mary Louise called her Dungannon brogue
a French accent; Maria Francesca prays outside
the clinic where I work; Mary Patricia (now M. Pat)
called me after thirteen years to ask, Is the pill
safer now? then got divorced and married my brother;
Mary Helen marched with me all the way
down State Street, holding Mary Magdalene
over our heads; and angry Mary Carol goes to Mass
for the music, the poetry, the rush of spirit,
crying in pure nostalgia: *They can't keep me out!*

MARTHA SILANO

Harborview

By the roots of my hair some god got hold of me
—Sylvia Plath

By the roots of my hair, by the reinforced elastic
of my floral Bravado bra, by the fraying strands

of my blue-checked briefs, some god's gotten hold of me,
some god's squeezed hard the spit-up rag of my soul, rung me

like the little girl who rang our doorbell on Halloween, took
our M&Ms *is your baby okay? Why did they take him away?*

Some god's got me thinking my milk's poison, unfit
for a hungry child, some god's got me pacing,

set me flying like the black felt bats dangling
in the hall, some god so that now I can't trust my best friend's

healing hands, the Phad Thai she's spooning beside the rice (ditto
to the meds the doctors say will help me sleep) *Poison poison!*

as if the god who's got hold of me doesn't want me
well, doesn't want my rapid-fire brain to slow,

wants this ride for as long as it lasts, wants to take it
to its over-Niagara-in-a-barrel end, which is where

this god is taking me, one rung at a time, one ambulance,
one EMT strapping me in, throwing me off this earth,

cuz I've not only killed my son but a heap of others too.

Some god's got me by my shiny golden locks, by my milk-

leaking breasts, got me in this hospital, wisps like white scarves
circling my head, wisps the voices of men *back to bed you whore!*

Some god till I'm believing I've been shot, guts dribbling out,
till I'm sure I've ridden all over town in a spaceship, sure

I'm dead, a ghost, a smoldering corpse, though not before I'm holding up
a shaking wall, urging the others to help me (a plane about to land

on our heads), though soon enough thrown down by two night nurses,
strapped to a bed, though for weeks the flowers my in-laws sent

charred at the tips (having been to hell and back), clang of pots,
hissing shower, the two blue pills my roommate left in the sink,

all signals of doom, though some god got hold of me,
shook and shook me long and hard, she also brought me back.

Motherhood

Suppose I emptied my flat of everything,
everything but my books? The elephants
would have to go. They'd be the first to go
– being the youngest – and the last, the plants
perhaps, relics of early motherhood.
I'd keep the piano, all my files and photos.

I'd keep my grandmother's chest to keep my photos
in, in and not on top of, everything
swept absolutely clear of motherhood.
Nothing shall move: no herd of elephants
proceed down my mantelpiece, spider-plants
produce babies, carpets moths, moths shall go

into the ether where all bad spells go.
I'm sick of the good. Of drooling over photos
that lie, lie, lie, breaking my back over plants
for whom – *Oh! for whom?* Not everything
I thought green greened. Not even elephants
consoled me for the bane of motherhood.

Therefore motherhood must go. Motherhood
must go as quietly as prisoners go
and all her things go with her, elephants
troop behind her, tapestries drown her, photos –
OK photos can stay but everything
dust-collecting goes the way of the plants.

Everything shall live in name only. Plants
now extinct shall be extolled, motherhood
shall be blessed but not mothers, everything
everywhere being their fault though they go

to the dock protesting, producing photos
of happy toddlers, citing elephants,

rashly, as preceptors since elephants,
however vicious they may be to plants
or photographers with blinding flash photos,
are the very model of motherhood.
Such are the myths of nature. They shall go.
There shall be room, time, space, for everything:

room in the wild for elephants and plants,
time to go rummaging a chest for photos,
space for everything cleared of motherhood.

Cloud Watching

Choose a continent, and in it, a country
            Doubled over itself on a postcolonial map,
As if a styracosaurus to the north of it
Had driven its horn into the belly – Imagine
The shade of cloud-watching,

The country a kidney-bean, a bi-lobed
Nucleus, the isthmus, two camel humps
            Or two breasts – And in it
Choose a grandmother and her daughter
Dancing and clapping for you around a cardboard box,

A makeshift incubator
That housed their preterm twins
Until the breasts were filled – And if a silver
            Thermal wrap, paper thin, lambent,
Is thrown on top of it all, box

With twins and blankets on grandma's head,
            There would be singing
The whole long walk home – Imagine
A clay-brick hospital with plastic sheeting for a roof,
And a skeleton rolls

In on a bicycle. A grapefruit-size uterus,
A fungus in the mouth – And when that mother
            Is dead and no breast
Will touch her newborn,
And if the father

Takes his son and your formula milk
Across the country, past the horn in the belly,
Searching for breasts, he would find them
Cumulus as clouds –
          One looking more like god.

Film Noir

At the Gare Centrale
She fingers the blue
Of her Canadian passport.

Wears the shoes she bought
From the marché aux puces.

Crimson, strapped at her ankles,
They once belonged to a dancer
With the Moulin Rouge.

At each city limit
A border to be crossed.
Every language a new currency.

At the hotel in Prague
She befriends the night porter.
Tells him secrets,
Intimate stories of her life.

She is conscious of the weight
Of inheritance
The heft of her mother's rubies
Sewn into the hem
Of her skirt.

Insured
She knows there is always
Someone willing to bargain for the past.

A Map to the Next World

for Desiray Kierra Chee

In the last days of the fourth world I wished to make a map for those who would climb through the hole in the sky.

My only tools were the desires of humans as they emerged from the killing fields, from the bedrooms and the kitchens.

For the soul is a wanderer with many hands and feet.

The map must be of sand and can't be read by ordinary light. It must carry fire to the next tribal town, for renewal of spirit.

In the legend are instructions on the language of the land, how it was we forgot to acknowledge the gift, as if we were not in it or of it.

Take note of the proliferation of supermarkets and malls, the altars of money. They best describe the detour from grace.

Keep track of the errors of our forgetfulness; the fog steals our children while we sleep.

Flowers of rage spring up in the depression. Monsters are born there of nuclear anger.

Trees of ashes wave good-bye to good-bye and the map appears to disappear.

We no longer know the names of the birds here, how to speak to them by their personal names.

Once we knew everything in this lush promise.

What I am telling you is real and is printed in a warning on the map. Our forgetfulness stalks us, walks the earth behind us, leaving a trail of paper diapers, needles and wasted blood.

An imperfect map will have to do, little one.

The place of entry is the sea of your mother's blood, your father's small death as he longs to know himself in another.

There is no exit.

The map can be interpreted through the wall of the intestine—a spiral on the road of knowledge.

You will travel through the membrane of death, smell cooking from the encampment where our relatives make a feast of fresh deer meat and corn soup, in the Milky Way.

They have never left us; we abandoned them for science.

And when you take your next breath as we enter the fifth world there will be no X, no guidebook with words you can carry.

You will have to navigate by your mother's voice, renew the song she is singing.

Fresh courage glimmers from planets.

And lights the map printed with the blood of history, a map you will have to know by your intention, by the language of suns.

When you emerge note the tracks of the monster slayers where they entered the cities of artificial light and killed what was killing us.

You will see red cliffs. They are the heart, contain the ladder.

A white deer will come to greet you when the last human climbs from the destruction.

Remember the hole of our shame marking the act of abandoning our tribal grounds.

We were never perfect.

Yet, the journey we make together is perfect on this earth who was once a star and made the same mistakes as humans.

We might make them again, she said.

Crucial to finding the way is this: there is no beginning or end.

You must make your own map.

Legends

for Eavan Frances

Tryers of firesides,
twilights. There are no tears in these.

Instead, they begin the world again,
making the mountain ridges blue
and the rivers clear and the hero fearless—

and the outcome always undecided
so the next teller can say *begin* and
again and astonish children.

Our children are our legends.
You are mine. You have my name.
My hair was once like yours.

And the world
is less bitter to me
because you will retell the story.

all the rivers of her red veins
move into the sea

Keine Lazarovitch: 1870-1959

When I saw my mother's head on the cold pillow,
Her white waterfalling hair in the cheeks' hollows,
I thought, quietly circling my grief, of how
She had loved God but cursed extravagantly his creatures.

For her final mouth was not water but a curse,
A small black hole, a black rent in the universe,
Which damned the green earth, stars and trees in its stillness
And the inescapable lousiness of growing old.

And I record she was comfortless, vituperative,
Ignorant, glad, and much else besides; I believe
She endlessly praised her black eyebrows, their thick weave,
Till plagiarizing Death leaned down and took them for his mould.

And spoiled a dignity I shall not again find,
And the fury of her stubborn limited mind:
Now none will shake her amber beads and call God blind,
Or wear them upon a breast so radiantly.

O fierce she was, mean and unaccommodating;
But I think now of the toss of her gold earrings,
Their proud carnal assertion, and her youngest sings
While all the rivers of her red veins move into the sea.

from Kaddish

For Naomi Ginsberg, 1894-1956

I

Strange now to think of you, gone without corsets & eyes, while I walk on
the sunny pavement of Greenwich Village.
downtown Manhattan, clear winter noon, and I've been up all night, talking,
talking, reading the Kaddish aloud, listening to Ray Charles blues
shout blind on the phonograph
the rhythm the rhythm—and your memory in my head three years after—
And read Adonais' last triumphant stanzas aloud—wept, realizing
how we suffer—
And how Death is that remedy all singers dream of, sing, remember,
prophesy as in the Hebrew Anthem, or the Buddhist Book of Answers—and my own imagination of a withered leaf—at dawn—
Dreaming back thru life, Your time—and mine accelerating toward Apocalypse,
the final moment—the flower burning in the Day—and what comes after,
looking back on the mind itself that saw an American city
a flash away, and the great dream of Me or China, or you and a phantom
Russia, or a crumpled bed that never existed—
like a poem in the dark—escaped back to Oblivion—
No more to say, and nothing to weep for but the Beings in the Dream,
trapped in its disappearance,
sighing, screaming with it, buying and selling pieces of phantom, worshipping each other,
worshiping the God included in it all—longing or inevitability?—while it
lasts, a Vision—anything more?
It leaps about me, as I go out and walk the street, look back over my shoulder,
Seventh Avenue, the battlements of window office buildings shouldering each other high, under a cloud, tall as the sky an instant—
and the sky above—and old blue place.
or down the Avenue to the south, to—as I walk toward the Lower East Side

—where you walked 50 years ago, little girl—from Russia, eating the
first poisonous tomatoes of America—frightened on the dock—
then struggling in the crowds of Orchard street toward what?—toward
Newark—
toward candy store, first home-made sodas of the century, hand-churned ice
cream in backroom on musty brownfloor boards—
Toward education marriage nervous breakdown, operation, teaching school,
and learning to be mad, in a dream—what is this life?

The Woman in This Poem

The woman in this poem
lives in the suburbs
with her husband and two children
each day she waits for the mail and
once a week receives
a letter from her lover
who lives in another city
writes of roses warm patches
of sunlight on his bed
Come to me he pleads
I need you and the woman
reaches for the phone
to dial the airport
she will leave this afternoon
her suitcase packed
with a few light clothes

But as she is dialing
the woman in this poem
remembers the pot-roast
and the fact that it is Thursday
she thinks of how her husband's face
will look when he reads her note
his body curling sadly toward
the empty side of the bed

She stops dialling and begins
to chop onions for the pot-roast
but behind her back the phone
shapes itself insistently
the number for airline reservations
chants in her head

in an hour her children will be
home from school and after that
her husband will arrive
to kiss the back of her neck
while she thickens the gravy
and she knows that
all through dinner
her mouth will laugh and chatter
while she walks with her lover
on a beach somewhere

She puts the onions in the pot
and turns toward the phone
but even as she reaches
she is thinking of
her daughter's piano lessons
her son's dental appointment

Her arms fall to her side
and as she stands there
in the middle of her spotless kitchen
we can see her growing
old like this
and wish for something anything
to happen we could have her go
mad perhaps and lock herself
in the closet crouch there
for days her dresses withering
around her like cast-off skins
or maybe she could take
to cruising the streets at night
in her husband's car
picking up teenage boys
and fucking them in the back seat
we can even imagine
finding her body
dumped in a ditch somewhere
on the edge of town

The woman in this poem offends us
with her useless phone and the persistent
smell of onions we regard her as we do
the poorly calculated overdose
who lies in a bed somewhere
not knowing how her life drips
through her drop by measured drop
we want to think of death
as something sudden
stroke or the leap
that carries us over the railing
of the bridge in one determined arc
the pistol aimed precisely
at the right part of the brain
we want to hate this woman

but mostly we hate knowing
that for us too it is
moments like this
our thoughts stiff fingers
tear at again and again
when we stop in the middle
of an ordinary day and
like the woman in this poem
begin to feel
our own deaths
rising slowly within us

my mother's hands

appear one afternoon as i peel potatoes for supper
the twist of wrist, a cupping of the palm
veins of garden soil in her thumb cracks
traces along the cuticle

sometimes they wear the stain of fall beets
peeled after boiling on the wood stove
the blunt fingernails, the memory of chalk dust
the strength of holding, of letting go

one saturday, her hands deep in wash water
the tongue of sheets passed through the wringer
with a gasp of air   I looked up to see
her fingers hand   arm

following the cloth into the rollers
until she sprung their grip and cried
get your father   with a hollow dark
in my chest i ran to the barn calling

now as her hands emerge from mine
i remember the day when i first knew
that she too was a passing force
a warm wind blowing outside my window

Anti-Mother Ballad

Long live Death
Falange Española Tradicionalista
—slogan, 1936

The young women
fussing with satchels of gear, with strollers,
awed and full of self-praise at
the accomplishment of their bodies,

at a task they watched, abetted,
then achieved with great pain: another helpless being
brought to term. The mothers
in their smug innocence

provide the sweetness of milk,
the comfort of dry, of warm noises
and softness, the knowledge
that these delights will vanish:

these mothers give birth
to death—*death*
in its baptismal gown
death on its tricycle

death taken hand-in-hand to a
first day of school
death who stares at
mewling, crawling kittens

now still: the shock that
death, too

is to die
Death discovering

in the anecdotes of its peers
the anatomy of the other accomplice
to death, sudden
alterations to death's body

to prepare it for death, the living dead
speak about a book that claims
death has been rescinded
for some, death

in love, death making
the death from which
emerges
the blessing

Grace

Once, when I imagined my child's face
in the hands of a killer, I felt the plates shifting

in my brain and the world darken. It was a time
when I was afraid I couldn't love the child

inside me as much as the one already born,
when the signs that madness had a mind of its own

were everywhere, like the young mother who believed
the bundle in her arms had become a rat,

its pointed face nosing for frail air while she held it
firmly under water. The world was sown

with half-buried cages of bone, and the moon was
a light left burning at an unlocked door.

It's night as I write this, as a man on screen describes
how he followed a boy into a restroom,

disarmed him with a smile, then held the boy's head
to his chest when he drove in the knife. If I write

how the blood on urinal walls seems holy for the way
it warms the man, it's because of a dream I have

of waiting for my child, of calling his name, his name
echoing in a silence that might be—No, I will say it—

that *is* death, and how I go back into the dream,
as though into a stranger's home, to change

the dead child into another, not my own.

LORRI NEILSEN GLENN

Combustion

And so the nuns put my little brother Jack into the furnace, and that was that. My mother doesn't know until she wakes, the white shoes a whisper by her bed, my father's voice cold sand in her ear. And I, at home, curled near the heat register, Gram despairing that I won't eat. Won't eat. Waiting for the baby. Snowball sits on the back of the chesterfield, watching what wind does in the claws of bare trees, drifts outside too high and wilding for her paws, too high for me and my snowsuit. Too high, too cold. And the black phone on the wall. And no baby. Fine then, no soup. *They decided,* she says now, fifty years away, as we sit on the deck, our skin inhaling summer-waning sun. *The holy Trinity. Doctor, nun, husband. Dead of winter. They could have waited until I saw my son's face.* She stuffs out her cigarette, rolls her head back. That distance—where she goes. I reach, grasp only the howl of storms in the small railway town, fist of cold at the door in winter, maw of Main Street under high clouds and summer dust. My father's voice at supper — *they fired the stationmaster today*: image of a man tied to a pole over a bonfire. The July parade: crepe paper, my white peaked hat and apron, the Old Dutch Cleanser woman. Joey, hobbling beside me, brown-fringed hat and holster. The water tower the highest thing in the world at the end of the road. Drums. And the Switzer girls on their tricycles ahead of us, gone the next winter. Fire, their whole house down. Clang of the coal stove, my father shoveling at dawn. Heat. Cold. Mother. Gram. Cat. And the empty space where a baby was going to be. I could pull out the old Brownie photos, crisp and snapping from their little crow-wing tabs, burn those into my mind. But how to go back on my own. To go where she goes, even to the edge. She pulls out her lighter again. The DuMaurier, a small white finger in her mouth, sparks. Ash. *Lying there, cut from my gut to my ribs. Sick from ether. Out cold. And he comes home from Hinton in time to tell them to go ahead. Dispose of the body. Small town. Small hospital. And you at home, waiting.* Stillborn. A brother. Out the chimney into the air, the whole town breathing him. Her smoke drifts off the deck toward the trees, white mark in the air, a wavering trail.

Small Passing

For a woman whose baby died stillborn, and who was told by a man
to stop mourning, "because the trials and horrors suffered daily
by black women in this country are more significant
than the loss of one white child."

*

I
In this country you may not
suffer the death of your stillborn,
remember the last push into the shadow and silence,
the useless wires and cords on your stomach,
the nurse's face, the walls, the afterbirth in a basin.
Do not touch your breasts
still full of purpose.
Do not circle the house,
pack, unpack the small clothes.
Do not lie awake at night hearing
the doctor say "It was just as well"
and "You can have another."
In this country you may not
mourn small passings.

See: the newspaper boy in the rain
will sleep tonight in a doorway.
The woman in the busline
may next month be on a train
to a place not her own.
The baby in the backyard now
will be sent to a tired aunt,
grow chubby, then lean,
return a stranger.

Mandela's daughter tried to find her father
through the glass. She thought they'd let her touch him.

And this woman's hands are so heavy when she dusts
the photographs of other children
they fall to the floor and break.
Clumsy woman, she moves so slowly
as if in a funeral rite.

On the pavements the nannies meet.
These are legal gatherings.
They talk about everything, about home,
while the children play among them,
their skins like litmus, their bonnets clean.

2.
Small wrist in the grave.
Baby no one carried live
between houses, among trees.
Child shot running,
stones in his pocket,
boy's swollen stomach
full of hungry air.
Girls carrying babies
not much smaller than themselves.
Erosion. Soil washed down to the sea.

3.
I think these mothers dream
headstones of the unborn.
Their mourning rises like a wall
no vine will cling to.
They will not tell you your suffering is white.
They will say it is just as well.
They will not compete for the ashes of the infants.
I think they may say to you:

Come with us to the place of mothers.
We will stroke your flat empty belly,
let you weep with us in the dark,
and arm you with one of our babies
to carry home on your back.

Listen

Here, in this scalding air/
My speech will not heal. I do not want it to heal.
—Eavan Boland

If the moon had been tatter and fog
(but the night air was sharp and clear)—

if I lived in green valleys of wheat
(but I live on this cratered square)—

*

I'd have unlocked the courtyard door
to my son's sweet, impatient face,

his white sleeves rolled to the elbow,
hands bearing the evening bread, the wine—

*

If the moon had been tatter and fog
if we lived in green valleys of wheat—

the crowd might have missed the cap,
the accent, the mark that betrayed him,

might have followed the guttering torches
to crush another's ripe seed —

*

(*Listen:* I thought that my son, like others',
was destined to see me to sleep,

to light the memorial candle,
to lift his voice to honor my name—)

*

(but the night air was sharp and clear)—
(but we live on this cratered square)—

what I heard . . . a brute noise,
a breaking. I snatched at the door—so—

and saw, not my child bearing blessing,
but the mob, like teeth as they took him,

in this square, in this cobbled street,
with no alley, no route for escape—

*

If the moon had been tatter and fog
(but the night air was sharp and clear)—

They broke him with cobble and board
shattered his bones (*my* bones)

with a plank, pinned me
fast to the courtyard gate . . .

*

If we'd lived in green valleys of wheat
(but I live, if it's live, on this square)—

They turned me to watch. (The bread
    stained red. The wine spilled,

bile on shale.) Forced me to watch
    as he drowned

            in the bitter lake of bad blood.

*

If the moon had been . . .
    (but the night air was . . .

                    Listen.

Listen to Her Face

Listen to her face, I whisper to my sister
we've come to fill the urn with geranium water
Listen to the sound of her chin, the slant of her eyelids
to prune back starchy branches and blood petals
Listen to the fine hair of her eyebrows
we drive my mother through a maze of tombstones
Listen to the pale lid over blue iris
looking for her parents, Glenn and Charlie
Listen to her calm yellow skin, the open throat
our eyes team with clouds of crosses
Listen to the curl of hair, lace beneath her chin
voices echo inside us like children calling through tunnels
Listen to her blue veins, flowers opening on desert
as if the dark ricochet of their voices can rescue us
Listen to the bruise below her left knuckle
how often we have broken the wishbone in two
Listen to her fingers warming my right hand
salvaged like a piece of scrap metal put to good use
Listen to the tender pulse of her neck
swearing in a language she's never used before
Listen to her voice as it rises from my past
reminding me, *Bring in the sheets if it rains.*

Lilies

That night smell of lilies when the moths come to make their bodies light.
Theirs are bright wings clad in pallor. They are the night and our only fear
when we sit vigil on the body in the wake room. And the white moths come
whose bodies are not made of blood. It is now we wish a fire to turn
thin wings to ash. We bring to the body our distress in quiet lament.
How like the moth's wings were my mother's hands upon my father's flesh.
In her throat was the guttural moan she called silence, her mother howl.
And everywhere are the lilies coming to life in darkness with their scent.
They are the flowers we will not have in the room where we lie awake,
our eyes white wings we fly to close, all ash upon the window
where what we see is nothing, seen again.

DAPHNE MARLATT

from *Seven Glass Bowls*

it was July, that radiant kind of morning when all of outside shines in, calling the body out to play, light pristine, rearisen, chickadee's two-note shrill euphoric, *here / i'm here* – this *joyant* pouring in with sun across a kitchen nook amist with memory smoke, his breakfast cigarette, my usual struggle with a five year-old, eat your cereal, you can't go out until you eat. while all three of us know, between sips of this and that, only two blocks away the waves are lapping tenderly at sand, at soon-to-be bare feet, a thrill of seaweed under the gulls' dip and shriek.

how it was, that morning of liquid flight when my father's call came: i can't wake her up, his voice like a child's, crushed, lost. i've tried, she won't wake up. & birds, out the corner of an eye i stared unfocussed at their sky-writing: flap flap, soar. their sanskrit.

why does the eye slide off? the mind refuse anything more than grabbing at keys, making quick arrangements, then tearing through the parkway across the bridge along the Upper Levels, thinking glorious glorious morning, everyone driving their usual cavalcade of must-do's and if only's, thinking how can this be? this sudden gap.

gape. a wound that is love and not love.

you can't do that, she told me over the phone when we'd come back to the city and i wanted to paint what would be the baby's room. you can't paint when you're pregnant. that limiting fear i bridled at. it's latex, Mom. we painted together in a memory loop from my childhood, water instead of turps, a splotch of robin's egg blue on the soft sag of her cheek, her perfection at cleaning brushes. paint moons at the root of our nails, and her latest conspiracy theory about her doctor, her dentist.

A pleasant glow of sentiment was shed by a light rosily shaded and suffused.

that too. its pleated shade, its fluted glass stem a little tippy, casting a glow to read by. a satin quilt pulled up to her chin, hands holding the well-used public library smell of plastic covering a queen's unbent head, the bloody intrigue of courtiers and kings, while all the while steam rose from the rose-patterned teacup beside her, twisted and thinned to nothing in the pinkpearl glow.

rapid overlay, one place-time on another, as if we're actually in the movement between, memory cascading its lightdrenched moments and then suddenly that single jet of recognition, parallel perhaps, that allows us to see, paradoxically, this place we're in the midst of...

incredible. conflicting with explanation.

underlay, as if
her body under the
lay of the city under
lies it

to feel at home in just that particular light before haze moves in – moments only – brightens Spode blue mountains dusted white today. Crown leaning its dazzle over the blue shoulder of Grouse. against their steady presence the restless filigree of leafless birch. a waver, tremble. still getting used to this particular sense of history as missed story, shadowing place.

alternatively, clop clop. the Grand Canyon Suite she'd iron to, that syncopated beat filling the house when i came in from school, dumping books on the camphorwood chest (*how many times have i told you…?*), fresh linen air of line-dried sheets seared now in the heat of the press (*did you eat your apple or give it away?*). not even turning her head, burn mark on the inner flesh of her forearm….

on, little donkey….

her loopy scrawled hand – *Just keep me – Guide & love me Lord – Just for today.*
inside *The Plain Man's Book of Prayers*. one day at a time.

we bring what there is to burn in the still of the morning, the trace of a smell for those who can only eat what is burnt. candle flame and water.

exit signs flashed by me, exit from the rapid urge to get there, reach the end (of what?). cars rushed by me in their focussed race to the ferry or to work, digital numbers rolling up on dashboards. time, that net, tightens in around us (just to know / i don't want to know), numbered exits adding up.

where's there's a will there's a way. one of the maxims she passed on from English children's books meant to curb bad temper and boredom. i still remember the child who had to gather every scrap she'd torn up in a pique. the girl who had to carefully unpick her own imperfect stitching. shadowy figures i tried *not* to pass on to Ange and Ben. those mauve goads dyed deep in her, and further back, mauve half-circles under my grandmother's eyes.

"*the incessant swing of our despair* between this love and its body."

what to do with the body? we didn't know.

PATRICK LANE

My Father's Watch

My mother, drunk again, her nightgown pulled up to her hips, raised her legs and scissored them in the still air of the room where we had all lived once in the great confusion of family. I didn't know what she did there alone in the years after my father's death, what mirrors she stared into or what she saw there, what rooms she paced or where she placed her hands as she gazed into the test pattern late at night, the rye whiskey bottle beside her and the golden glass she drank from. Bare calves and thighs and the dark willow smudge of wet leaves between her legs. Daddy loved my legs, that coquette wince of voice, the sound like something dropped among steel blades and minced there. I didn't know then it was not my father she spoke of but her own. Or perhaps it was both and she was only drunk again and lost in time, her memory a face she might have known and did no longer. There are stories so simple they elude me, their meaning lost in the telling, so that even now I miss the words, the or and if, the but that makes all questions possible.

Or was it the willow above the pond
where I saw her last, that flash of red babushka
above her hands deep in the earth?

If, if, if? In time I will tell you of the wind
in the willow if you hurry to the garden,
if she is still there on her knees by the pond.

But you didn't see her, did you? So furious
her scraping at the earth, the willow flailing
in the last great winds of spring. Oh, yes.

My return to her was to a garden, the orchards of the desert hills. I would pick my steady way through the trees above the lakes in the fall until the cold branches were empty of fruit. A dead marriage, children gone, a continent to wander, and always leading back to her. What if, I might have said. Nights after the bars closed I would walk drunk the miles back to that dark house, the only light from the window a flutter of blue, the comedies and tragedies over, the news finished, the test pattern a flicker on the screen in front of the couch where I knew she sat with her whiskey and her glass. How I would wander outside saying this was the garden of my father, that is his tool shed, there is the place where he parked his car, and here is the well, the root cellar, the sawdust bin, the steps leading down into the basement—here, there, this and that, and not going, yet, into the house.

I wanted to place the word *sorrow*
in a poem so that it was no more
or less than *and, if*, or *but*.

One crow for sorrow, two for mirth…
I know I have it wrong, but willow leaves,
are they what fall among her slow fingers?

It is not a willow leaf, nor can it be, but that I
make of it a sorrow. The form of, how I know
the wind by the shape willow leaves make in fall.

I don't think she waited for me. I was a ghost as much as anyone was in that cold autumn. I could tell by the way she looked at me I was a stranger kind of son. It wasn't a question I could reach into. *Oh, it's you*, she'd say, as if there was anyone else who might have come. I'd drink her into dawn. I'd drink her into sleep, my body folded on the faded couch, dreams of apples tumbling from my hands into bins that never filled. Each fall I'd come and stay the harvest month. The living room was full of the gone, too many to count, the shadows of my family, my father, his breathing quiet in the chair I never sat in. *That's the man's chair. Sit there, sit there*, she'd say. I could hear his lungs hiss, quartz crystals like stars inside his chest. When she pulled her night-gown up and raised her legs it was as if she fell backwards into a darkness all her own and the flutter of her calves and thighs what a body does before it dies.

So white, so white, her dance
in that room of fluttered light.

Dark earth, a staghorn's prance

among the fallen leaves at night.

How small her gentle feet, her glance,
wet willow leaves, her hands, their slight.

Should, must, will, all words. Who was it I served as I stared at her white flail and the damp I call now leaves for lack of a better, other word, between her legs? *Daddy loved me*, she'd say, her flirtation not with me but with some ghost that walked inside her eyes. A father's night in that steady sorrow of straggled lipstick, the giggle of a girl as she lowered her legs, her nightgown awry, and looked at me as if I knew. Flirtatious, thin coquette, she stood and walked to me, and dropped into my lap my father's watch, then swirled around the room until she slumped into my arms, a little thing, her body like a child's, thin bones and wretched flesh.

A stone fell five thousand years through ice
to find its way to this garden. First things,
where nothing is that is not nothing.

I crawl on my knees to find the trace
of her hands in the wet earth. I have a stone
to place among willow leaves and rain.

Her ghost in the garden again today.
Sleep son, little mother. Go to spirit
that this world at last might rest.

I carried her then to the bed she had shared with my father and covered her, her face slack and wet. I sat in the light coming over the blue hills, the watch on my wrist. It had begun again, the hands starting their slow, methodical measuring. In the bracelet's chain his sweat had congealed in thin grease mixed with dust, the fragile tick of seconds counting the night into the day, my thumb moving across the scarred face and hinge of links that bound me.

SUSAN GLICKMAN

The Reproof

When was it that you first heard Mother groan
I want to die. When?

Before words were more than alluring syllables
while they were still ambient air
hushed as the rustling of leaves
distant and familiar
as the rustling of leaves

before translation
before conjugation of the verb *to die*

when each thing was singular and new
and so was each day
so that this groan, this body of grief
was absolute reproof
of your very mode of being

which was joy

so that this pain, which you understood,
and for which no translation was needed
this pain before words which you saw in her body
and felt in her rejection of your singularity
and of your mission

(which was joy)

entered deep and split each thing
from its welcome self
into strangeness and threat
the bright polyphony of leaves

the play of dust-motes in the sun
in the shaft of sun which had been your companion
now swirled randomly, their dance broken

and then it was that you knew you too
could be lost and forsaken and forgotten
and already were

The Fare

Bury me in my pink pantsuit, you said – and I did.
But I'd never dressed you before! I saw the glint
of gold in your jewelry drawer and popped
the earrings in a plastic bag along with pearls,
a pink-and-gold pin, and your perfume. ("What's this?"
the mortician said... "Oh well, we'll spray some on.")
Now your words from the coffin: "*Take my earrings off!*
I've had them on all day, for God's sake!"
You've had them on five days. The lid's closed,
and the sharp stab of a femininity
you couldn't stand for more than two hours in life
is eternal – you'll never relax. I'm 400 miles away.
Should I call up the funeral home and have them removed?
You're not buried yet – stored till the ground thaws –
where, I didn't ask. Probably the mortician's garage.
I should have buried you in slippers and a bathrobe.
Instead, I gave them your shoes. Oh, please
do it for me. I can't stand the thought of you
pained by vanity forever. Reach your cold hand
up to your ear and pull and hear the click
of the clasp hinge unclasping, then reach
across your face and get the other one
and – this effort could take you days, I know,
since you're dead. Let it be your last effort:
to change my mistake and be dead in comfort.
Lower your hands in their places
on your low mound of stomach and rest, rest,
you can let go of the earrings. They'll fall
to the bottom of the casket like tokens,
return fare fallen to the pit
of a coat's satin pocket.

The Chain

My mother's insomnia over at last,
at dawn I enter her bureau drawers.
Under the petticoats, bedjackets, corsets,
under the unfinished knitting that crossed
continents with her, an affable animal,
I come on a hatbox of type-O any-hair,
heavy braids that have lain fifty years in this oval.
Between them, my mother's mother's calling card
engraved on brittle ivory vellum:
Mrs. Abraham Simon, Star Route 3, Radford.

Radford, Virginia, three thousand souls.
Here my mother spent her girlhood, not
without complications, playing
the Methodist church organ for weddings,
funerals, and the Sunday choir.
Here her mother, holding a lily-shaped
ear trumpet, stepped down from the surrey
Grandfather drove forty miles to Roanoke
to witness the blowing of the shofar
on Rosh Hashonah and Yom Kippur.

Affirming my past, our past in
a nation losing its memory, turning
its battlegrounds into parking lots,
slicking its regional differences over
with video games, substituting outer
space for history, I mourn
the type-O any-deaths of Mecca,
Athens, Babylon, Rome,
Radford, country towns
of middle-class hopes and tall corn.

Every year a new itinerant
piano teacher. New exercises
in the key of most-flats. 1908,
the first indoor toilet. The first
running hot water. My mother
takes weekly elocution lessons.
The radio, the telephone,
the Model T arrive. One by one
her sisters are sent north to cousins
in search of kindly Jewish husbands.

Surely having lived this long confers
a kind of aristocracy on my mother,
who kept to the end these talismans,
two dry links in the chain of daughters.
In the land of burley tobacco,
of mules in the narrow furrows,
in the land of diphtheria and strangles,
of revival meetings and stillborn angels,
in the land of eleven living siblings
I make my mother a dowager queen.

I give her back the chipped ruby goblets.
I hand over the battered Sheffield tureen
and the child I was, whose once-auburn hair
she scooped up like gems from the beauty-shop floor.

STEVEN HEIGHTON

2001, An Elegy

First scene:

I was the child
plucked from Miss Porch's kiln of a second grade
classroom, Indian summer 1968, the getaway Datsun
panting at the curb, Dad at the wheel—and you, like Jackie O,
with gangland shades and auburn bouffant, gold
drachma profile, making me your merry truant,
secret suitor. And for a matinee. (Miss Porch,
I think, subsequently disapproved.)
Decades later you would recall nothing of this,
and then, at the closing, nothing at all.
But the film lingers. How HAL's robotic voice
resembled Vice-Principal Hoop's ominous monotone,
Just what do you think you're doing . . . Dave . . .
and the spacemen in their plastic hibernacula
as futuristic pharaohs, LIFE FUNCTIONS
TERMINATED . . . and how, for thirty-three years,
that science-fiction date '2001' reared, monolithic
though distant as Jupiter, black parsec-stone or
postmodern tower, where I'd make it
to forty years, my parents
a Paleolithic sixty-five.

Later scene:

The deep space of Mt Pleasant
Theatre smudged with sweet, unfamiliar fumes
(unlike the Pall Malls you're smoking) and I press close,
peer up as Kubrick's chromatic vortices make violent

kaleidoscopes of your cat-eye lenses, the capsule
like a pill plummets through psychedelic voids, and
you and Dad (I think now) wonder if maybe
Fantasia would have been better. . . . Now see the hero,
retired, sexless, mummified in his final bed—
hard to conceive, from inside the living
frame of family, such mythic age,
and solitude. There are losses beyond losing.
The one closing I never foresaw:
that 2001 would be your year to leave, and me
in the "dark wood" of halfway through, commuting
fear to fear, until I reach your cribside (yes,
just that) and recite—since hearing's always last
to lapse—your favourite Hopkins—*I desired to go*
where springs not fail, where flies no . . .

Cotside. Coffinside. *Wait for me wait for me*
wait for me the widower said—

Closing scene:

Bed in a white room
where I sit by your side for a last *again*, read you more,
No sharp and sided hail, and a few lilies blow.
From a lampless house in high-flung fallow
you've the metropolis for starfields, high-beams
of cars on concession roads cruising slow
and straight as satellites, space probes.
In New Year's
smallest hours, you do hear a child deep inside
your ear, murmuring, *Mama,*
listen. It's 2001.
We made it.

Lenox Hill

(In Lenox Hill Hospital, after surgery, my mother said the sirens sounded like the elephants of Mihiragula when his men drove them off cliffs in the Pir Panjal Range.)

The Hun so loved the cry, one falling elephant's,
he wished to hear it again. At dawn, my mother
heard, in her hospital-dream of elephants,
sirens wail through Manhattan like elephants
forced off Pir Panjal's rock cliffs in Kashmir:
the soldiers, so ruled, had rushed the elephant,
The greatest of all footprints is the elephant's,
said the Buddha. But not lifted from the universe,
those prints vanished forever into the universe,
though nomads still break news of those elephants
as if it were just yesterday the air spread the dye
("War's annals will fade into night / Ere their story die"),

the punishing khaki whereby the world sees us die
out, mourning you, O massacred elephants!
Months later, in Amherst, she dreamt: She was, with dia-
monds, being stoned to death. I prayed: If she must die,
let it only be some dream. But there were times, Mother,
while you slept, that I prayed, "Saints, let her die."
Not, I swear by you, that I wished you to die
but to save you as you were, young, in song in Kashmir,
and I, one festival, crowned Krishna by you, Kashmir
listening to my flute. You never let gods die.
Thus I swear, here and now, not to forgive the universe
that would let me get used to a universe

without you. She, she alone, was the universe
as she earned, like a galaxy, her right not to die,
defying the Merciful of the Universe,
Master of Disease, "in the circle of her traverse"
of drug-bound time. And where was the god of elephants,
plump with Fate, when tusk to tusk, the universe,
dyed green, became ivory? Then let the universe,
like Paradise, be considered a tomb. Mother,
they asked me, *So how's the writing*? I answered *My mother*
is my poem. What did they expect? For no verse
sufficed except the promise, fading, of Kashmir
and the cries that reached you from the cliffs of Kashmir

(across fifteen centuries) in the hospital. *Kashmir,*
she's dying! How her breathing drowns out the universe
as she sleeps in Amherst. Windows open on Kashmir:
There, the fragile wood-shrines—so far away—of Kashmir!
O Destroyer, let her return there, if just to die.
Save the right she gave its earth to cover her, Kashmir
has no rights. When the windows close on Kashmir,
I see the blizzard-fall of ghost-elephants.
I hold back—she couldn't bear it—one elephant's
story: his return (in a country far from Kashmir)
to the jungle where each year, on the day his mother
died, he touches with his trunk the bones of his mother.

"As you sit here by me, you're just like my mother,"
she tells me. I imagine her: a bride in Kashmir,
she's watching, at the Regal, her first film with Father.
If only I could gather you in my arms, Mother,
I'd save you—now my daughter—from God. The universe
opens its ledger. I write: How helpless was God's mother!
Each page is turned to enter grief's accounts. Mother,
I see a hand. *Tell me it's not God's.* Let it die.
I see it. It's filling with diamonds. Please let it die.
Are you somewhere alive, somewhere alive, Mother?
Do you hear what I once held back: in one elephant's

cry, by his mother's bones, the cries of those elephants

that stunned the abyss? Ivory blots out the elephants.
I enter this: *The Belovéd leaves one behind to die.*
For compared to my grief for you, what are those of Kashmir,
and what (I close the ledger) are the griefs of the universe
when I remember you—beyond all accounting—O my mother?

RUTH PANOFSKY

Laike's Loss

1
Lazar at two
falls to his death
from our balcony

Hannah at five
watches him land
on the concrete

I at thirty-two
warm soup
at the stove

2
Six children
minus one

I count
and count again

Five boys
Jacob, Isaac, Abraham, Lazar, Saul
and one girl
Hannah

One is missing
gone

3
Dreams of children

plummeting
through pitch of night
buried by dawn

conjure the ghost
of Lazar
tiny among boys
grown tall and bold

4
Five boys and one girl
                    one boy missing
                    small boy

light and noise
of a hospital corridor
disrupt my rest

                    two flights up
                    iron balustrade

the nurses are kind
they calm me
with pills
and soothing words
chère Madame, ces mauvais jours will pass
they will pass, Madame
dormez Madame, dormez

                    two flights up
                    iron balustrade
                    Hannah watching
                    Lazar falling

five boys, one girl
                    one boy missing
                    small boy

5

We move one last time
to a ground floor flat
no balcony
no climbing
no falling
no

in memory of Gracie: still shaken by the stillness of your name

unnerving and delicate

as the indentation of a nib on parchment
or the sheen of oil on lamp-lit insects' wings.

Talk to me
though your voice

was never heard yet—
complicate

this single note of grief,

I need something to declare
other than the shape of you,

avian, streaked with blood,
soft skull still porous,

something to record
other than the weight of you

falling into dissonance—
that swallowed hive, my tongue

your final nursery—dear melted zipper
in a bag of ash.

Sad Rite

Because I was empty
my body got me a child,
the small idea of a child—
some pearly cells and light.
I thought of it all night.
It still lacked hands
or a face with which to fill
its hands, or another, livelier
face to fill its heart.
Because I tend
to take myself apart, I planned
to scoop it out, this child, but keep
the idea, being cursed
with keeping and ideas,
with emptiness. And so I did.
And so I keep
a small abyss inside
until the moon is right.
And then I find a bar, a man
who'll neatly stack my empties
while he drags his sour cloth
across my place, and I read omens
in the clouds he makes, until the moon
comes down when I rise up, its red light
a blade; inside me bloody flame.

The Mother

Abortions will not let you forget.
You remember the children you got that you did not get,
The damp small pulps with a little or with no hair,
The singers and workers that never handled the air.
You will never neglect or beat
Them, or silence or buy with a sweet.
You will never wind up the sucking-thumb
Or scuttle off ghosts that come.
You will never leave them, controlling your luscious sigh,
Return for a snack of them, with gobbling mother-eye.

I have heard in the voices of the wind the voices of my dim killed children.
I have contracted. I have eased
My dim dears at the breasts they could never suck.
I have said, Sweets, if I sinned, if I seized
Your luck
And your lives from your unfinished reach,
If I stole your births and your names,
Your straight baby tears and your games,
Your stilted or lovely loves, your tumult, your marriages, aches, and your deaths,
If I poisoned the beginnings of your breaths,
Believe that even in my deliberateness I was not deliberate.
Though why should I whine,
Whine that the crime was other than mine?—
Since anyhow you are dead.
Or rather, or instead,
You were never made.
But that too, I am afraid,
Is faulty: oh, what shall I say, how is the truth to be said?

You were born, you had body, you died.
It is just that you never giggled or planned or cried.

Believe me, I loved you all.
Believe me, I knew you, though faintly, and I loved, I loved you
All.

Appendix to Ordinary Time

My mother died the autumn I was writing this. And *Now I have no one*, I thought. "Exposed on a high ledge in full light," says Virginia Woolf on one of her tingling days (March 1, 1937). I was turning over the pages of her diaries, still piled on my desk the day after the funeral, looking for comfort I suppose—why are these pages comforting? They led her, after all, to the River Ouse. Yet strong pleasure rises from every sentence. In reflecting on the death of her own father, she decided that forming such shocks into words and order was "the strongest pleasure known to me" (*Moments of Being* [London 1985], 81).

And whom do we have to thank for this pleasure but Time?

It grows dark as I write now, the clocks have been changed, night comes earlier—gathering like a garment. I see my mother, as she would have been at this hour alone in her house, gazing out on the cold lawns and turned earth of evening, high bleak grass going down to the lake. Or moving room by room through the house and the silverblue darkness filling around her, pooling, silencing. Did she think of me—somewhere, in some city, in lamplight, bending over books, or rising to put on my coat and go out? Did I pause, switch off the desklamp and stand, gazing out at the dusk, think I might call her. Not calling. Calling. Too late now. Under a different dark sky, the lake trickles on.

How vanished everyone is, Virginia Woolf wrote in letters to several people in 1941. And to Isaiah Berlin, *Please knock on my little grey door.* He did not knock; she died before. Here is a fragment from February of that year:

> It is strange that the sun shd be shining; and the birds singing.
> For here,
> it is coal black: here in the little cave in which I sit.

> Such was the complaint of the woman who had all her faculties entire.
> ~~She did not sufficiently. She had no grasp of~~
> (Berg Collection of the New York Public Library)

Reading this, especially the crossed-out line, fills me with a sudden understanding. Crossouts are something you rarely see in published texts. They are like death: by a simple stroke—all is lost, yet still there. For death *although utterly unlike life* shares a skin with it. Death lines every moment of ordinary time. Death hides right inside every shining sentence we grasped and had no grasp of. Death is a fact. No more or less strange than that celebrated fact given by the very last sentence of her diaries (March 24, 1941):

> L. is doing the rhododendrons.

Crossouts sustain me now. I search out and cherish them like old photographs of my mother in happier times. It may be a stage of grieving that will pass. It may be I'll never again think of sentences unshadowed in this way. It has changed me. Now I too am someone who knows marks.

Here is an epitaph for my mother I found on p. 19 of the Fitzwilliam Manuscript of Virginia Woolf's Women and Fiction:

such
abandon ~~Obviously it is impossible, I thought, looking into those~~
ment ~~foaming waters, to~~
such ~~compare the living with the dead make any comparison~~
rapture ~~compare them.~~

Mother tongue was a pang

NICOLE BROSSARD

The Garden

During the same year, the two women saw each other again, in the East this time. On the other side of the Atlantic. The young woman now spoke a foreign language that she alternated with the mother tongue linking her to the other woman. They were sitting in the garden. Around them, summer reigned with the sounds of cicadas and crickets, the perfume of roses and azaleas. Their soft voices floated above the grass and flowers. They were astonished that their voices were so rich in echoes and intonations.

"I'm expecting a girl," the young woman said delightedly. It was culturally possible for her to think it natural that nothing could be more joyous than to give birth to a daughter. To want a girl and declare it loudly was a recent phenomenon limited, nonetheless, to a tiny part of the globe. Elsewhere still daughters were a source of humiliation for fathers, a burden and by-product of humanity. So they got rid of girls before birth, during childhood, adolescence, or even later if they became infertile wives or incapable of producing sons. Girls, women, disappeared, burned, decapitated, strangled, sold, or simply abandoned to the cold and hunger.

In the garden, night fell. The older woman could not manage to conceal her emotion. The young woman took her hand, placed it on her belly. The mother dissolved in tears, incapable of uttering any words when her feelings made everything tremble, collapsing the arrangement of roles everywhere. Mother tongue was a pang, the ultimate oath of allegiance. Inalterable language.

Translation by Barbara Godard

To An Autumn Mother

A soldier chalks two words on sidewalks, no other hector in his hand. They are "love" and "heals." Crowds gather, crowds soften like an herb that's pounded into poultice for a shattered bone to knit it. "Love heals" remains. It rains.

In the rain, and when the healers are gone who heals when they are gone and who heals the gone in Autumn, where is my bed and what is the work of love, its dark attacks and rescues, poultices or words,   what work is emptiness where peace was, how do you know that love heals   it turns, in the earth   in the promise   in our air.

Without question marks we lie in the question. Its unmarked longing. No rain erasing.

a. and *b.* and *c.*

In zealot tides I dream of dead healers.
Kalua, in Lahaina. Empedocles, in Sicily.
This year of wars that have not died, no matter
how many healers. This mouth that spouts like birthing
whales in a poisoned sea, but wordless.

In a corner of the dream, in the corner is a dwarf old woman
curled up in fetus, she is stiff and iridescent flies are at her eyes,
you have to bury her.

I am asleep beside an island pine, its wide twined root,
this is where I shovel-break the dirt to make a bed for her,
soiled clothes,   felt hat,   flies.

I'll sleep where she slept now, on flat stones, near the wall,
she, in the softened earth. The healers are—I don't know where but gone.
Is it time to speak of how it flowed from our hands for the calling
like falcons, come, please come,   is it time to speak of helping?

Healing haunts my walls.
Are you a healer?

Sometimes.
If healers taught you,
what do you know?

a.   *b.*   *c.*

Am doe in car lamps, knees locked,

suspect there is a word for faith,
its truth, its trial, its wall.
I want there to be such a word.
To trust it. Suspect, they taught us trust.

a.   *b.*   *c.*

For faith, I suspect its cell   its mustard grain and mountain may
be lost. Suspect there is still love. And air, for the airless, promised.
a.   *b.*   *c.*

Trust me, I want to say,
I can wear blood like child soldiers do,
bright finger paint across our souls—

Autumn mother, mere challenger—I can close your eye.

I give you my on-fire palms.

Trust me I can hold your terrible hand when you bleed and are afraid.
Trust when the God-name has become a sorrow. over used. vain.
Why, one asks.
Longing, I say.

Light, I say, come with my woman's welcome I have to offer.
We don't know what heals. But know the miracle that is loved
and gone. Spontaneous. And gone. Say come to this heat I have
and I can help you burn. I can help you paint. I can help you cry.

You cry in vain. When one fight's done, another crouches ready.
In the corner of a dream, the dwarf. In another, the lover like a giant.
Dying's in our bodies, as normal as a war and leaf fall. Normal as
longing. *a.* and *b.* and *c*.

In the Musée de la Vie Romantique are two framed locks of George Sand's saved white hair, glassed gold, her gifts of tiny rings, ash pearls. "I only care about things that come from the people I loved and who are gone," she said. An Autumn thorn is rooting in a black torrential rain where she is gone and her love is gone, dour Chopin's piano haunting soft cloth walls, as though it could not quiet.

Here is my hand, my hand because I have no more to give. Here my broken
art, for the same reason. Autumn mother, is there a wailing wall anywhere
 that
cannot answer your solemnity? We are being taught to cry.

Oh soft Autumn, come. I have no son for you.

*

ANDREA POTOS

Mother/Reader

After the last section of countertop has been scoured,
the sodden rag slung on its rod,

after the last toothbrush has been rinsed
and propped in its slot,

on the other side of her children's sleeping,
she imagines the book splayed open on her belly,

the drape of her grandmother's crocheted shawl around her.
After the last goodnight is given,

their breathing rhythmic and safe,
she travels to her room at the top of the house

as if she were hiking through the poppy field toward Oz,
wrestling with her fatigue, the phantom weight in her arms.

MICHELLE MOORE

Whitman by Candlelight

Tonight, my sadness has to do
with the candle on my bedside table
dancing in its own light,

and this Whitman poem,
its live oak uttering joyous leaves
though it stands alone,

no friend or lover near.
I was twenty when I read it first,
newly divorced and bringing up

a months-old daughter badly,
surviving as best we could
on canned stew and candlelight,

and when the flame went still
upon the page, as if startled to find itself
said that way,

I, too, felt I was changed—
how many lives have I burned through
since then, how many men

have I tried to love
against history, smolder and ash,
dancing, in spite of the shadows I cast.

Burning Day Behind "Country Books"

On a guilty evening
just as the light from the fire
begins to mock the low-lying sun,
she flicks coverless paperbacks
into the red roar of copyright law.

She always ripples through the convicted:
those missing her "must-read" pile
harder now to discriminate without archer's biceps,
and ripped bodices.

She's a southern girl,
former, she'd tell you, but this
fire begins to boil her,
begins to singe the same as
the library fire, same as
the Alamogordo book burning.

By the time the fire department
volunteers, paged from their early beds,
chase hot print across the empty lot,
Mother is still leaning into the barrel,
pulling out survivors.

Between God and Evil

is the title of the book review in the Saturday paper
which I am trying, ineffectually, to read
with Rachel on my lap, coffee cooling just out of reach.
She grabs a blue pencil (*turquoise*, she corrects me,
turquoise and violet being her two favourite colours)
and methodically circles all the words she recognizes:

> *to, the, and, in,*
> *look, little, one,*
> *me, you, or,*
> *love, lost* and *garden.*

She skips over *Nazis* and *Hildegard of Bingen*; ignores *destiny*
and *hallucinations*; turns her pyjama-clad back righteously
on *fundamentalism*. And maybe she's right.
None of those words have brought you and me any closer
to love; or to the little one lost
in the garden.

The Tui, Beloved of Crossword Constructors,

Is native to New Zealand, Aotereoa of the Maori,
who themselves appear with greenstone frequency
somewhere in the Arts section of the New York Times,
companion there of the adolescent eft,
bright pumpkin crawling among duller fallen leaves
(Massachusetts woods, beaver pond, gray stone to mark where New Hampshire begins).
Four of us to kick the leaves,
four marriages, seven childbirths, two divorces, and two dead sons among us.
Solve that puzzle, solve for the unknown, for what any four women will know
about Sub-Zeros, wild mushrooms, and colder, darker things.
But never underestimate the crossword puzzle.
The linked chain, geometry of language, the comfort of grammar,
resolution of chaos and loss in the time it takes to drink a cup of English Breakfast tea.

Fifty-four across, the tui, drops its amber song along a hill
one continent, one cold ocean away, and fifty-four down is time.

A Woman and Child

Sharp-eyed, in multi-coloured skirt
and high heels, with her free hand
she holds out roses and takes coins,
with the other, clutches and breast-feeds
her linen-swathed infant.

The instant collapses, and the clear
morning sunlight is dream
of the foetus in the womb –
the watery mystery knitting
a lightning of flesh and bone –

now of the milk of eternity
suddenly flowing freely
over tables, into stalls, alcoves,
through clothing racks set up
along the aisles of the bazaar.

She draws her blouse, turns,
quick, musical speech on her lips,
and the world flashes, her earlobe's bangle.
Every word I have learned
goes after her, clinging to her neck.

Cartographer of the Most Serene Republic

The four wild blonde-headed kids were moving seat to seat
around the train, and the mother who was commanding them
to sit still – to get back – to follow her from the moment they
boarded, her voice the sort of voice you could hear above any crowd,

said to them *sit right there, I have to see where you are.* It's the city,
the underground, the subway, the great escalators rising out of the earth
straight up and down and the tunnels vast. *If I get off
and leave any of you on the train,* she said, *I don't want to be hearing about it,*

and I was wondering how you could hear about it
if the wild kids are on the train riding toward Maryland bouncing seat
to seat and reckless with themselves, and you gone off someplace
without them. Or was it she didn't want them to show up

sometime later with the story about being left behind on the train,
which is what any mother wants – not to have the story
come back at her. How she left, got off the train, what have you.
She had the pinching finger mother voice

of long range and lots of trouble, not enough money, something
scrapping in her. The children over active, refusing to stay in sight.
I was sitting on the train in a strange city having
done something that day that might change my life.

Done it as easily as I had boarded this train. Doors opened
and I got on and went. Which we do sometimes
and find ourselves gone – *Who knows where you'll end up*
she said, reaching down the train, grabbing one of the round

headed kids by the ear, *sit down, and stay down.*
I got off the train before them, and I can still picture those kids
out there somewhere ricocheting by themselves through D.C. tunnels,
station by station lighting their blinking faces.

MARTHA MARINARA

Reflection in a Well House, Tuscumbia, Alabama, 1887

Non plus seulement connaitre, mais se connaitre; non plus seulement savoir mais que l'on sait.

—Chardin

It was cool in the well
house. Annie Sullivan pulled
her pupil inside, away
from the hot Alabama
summer. Bone tired when she lifted
the pump handle and forced Helen's
hand under winter cold water
water spilling spelling words
until Helen heard the rhyme lit wonder-
full flash clap of sense
and knew *water.*
Helen Keller became newborn
named her creatures
the apples no longer unknown.

It is what happens
the second a child leaps from instinct
to knowing as the center explodes
hard and clean as Eve's new teeth in fruit.
My daughter reached through space and time
and through the ringing air
to know the word *blue*
was the sky
and the waters rising blue
upon blue.

Two Rivers

The spirits are raining. This is true because of airplane breath.

A "day" slips back and forth in time.

I make numbers, my mother's darkness to the left, soon she'll be
the curve in a 5.

A secret can be used in public if not done in a row. Fix your face
so they know you are listening, then think your new word.
Today's new word is stewardess.

In the now of this she points from the airplane: the lines of Brazil
are simply there

where the dark & lighter rivers join, the joining is

a tiny slash (/).

For a time I dissolved upon my mother's tongue…

Rio Preto, she says. Amazon from the right (girl / boy, dark / light
which should I prefer)

Both rivers have fish that could eat a girl in minutes.

It's not that I can't choose between them but why bother—

If I'm made to decide…

(which is why I begin to love metaphor)

(was it "post-colonial"?)

Whitewash of Houston

Who would have thought of her as mother small
town raunchy with cowhands coming and country
girls and boys not knowing Dr. Freud but
Moses very well as big-nosed Bach pumped both
organ and wife scattering music even
more than her cattle safely graze those meadows
of midnight and darknesses presences surrounding
her with cloud by day and night also going
before her where she only stumbles in
imagination fearing that they are
only dry holes reverberating with
some ancient terror tutored by none
but teachers' voices like a piece of chalk
scratched white across the face of midnight breaking?
Who would have thought of her as mother sleek
big-butted like black cars that bulging slickly
swim over pavement and pothole splattered with
delicate bone and gut of squirrel none
except poor folk afoot or else on bike
would ever notice much less mourn on grounds
as female as the moon her son tromped on
galumping ghosts crumpling that most dainty
fingernail of poetry into a
fist fondling their rod that flaunts their flag
dribbling oil and slime and muck that ooze
from under her armpits as she stuffs her mouth
with garbage drooled onto her front until
she drops dead in her tracks to bed hot for
that prick and prong of sleep's sweet long and hard?
Who would have thought of her as mother gunning
down eerie corridors of her dark self
dented and bent the shape of truth no meaning

can measure and that has no end but life
to cradle whether for its good or ill
nobody knows however life may teem
with fact outwearing pint-sized brains made all
she ought to stand up straight behind her shame
before the world that tossed her to the dogs
as innocent as she once seemed with knowing
what shadow loops its coil about her legs
quickened with light and slowed to dusk on seeing
her terror driving all her children dumb
down the long chute of death and safely home?

II

Who would have thought of her as mother mad
at morning and mad with mourning and merry
as the scissor grinder's whistle blown far dodging
February currents and her memories
bouncing it up and down like a fey bell on
her cars as keen as gray chill cuts and leaner
than Lent has stripped away the clover blossoms
long ago vanished with the honey bees
that horny fingers of the rain uncoiled
March and April meandering across
the vacant lot of Easter and back home?
Who would have thought of her as mother fed
and fudged till fattened on her lentil vigils
as open as her covert cesspools ripe
with the rich grain of avarice and April's
froth of green and dogwood's lace hung over
the land and greening all her lawns until
she lies down with her apron smelling of summer?
Who would have thought of her as mother light
could lift into corn cribs to lie until
curious as a calf she grows and swells
with moonstruck offspring pushing all awry
who have not known the hollow of her womb
more hollow than the opening leading to it

to gobble down her shacks and spires till time
has hulled them all like winter's dried pecans
dropped to her earth leaning and lurching fawnwise
mulched with the sunshine long since loamed with darkness?

For the Color of My Mother

I am a white girl gone brown to the blood color of my mother
speaking to her through the unnamed part of the mouth
the wide-arched muzzle of brown women

at two
my upper lip split open
clear to the tip of my nose
it spilled forth a cry that would not yield
that traveled down six floors of hospital
where doctors wound me into white bandages
only the screaming mouth exposed

the gash sewn back into a snarl
would last for years

I am a white girl gone brown to the blood color of my mother
speaking for her

at five, her mouth
pressed into a seam
a fine blue child's line drawn across her face
her mouth, pressed into mouthing english
mouthing yes yes yes
mouthing stoop lift carry
(sweating wet sighs into the field
her red bandana comes loose from under the huge brimmed hat
moving across her upper lip)

at fourteen, her mouth
painted, the ends drawn up
the mole in the corner colored in a darker larger mouthing yes

she praying no no no
lips pursed and moving

at forty-five, her mouth
bleeding into her stomach
the hole gaping growing redder
deepening with my father's pallor
finally stitched shut from hip to breastbone
          an inverted V
          Vera
          Elvira

I am a white girl gone brown to the blood color of my mother
speaking for her

as it should be,
dark women come to me
                              sitting in circles
I pass thru their hands
the head of my mother
painted in clay colors

          touching each carved feature swollen eyes and mouth

they understand the explosion, the splitting
open   contained within the fixed expression

they cradle her silence

                              nodding to me

Morning Laughter

To my mother, Elsie MacEwen

umbilical I lumbered
trailing long seed, unwombed
to the giant vagina, unarmed,
no sprung Athene
—cry, cry in the sudden salt
of the big room, world
—I uncurled plastic limbs of senses,
freed the crashing course of menses,
                                        —hurled

I hurled the young tongue's spit
for a common coming, a genesis
sans trumpets and myrrh, rejected
whatever seed in love's inside
fought and formed me from
an exodus of semen come
  for the dream of Gwen,
  the small one,
  whose first salt scream
heralded more and borrowed excellence.

years have tied the sweet cord;
morning laughter, ships of daughter
and of mother move together
in clumsy grace:
you look to a roof of brass clouds
crash loud as the known world knows us;
and each motion's intrinsic as I reach
beyond roofs for a clutch of that first seed.

wary we speak from a fringe of meanings,
circle and pat-a-cake in cat-paw diplomacy,
each hope hoisted to a veined rainbow,
our common denominator, whose colors
are all blood and bone,

wary we speak from a fringe of meanings,
each tongue censored with love and its
cat-paw circling
            ,now foetal in the world's wide womb
            ,now known in my own rebellious belly
             the stuff to people further days
            ,now forced by some grim reason
             to hark down the bonds of the blood
            ,can still remember from that womb walking,
             sideways out of that womb,
             glorious from that womb, bent and insolent.

—morning laughter with your young daughter—
smile at the pen she picks, armed to bring light
into terrible focus
and the paper builds worlds but makes
no prodigal…

who would erase the scribbled slate
of gone years, their jumbled algebra,
their rude designs
junked under a rainbow, all blood and bone
that links the mother and the morning daughter—
and acknowledge now, armed and still insolent
that what is housed in the fragile skull
—light or learning or verbal innocence—
grows from the woman somehow who housed the whole
body,
who first fed the vessels, the flesh and the sense.

from "My Bag of Broken Glass, 1939-1978" (Poland 1939 / Canada 1978)
6. a woman is a drawer — a keeper of threads —

she is making likenesses, recreating us, right foot on the treadle conducts the plaintive purr
of her singer, its back up as if spooked by the spectacle (the specter) of west
sun haunting the windows — the singer shines on all fours, a gold ring around its neck,
on point on its wooden desk in which sleep comes cool, sound and up-side-down
— and drawers emit alizarin crimson tangled in rose madder — thread drowned,
inseparable from cerulean and boysenberry, my mother sings and plays her singer

she is shaping a motherland in her mouth, freeing space — but if the self's a homeless singer,
the better self at home in exile — think of what a border costs — scattering, dispersion
— if boundaries are sharp things, edges scissors, my mother a hive, margin and pit, drowned —
a straw bent in a glass of water — then may each carapace sink like a western
sky's light, shatter like an ice-cube between uneven erosions of teeth, fall down
from the tongue's precipice, a glossary of stains, along the canals of our necks

because we wanted no edges between us, we knew they were there, obstructing like a bottleneck
the highway of her body to mine — fragile, her torso, the most slender vase, obsolete singer
sewing shadows to our landscape without perspective, vanished to no point, up-side-down
— a woman is diasporic, atomized scent of clean hair braided in a mirror, perfectly
black and straight inside a harbor of hot light on a back scrubbed and bare — she goes west,
my mother motherless, crescent and want, formed formlessness — history drowning

her singer pertinacious, she stitches relief, a crib of petals issues from her throat to drown
our dislocations — we are up to our necks in scissors and threads, in exile, up-side-down
inside-out — we gash the caul — we scavenge for language in a place where we will always be guests —

SHANA YOUNGDAHL

To Have

The noises of the house; door slam, dog bark, our slow pulse of domestic excitements tick, keys under unkempt finger nails. I am drowned of lingo and claims to one word lines holding their own radioactive power. See the haze eyes of women given up on monologues in favor of ornithology. Not a bad substitute. We are all mesmerized by the power of flight. I am here wiping my finger on the softest monogrammed towels as each reality kisses the next. I want nothing more than to somehow live with this child under my arm and you, leaning against the door frame.

I'm not sure this is sacrifice. I won't bow to abandonment. I promise to throw out their notes. I will to continue stack vowel to vowel lay the child in her crib, pass my body under your hands. Speak.

Mother Love

Mother Love

Who can forget the attitude of mothering?
Toss me a baby and without bothering
to blink I'll catch her, sling him on a hip.
Any woman knows the remedy for grief
is being needed: duty bugles and we'll
climb out of exhaustion every time,
bare the nipple or tuck in the sheet,
heat milk and hum at bedside until
they can dress themselves and rise, primed
for Love or Glory—those one-way mirrors
girls peer into as their fledgling heroes slip
through, storming the smoky battlefield.

So when this kind woman approached at the urging
of her bouquet of daughters,
(one for each of the world's corners,
one for each of the winds to scatter!)
and offered up her only male child for nursing
(a smattering of flesh, noisy and ordinary),
I put aside the lavish trousseau of the mourner
for the daintier comfort of pity:
I decided to save him. Each night
I laid him on the smoldering embers,
sealing his juices in slowly so he might
be cured to perfection. Oh, I know it
looked damning: at the hearth a muttering crone
bent over a baby sizzling on a spit
as neat as a Virginia ham. Poor human—
to scream like that, to make me remember.

Repetitions For My Mother

I want my mother to live forever,
I want her to continue baking bread,
hang the washing on the line, scrub
the floors for the lawyers in our town.
I want her fingers red with cold
or white with water. I want her
out of bed every holiday at six
to stuff the turkey, I want her to cut
the brittle rhubarb into pieces, to can
the crab apples, to grind the leftover roast
for shepherd's pie. I want her to grab me
and shake me out of my boots when I come home
late from school, I want her to lick her fingers
and wipe the dirt from my face. I want her to
put her large breast into my mouth,
I want her to tell me I am pretty, I am sweet,
I am the apple of her eye. I want her to knit and knit
long scarves of wool to wrap us in like
winding sheets all winter through. I want her
to sing with her terrible voice that rose above
the voices in the choir, to sing so loud
my head is full of her. I want her to carry
her weariness like a box of gifts up those stairs
to the room where I wait. Sleep, I will croon
at the edge of her bed, sleep, for tomorrow is
a holiday. Her hands will move in dream, breaking
and breaking bread. Not pain, not sorrow or old age
will make my mother weep. But the sting of onions
she must slice at six a.m., the bird forever
thawing in the kitchen sink, naked and white,
I want so much emptiness
for her to fill.

My Mother in Old Age

As my mother ages and becomes
Ever more fragile and precarious
Her hands dwindle under her rings
And the freckled skin at her throat
Gathers in tender pleats like some startled fabric.
The blue translucence of her veins gives
The texture of her skin an agate gleam
And the dark-blue, almost indigo
Capillaries of her cheeks and forehead
Resemble the gentle roots
Of cuttings of violets
In sheltered jars.

I love her now more urgently
Because there is an unfamiliar and relentless
Splendour in her face that terrifies me.

"Oh, don't prettify decrepitude,"
She demands. "Don't lie!
Don't make old age seem so *ornamental*!"

And yet, she abets her metamorphosis
Invests herself in voluminous costume
Jewels and shrill polyesters

—ambitious as a moth
To mime the dangerous leaf on which she rests.

Pumpkins, for Claire

When you spin on heels and stare
into past sizes of self, this

when you're thirty-five or forty-
five increments older or more tired

as we "softening" adults seem (sometimes even
slightly bruised or blasted by simple soul-

bumps) well, then you'll know: the girl we adore
at twelve did plod and probe interior fields

for left-behind, missed-over meanings.
The other children her age—yes, *some* wore the same

searching head-lamp into the dark field, but
many go, by blatant day, trading the search itself

for standard behemoth fruits, bicep-round
golden squash, squawking out from the foliage

festering in self-display, as orange as rubber.
But she, you, lift fan-shaped leaves, looking

for what's been leap-frogged by the harvest's obvious
ease. What of the smaller melon-shaped heads,

dud pumpkins so bubbled they are molten and
folding into themselves, shy introverts

double-chambered in desire for sky *and* soil,
for largeness and smallness, coiling away from *and*

toward wrist-thin stems, attachments too involved
for the snappish pickers before, still: all marvels.

Claire at twelve would put her palms on these.
Find their hide chilled, *watery*, or warm from September's

canny cool-hot sun, tomato-yellow toss-aways
piled on each other like lonely molecules, all together

a globular bouquet, she might cheerily
announce, the way the spherical structures

seem to buckle in front of you, blossom
in vision like sorceress flowers, although they

are pumpkins! And you would giggle, fill
your basket with carrot-rouge images, magic

mirrors of your irises like two tiny pumpkins
tucked inside that original mane we all

carry with us like October. Claire's hair
like the perfect fall day, flamboyant

blue air, maple leaves drifting like stop-gapped
honey from heaven, red-pepper flecks in wheat.

Remember how big your hands will be. Recall
at twelve you watched them grow, month by

month, changed mitt size for consequent winters.
For adults that's always the reverent wonder
of our children's birthdays, how you are
growing before our eyes like pumpkins in fields

as we keep vigil, watching the farm bear visitors,
carloads of seekers who come and leave quickly

clutching their Hallowe'en prize, prouder about it than
about their own staggering development, for they

are each miraculous, like the entire field that grew again
from scratch this year, and like Claire who by moonlight

and candelabra crown is crouching with blankets
in the pumpkin patch, reading *Rumpelstiltskin* to

baby pumpkins, brewing savoury soup in a large
kettle-shaped pumpkin, a country-bumpkin girl

tonight, all costumed and in character, tending
to the little ones left there, and maybe

they are happier for it, rosier by morning, more
confident, since they have Claire, at twelve

RAY HSU

Traitor

Running in the family is the capacity
to bruise
over a long time. Naturally,

you try to heal. Harm should, at best, be
small enough
to mistake. The eye whose vision is touch

never sees it coming. Who are these
incompatibilities:
mother, aunt, daughter, the last to grow

to accountancy. You cross one out
for every three.
What relief

to go from what you see. Soon nothing
will soften it.
Happiness, now, must be something

else. That which spreads within. On paper,
everything.
equals out.

PRISCILA UPPAL

My Mother is One Crazy Bitch

How do you write that on a postcard?

How will I tell my brother, that yes, yes, I found our mother
after twenty years and she's about as lovely as an electrical storm
when you're naked and tied to the highest tree in the county.

She has tantrums when we wake in the morning,
tantrums when we catch our cabs for the day,
outside the theatre, inside the theatre, after the theatre,
then again on the ride home. She has several more
when I am hiding in the washroom, washing
my underwear in the sink.

You don't love me enough! is her main point of contention.
So, we battle this love thing out as if it were some native Brazilian dish
I am supposed to swallow until my stomach spasms,
until I learn to crave it. But I am a teacher now, not a student.

My mother switches off the television and starts to snore. Even at night,
she accosts me, even in the middle
of my across-the-ocean nightmares she makes sure
uncredited appearances.

At the checkout desks of my subconscious I am writing postcards
to all the dead mothers out there, all the dead daughters
who never had a chance to meet in this life. I collect
their tears the way I have been hoping to collect my thoughts.

Unknown grief is sweeter, I write. *Stay on your side off-stage,*
let others stay on theirs. Only then can we indulge
in the luxury of applause.

LOUISE GLÜCK

Brown Circle

My mother wants to know
why, if I hate
family so much,
I went ahead and
had one. I don't
answer my mother.
What I hated
was being a child,
having no choice about
what people I loved.

I don't love my son
the way I meant to love him.
I thought I'd be
the lover of orchids who finds
red trillium growing
in the pine shade, and doesn't
touch it, doesn't need
to possess it. What I am
is the scientist,
who comes to that flower
with a magnifying glass
and doesn't leave, though
the sun burns a brown
circle of grass around
the flower. Which is
more or less the way
my mother loved me.

I must learn
to forgive my mother,
now that I'm helpless
to spare my son.

Mother Fear

The fear of ending up like her,
alone, removed from life,
numb to the world; the fear
of finding out that she chose this

That she didn't

The fear that it's latent in the genes,
this disease of the heart,
this soul ailment; that one day
(whether I expect it to or not)
it will strike me down

The fear that loving you
will hasten it, the fear
that not loving you will hasten it

The first greater

LATE

For Marie Candee Birmingham, my mother

1

Dark on a bright day, fear of you is two-poled,
Longing its opposite. Who were we?
What for? Dreaming, I haunt you unconsoled.

Rewarded as I force thought outward, I see
A warbler, a Myrtle, marked by coin-gold—
I feel lucky, as if I'd passed a test,
And try my luck, to face the misery
Of loss on loss, find us, and give us rest.
Once we birdwatched, eyeing shrub & tree
For the luck beyond words that was our quest;
Your rings flashing, you shoed me day-holed
Owls, marsh blackbirds on red wings, the crest
Kingfishers bear. Mother, dreams are too cold
To eye the dark woodland of your bequest.

2

To eye the dark woodland of your bequest
I wear the fire of diamond on my hand,
Flawed extravagance of your first love expressed
In a many-faceted engagement band.
Recklessly cut with the blaze I invest
In my dazzling flaws, careless of weight,
The fiery cast of mind that I love planned
To sacrifice carat-points for this bright state.
It is yours still, and I go talismanned

By you to find you, though I'm lost & Late.
You left this for me; ringed I go dressed
To mother us, mother, to isolate
And name the flight of what, mouth to rich breast,
We meant while we were together to create.

3

We meant while we were together to create
A larger permanence, as lovers do,
Of perfecting selves: I would imitate
By my perfections, yours; I would love you
As you me, each to the other a gate
Opening on intimate gardens and
Amiable there. Mother you were new
At it but when you looped us in the bands
Of clover hope to be each other's due,
The hope at least lasted; here I still stand
Full of the verb you had to predicate.
Though you as subject now are contraband
Half hidden, half disguised to intimidate,
I recognize your diamond on my hand.

4

I recognize the diamond on my hand
As the imagined world where we were whole.
Now among boxes, pine roots, & Queens sand
You have changed places with this bit of coal,
Dark to light, light to dark. To understand
The dark your child never was afraid of
I go lightless sightless birdless mole
In the dark which is half what words are made of
I enter the dark poems memories control,
Their dark love efficient under day love.
Down I go down through the oldest unscanned
Scapes of mind to skim the dim parade

Of images long neglected lost or banned,
To root for the you I have not betrayed.

5

To root for the you I have not betrayed
I hunt the ovenbird we never found—
Or guessed we'd found when something leafbrown strayed
Under the trees where soft leaves lay year round.
When you'd said, "Hush," and we'd obeyed (obeyed
Lifelong too long) "Tea/cher!" we heard; the shy
Bird spoke itself, "Tea/cher!" from the dim ground
The call came plain enough to recognize
And we went out following the sound.
It went before us in the dusk; its cries
Go before me now, swerve & dip in shade
Woman daughter bird teacher teach me. Skies
Boughs brush tufts; blind I have lost where we played
All trust in love, to the dark of your disguise.

6

Trust in love to the dark of your disguise,
I forget if I loved you; I forget
If, when I failed, you requisitioned lies;
Did we make believe we saw the bird, and set
On my lifelong list what my long life denies:
That we found what we wanted side by side?

But I did see you bird I see you yet
Your live glance glinting from leafdust; you hide
Calling, colorless, your brief alphabet
Sharp. Wait, wait for me. Flash past, dusty bride,
Stand safe, rosefooted, before my finite eyes.
Sing, undeafen me. Bird be identified.
Speak yourself. I dread love that mystifies.
Say we wanted what we found side by side.

7

I say I wanted what I found at your side.
("Is that your mother?" Yes. "But she's a tea/
cher." Yes. I see that.) Reading, sunned, outside,
I see your lit hand on the page, spirea
Shaking light on us; from your ring I see slide
A sun, showering its planets across skies
Of words making, as you read or I or we,
A cosmos, ours. Its permanence still defies
The dark, in sparkles on this page; fiery,
It makes its statements clear; light multiplies.
No matter on whose flawed hand what jewel rides
Or who quickens to what bird with jeweled eyes,
The light of the planet is amplified.
Bird your life is diamond and amplifies.

REPLAY

The luck beyond birds that was our quest
I find in you. Although I'm lost & late
Our hope at least lasted; here I still stand
In your dark love, efficient under day love:
It goes before me in the dark, its cries
Sharp. Wait, wait for me. Flash past, dusty bride,
Make your statement clear: light multiplies.

NAN BYRNE

Love Me Tender

I've said it before
And I will say it again
I feel close to Elvis
I always have
Ever since I heard
About Gladys
How she raised that boy
to love her
like no one else could
Not even Vernon
came between
the two of them
Gladys wrapped and
tangled that boy up
with the strong thread
of her mother love
Think about that
How a thread
becomes a string
and the string
becomes a rope
and the rope
becomes a noose
and the noose
The noose
becomes the connection
Then you will know
why I feel close
to Elvis

Then you will know
why some people
stumble through life
It's cause
Their feet are swinging

LEON ROOKE

Bonnie Dressed to Kill (Sam)

Hat from Panama
boots from Gibralter
(spurs, Wyoming)
stockings from Brazil
dress the Americas (Bergdorf & Goodman's)
panties (pink blue clouds over each fanny)
from Your Sister's Coming
belt from the Navaho Nation
(silver buckle bearing label 'Made
by Pauper's Hand, Tuscon')
dangling figures vaguely Moroccan
chaps Francine of Bollywood
pearls (the Orient)
hair by Brubecler
eyes by Miro
lips Miro's brother
gloves (Duchamp)
purse a Hell For Leather Creation
of the Dobson twins of New Plymouth
perfume unknown though known
to be reliable
in Bonnie's purse a white pistol
(yellow barrel) a two-shooter
a new saltshaker (Buddhist model)
mints, tissue to catch the sobs,
proper reading matter for a woman
intent upon murder, a letter
from an admirer (descendant, Royal lodge
of the Upper Shelter),
scissors, Grimsby grass seeds in
Nantucket packet, fourteen
dollars (Canadian) in coins.

Rogue. Rake. She would say.
Then... Bang.
Bang.
Afterwards ... I think (she would say)
strong drink – sanguine dispatch
of the killer instinct never,
let's say, rarely – acted upon,
post-death theories rising
with every moon:
'Well, mother, I loved
him enough to carry his best suit
through nettle fields. I sang him melon songs
in the nude. I danced entire nights
to *Wabash Cannonball.* The suit
on those sticks look better than they do
on him. Crows squawk his name,
fierce-tempered, blackened by the smell.
So that, mother, is it for now from me here
suited-up with mother love.'

rubble and sorrow

SUSAN TERRIS

Josephs, In a Time of No Peace

A gnarl of streets
and Purim boys—my sons with striped towels
for their many-colored coats—roam them
until a rock, a boom, debris.

Then a rain of flesh on a door in a city

Because my father's father's
father stole a goat, the child of that goatless
father's father's father throws a rock, a bomb
past a door in a city.

Time's debris: both rubble and sorrow

MINNIE BRUCE PRATT

At the Vietnam Memorial

A black wall, grass rooting on top, sod over a grave, a mirror,
a bank of black clay, a granite gravestone with names, 50,000,
gritblasted, almost all men, names, sons of some mother.

I shimmer in the wall like a ghost in a dimension of death.

The other tourists rush around me, people with ice-cream cones,
bicycles, with baby carriages, with metal taps in their shoes because
they are Marines;
                                        people leaving white peonies, carnations, roses
dyed black, stuck in the cracks of the wall,
                                                                                leaving propped
in the dirt an engraved announcement, an Episcopalian funeral,

leaving taped to the granite a newsclipping, death by land-mine;

the people leaving *yahrzeit* candles, burning shimmering flames;

the people with their heads propped against the wall, looking
for the one name;
                                    the people who have left behind letters
wrapped in plastic baggies against rain.
                                                                        I find a letter
that's been left for me, from a mother to her dead son:
how on the dead wall she has just read his name, the one
she gave him when she held him the hour after birth.

How am I to answer this letter?

Dear mother of a dead son:

I have two sons, and I am afraid that, as with yours, so with mine:

that the two wings of this death bird the two arms of this grave
will meet around them:
and their names that have rolled out
of my mouth like peonies, like the tapping sound of woodpeckers:

that the sound of their names will one day be nothing but grit-
blasted marks on a wall propping up the dirt, their rotting bodies.

Gulf War and Child: A Curse

He is sleeping, his fingers all curled,
his belly pooled open, his legs gathered, still
in their bent blossom victory.

I couldn't speak of "war" (though we all do),
if I were still the woman who gave birth
to this soft-footed one: his empty hand,
his calling heart, that border of new clues.

May the hard birth our two heartbeats unfurled
for two nights that lasted as long as this war
make all sands rage, until the mouth of war
drops its cup, this bleeding gift we poured.

DEEMA K. SHEHABI

Curves in the Dark

There will be no creeks left
in the hills below Diablo mountain.
No almond orchards
or rust-purple grass before green;
No-one will come to us and ask:
Do you recall the struggle
of moon-veined blossoms
and the carnage of squirrels
in this thinned-out valley?
No gray-haired woman will be left
to tell a flood of warm-eyed children:
Weave those acorns back through the leaves
so they can be found by winter-starved animals.
And you thought the Iraqi moon
high above palms
would fall over our fragments,
and this live oak you placed in California earth
would give us refuge
against shadowed rustling,
but this moon is neighbor to everyone,
barefooted blade of silver
searching for a flawed heart to swell.
I touch the chill in my forehead
and wonder what it would be like to lose all my hair:
Jasmine with your knife of scent:
I hope my child never has to kneel
over my grave and weep
beneath a sleepless flesh of sky.
And you thought these weight-filled branches
would braid themselves
against the roof and root this house to earth,

but how often have we tugged
at curves in the dark
to remake our scars and slay our death?
Here the truck sounds are unhealed,
like all our comings and goings,
but what of making a home, you ask?
while across the street the blood-red bulldozer
flattens the torso of the last almond tree.
Tomorrow they will flatten Fallujah,
the newswoman says swiftly—no sign
of carnage in her eyes,
and through the stomach
of dark, my child is asking:
how many moons did we leave behind?

GLENNA LUSCHEI

Trailer

When you moved
into the trailer with your father
you charted a map
on four pieces of spiral paper
and with a magic marker traced
a purple trail,
glued it to my door.

Now

if there were a guerrilla shoot-out
and my house
went for headquarters
would their leader—
a specialist on maps and hideouts—
reconnoiter
and know you were my daughter
and not investigate
your move away from me
but consider
between every child of revolution
and her mother
there's a magic marker
a persistent and severed trail
through notebook holes
through stops and goes
past the shopping center.

Bomb

I have not tasted
that name in my mouth
for so long
I am jealous
of a young woman soldier
pinned
in army bus wreckage

like white winged storks
sheets unfurl
and roost on the street
blood
weeps her face
her friends' flesh decorates
her dark hair

open eyed
amongst twisted metal ribs
dismembered arms
she calls
mummy mummy help me I can't see

she names a luxury
mother
the word a cushion
on the hip of death

The Wall of Horror

I've heard the March leaf of the calendar belonging to the girl next door fall. For hours she looks at her big stomach as at a wall behind which moves a being nailed to her womb by drunk soldiers in a camp on the other side of the river. She stares at the wall of horror behind which a disease begins, a terrible disease which lives on images and silence. Perhaps she sees her maiden dress fluttering on a pole like a flag. Perhaps she feels the steps of the murderer in the sound of the falling leaf, the one she will recognize when the child starts to resemble something she will try to forget all her life. I don't know. All I heard was the March leaf of the calendar fall.

Translation by Amela Simic

DEEMA K. SHEHABI

Of Harvest and Flight

Beneath a wet harvest of stars in a Gaza sky,
my mother tells me how orchards
once hid the breach of fallen oranges,
and how during a glowing night

of beseeching God in prayer,
when the night nets every breath
of every prayer,
my uncle, a child then, took flight

from the roof of the house.
The vigilant earth had softened
just before his body fell to the ground,
but still there's no succumbing to flight's abandon;

our bodies keep falling on mattresses,
piles of them are laid out on living room floors
to sleep multitudes of wedding visitors:
the men in their gowns

taunt roosters until dusk,
while women taunt
with liquid harvest in their eyes,
and night spirits and soldiers

continue to search the house
between midnight and three in the morning.
On the night of my uncle's nuptial,
I watch my mother as she passes

a tray of cigarettes to rows of radiant guests
with a fuschia flower in her hair…

Years before this, I found a photograph
of her sitting on my father's lap,

slender legs swept beneath her,
like willow filaments in river light.
His arm was firm around her waist;
his eyes bristled, as though the years of his youth

were borders holding him back
and waiting to be scattered.
Those were the years when my mother
drew curtains tightly over windows

to shut out the frost world of the Potomac;
she sifted through pieces of news
with her chest hunched over a radio,
as though each piece when found

became a story and within it
a space for holding our endless
debris. But in truth,
it was only 1967, during the war,

three years before I was born…
But tonight, in Gaza beneath the stars,
I turn towards my mother
and ask her how a daughter

can possibly grow beyond
her mother's flight. There's no answer;
instead she leans over me
with unreadable long-ago eyes
and points to the old wall:
the unbolting of our roots *there,*
beside this bitter lemon tree,
and here was the crumbling

of the house of jasmine

arching over doorways,
the house of roosters
and child-flight legends,

this house of girls
with eyes like simmering seeds.

Ghazal: My Son

He's wearing a red silk shirt, my son.
He's done me a dreadful hurt, my son.

Now that the devil has shown his face,
he's hiding under my skirt, my son.

A mother is earth, but earth is sick.
A mother's nothing but dirt, my son.

The floor of the gym is strewn with limbs.
Children are lying inert, my son.

I see lights, he says, *hear voices too!*
Obscenities to pervert my son.

Don't look at the lights, the voice is yours.
What can I say to alert my son –

Don't look at the world, a beast that kills,
a savage you can't convert, my son?

What's happened to trust? Don't screen your eyes,
green eyes you always avert, my son.

White roses have buried Beslan's dead.
Mother, don't let me desert my son.

Mother

I set out to find home. The road was
full of ruins, one could see only fallen walls
and rubble, and there wasn't a person around.
Then my bedridden mother appeared.
She was never so well, full of energy and strength,
she took me by the hand and we made our way home
to the only decent room available.
I began crying, crying gently…
And she said: Don't cry, this is happening to everyone.

Translation by Evan Jones

The sound of your blood
crossed into mine.

Down the Little Cahaba

Soundless sun, the river.   Home in August
we flow down the Little Cahaba, the three of us,
rubber inner tubes, hot laps, in water so slow
we hear the rapids moving upstream toward us,
the whispers coming loud.
                                        Then the river bends,
the standing water at the lip, hover, hover,
the moment before orgasm, before the head emerges,
then over suddenly, and sound rushing
back from my ears.
                                The youngest caught in the rapids:
half-grown, he hasn't lived with me in years,
yet his head submerged as a scrape of rock pushes
pain through me, a streak inside my thighs,
vagina to knee.
                        Swept to the outside curve,
the boys climb upstream to plunge down again.

I stand at the mud bank to pick up
shells, river mussels with iridescent inner skin,
with riverine scars from once-close flesh.

  Years back, at the beach, with piles of shells
  in our laps, with the first final separation on us,
  one asked: *How do we know you won't forget us?*

  I told them how they had moved in my womb: each
  distinct, the impatient older, the steady younger.
  I said: *I can never forget you.   You moved inside me.*

I meant: *The sound of your blood crossed into mine.*

Wandering Womb

Painfully I have learned, achingly
come to believe, as the ancients did,
that the womb is unattached: wandering each night
– hysterical little organ –
the length of a woman's body,
capturing stray homunculi in its folds.

The first time my womb met open air,
I was numb from the neck down;
to check they ran pins over my shoulders.
My arms: spread and strapped down.

Though my lips were parched
no one would bring me water.

Doctors sheeted the space between my face
and that dangerous organ.
They said the sterile barrier must
be maintained. Watching the cut
might make me believe
I felt it.

To know they could rend me in two
and I would feel nothing: the first miracle.

Just picture the quick slit!
Bowel shifted
out of the way, gaudy pink garlands looped
lustrous as a holiday display. Then

the centerpiece: baby
tightly folded, coated in white vernix.

The rub to flush,

fast transfer to some
more reliable oven.

Prayer for crying,
answered.

Wet and shining as a Christmas ham,
the womb, lifted out to have its new mouth stitched,
secrets sewed away.
Dark placenta, what the ancients called
cake—
sloshed in the trash
behind the blue drape.

All the weeks after, when laughter brought me to tears,
bent me double, when the womb showed me its place
in the primacy of my anatomy. I began to understand
what the Victorians taught

was perhaps true: If I thought too hard
in this hysterical state about how it all began,
infinity and conception, stretch marks
and impending death, I'd suffer Sprained Brains.

Step by aching step I came to revere the ancients:
how did they know
that at night my womb went out
to gather flowers?

Every morning I woke,
throbbing
like the princess who had stolen away
to dance holes through her slippers.

Remembering nothing of my dreams,
every morning

beginning again: breasts rolling
    their vacant, milky eyes,
new scar smiling its crooked grin,
    the disparate pieces of my body
bound with black thread, crusted with blood.

Beside my arm, the slumbering dark head.
To know God is
    to wander,
            cleft in two. To know precisely
the cost—
                God
—of the wet head that fits perfectly in your hand.

The Birth

What the red womb, torn
open, exposed, he enters
and finding no cradle, no
ready nipple, does not
think birth and feels
only strain, rawness where
nothing, no one should
have lived. He enters

and even here without
a name he finds his story,
older than the hills—
it is familiar, dirt
beneath his nails familiar.

. . .

And throughout, his cry,
forcing movement
of the Adam's apple in his throat,
echoes: For he would be
the sun risen, a tree
rooted, the cry in pleasure
released. For he would be—

except the seasons run cold.
The hot sun grows tired,
distance—an unwashed star,
a destroyed part. He enters
to find his will assumed broken,

to find his spirit swollen,
and the climate mean.

. . .

O glacial moon, O shadowed tide,
a man arrives
and the world asks him,
(as if he is the first)
what is your weight, the burden of you?

To which he replies: *If I as human*
am meant to live this way
then I will die or am dead
and some night in my decay,
this, my load, come down.

. . .

Overtaken sky. Disgorged rain.
Shivering. Spent. Always he was,
is here, is the land's bruised
utterance, stillborn in the back
of naked, stark—far from
a mountain top. What echoes across,
his cry—a shower of stones,
a tight rip, a hot loss.

And his birth, the taste of blood
in his mouth and freedom—
it is this truth (*O freedom*)
that binds him up (*yes freedom*)
ties him up (*dear freedom*).

. . .

In humanity—
into its strange house,

he enters—with will, more
brave than true, he enters
to find himself held in
by skin meant to restrain
the breaking heart.

And always the hurt
is all the same,
even if he wouldn't take it,
even if he wouldn't make it home.

I Can't Write

about her birth—about the way, when finally, after an eternity
of curling in and screaming, they plopped her on my chest

like a hot, wet seal, like something straight out of a warm
long-ago ocean, something slippery and covered with fur—

but I can write about the clock and its second hand,
how I gauged my progress by its slow and gentle circling

while I bounced on a blue ball, brought my cervix inch by inch
to ten. But I can't write, exactly, about dilation—how I stayed at three

till long past twelve, how progression didn't really begin
till after the almost-full moon had risen high enough to view it,

if we'd wanted, from that 5th floor brimming, overbrimming, with moaning
or pacing, passing again and again that giant yellow and red mangle

of a Deborah Butterfield horse, where instead we occupied ourselves
with ice water, heat packs, string cheese, spray from a Jacuzzi's jets—

or the number of times I pushed, but I can tell you that later that morning,
from three mini-blinded windows, I could hear the voices of children,

of mothers telling them to settle down, how I wished my womb, like theirs
(I presumed) had returned to the size of a fist. And I can tell you about

my bed, how I could lower it, how I could make it rise like a chair,
a ready-made chair for nursing, how in that bed I wished my daughter

were older than half a day, where both of us smelled not only of yeast
but of the acrid, earthiness of colostrum, of colostrum and vernix

and blood. I can't write about the lighting or give you anything close
to a time frame, but two of the nurses were named Sharon

and each of them told me, as I begged for an epidural,
you don't need one, *this is your birth and this is your labor, feel that* (the long

wait begun in late July nearly up). I wanted to keep detailed notes
about hazardous waste dispensers, my first try at aspirating

my baby's nose, about the breakfast of Cheerios and tea and French toast,
but instead these loosely woven undies one of the Sharons dubbed

"Madonna lingerie"—wear and toss—instead, the doula and my husband
walking me to the bathroom to get those panties on and off.

And I can tell you about the luxury, on a Friday night, of popping
two Ibuprofens, taking my first unfettered, unfetused shower in months,

but I can't remember much about that art on the third floor
where they made me walk and walk. All I can see is a cow

in the middle of a stream, on either side of her that blurry green of spring,
are two blue doors, one marked THE TRUTH, the other, EVERYTHING BUT.

NICOLE BROSSARD

from *Intimate Journal*

Water, when the waters break and I'll know nothing about it, stretched out on the operating table, because Sesame, open up, flounders in wombs during caesarians and mothers sleep with exemplary soundness. Anaesthetized. Mothers in hospitals are hot, cold, tremble, revive, writhe, and bellow in rut. Mothers sign with a big X over the eyes of their children, sign the end of the eternal recommencement when they leave the hospital or when they leave reality or when they leave with a big X on their bellies. Yes mothers have all the attractions and all the trumps for the Xs that dance in their eyes, mothers have obligations, rendezvous, mothers draw inspiration from the deepest silence. Mothers suddenly desire the sea and the salt just like the amazons, gazing on the sea, must have tasted the salt of their lovhers as reality, mothers become grave and gravitate around their centre of gravity and then float, aerial, mothers who invent humanity in inventing their daughters in their own image and in the fuzziness of this image, mothers invent their life like tigresses, mothers put fire in the eyes of the she-wolves on the uttermost patriarchal steppes and the she-wolves become women in the crystalline curve of humanity. When this has been accomplished, the mothers say they have no time to keep their journals. Only their voice is heard then and their voices are never quite their own voice. They are voices that have travelled to the horizon like little clouds. And life gets ordered in spite of their sentences of love, and life erases their sobs.

Translation by Barbara Godard

JENNIFER MERRIFIELD

American Proper

At birth the umbilical cuts close to the ideal
woman: chases her
down the same path, bodies turning into bodies,

children springing from the floor. Not scissors
echoing down.
Not tintinnabulation emptied

of pot-and-pan parades. The delicious thump
her headache wants:
Wear the heart like a home.

When this reaches her, the prick and sting
might bring her
to dog-ear every safari: coax a busy oasis

out from under the rug: excavate
fossilized pollen:
order a backhoe to re-smooth the scene.

She's pineapple and lace.
A corset grove.
She's American proper and well-read.

Untitle her, please—peel her
off powdered milk and embroidered duvets.
Give her loose sand

and pea gravel, a container that won't break.
Tell her *turn here.*
Here. Tell her the light is hot because it pushes

away. Give her a book of synonyms
with lines to fill in:
insomnia. Like *chronic. hypnotized. revived.*

Tell her to dream away from her dreams.
When the light's last glimmer
is a secret pink she holds on her tongue, ask her

to pry her knees apart and lie
down beside her:
seventy-two names for god waiting between.

Birthday Tales

They were living, she tells me,
in one room, upstairs.
They tied strings to the ceiling,
strings and strings again,
overlapping them into
a lattice of shadows,
a web to hang their lives from –
lights, mobiles, clothes –
and then, my cradle.

She won't say much about the birth,
about nausea, pain that wracked
the bones of her back
till they blanked her with gas,
white shadows descending
from a thick black ceiling –
though she'll tell me how
he pushed past nurses,
was only stopped
by the last, locked door.
And how he brought roses.

She doesn't describe the first teating –
how that toothless small mouth
grabbed with surprising bone
at transparent skin, that reddened,
cracked, finally yielded
to the rhythmic, gentle draining.
Instead, she shows me photos
he took through the glass,
the card from my wrist
he pasted beside them.

Now, on my birthday, if I ask her to,
she'll tell me again of the room,
cradle, photographs, roses –
what she now remembers.
All she chooses now to know –

As I, today, tell stories for my daughters,
but also for her,
of the cramping, the tearing,
the suckling, the cries,
the man beside the birthing bed,
teethmarks on his hand.

And then we'll both recall
how they held our daughters out to us –

placed them in our arms
like chrysanthemums.

from *The Adoption Papers*

I always wanted to give birth
do that incredible natural thing
that women do – I nearly broke down
when I heard we couldn't,
and then my man said
well there's always adoption
(we didn't have test tubes the rest then)
even in the early sixties there was
something scandalous about adopting,
telling the world your secret failure
bringing up an alien child,
who knew what it would turn out to be

I was pulled out with forceps
left a gash down my left cheek
four months inside a glass cot
but she came faithful
from Glasgow to Edinburgh
and peered through the glass
I must have felt somebody willing me to survive;
she would not pick another baby

I still have the baby photograph
I keep it in my bottom drawer

She is twenty-six today
my hair is grey

The skin around my neck is wrinkling
does she imagine me this way

Chapter 6: The Telling Part from *The Adoption Papers*

Ma mammy bot me oot a shop
Ma mammy says I was a luvly baby

Ma mammy picked me (I wiz the best)
your mammy had to take you (she'd no choice)

Ma mammy says she's no really ma mammy
(just kid on)

It's a bit like a part you've rehearsed so well
you can't play it on the opening night
She says my real mammy is away far away
Mammy why aren't you and me the same colour
But I love my mammy whether she's real or no
My heart started rat tat tat like a tin drum
all the words took off to another planet
Why

But I love ma mammy whether she's real or no

I could hear the upset in her voice
I says *I'm not your real mother,*
though Christ knows why I said that,
If I'm not who is, but all my planned speech
went out the window

She took me when I'd nowhere to go
my mammy is the best mammy in the world OK.

After mammy telt me she wisnae my real mammy
I was scared to death she was gonnie melt
or something or mibbe disappear in the dead
of night and somebody would say she wis a fairy
godmother. So the next morning I felt her skin

to check it was flesh, but mibbe it was just
a good imitation. How could I tell if my mammy
was a dummy with a voice spoken by someone else?
So I searches the whole house for clues
but I never found nothing. Anyhow a day after
I got my guinea pig and forgot all about it.

I always believed in the telling anyhow.
You can't keep something like that secret
I wanted her to think of her other mother
out there, thinking that child I had will be
seven today eight today all the way up to
god knows when. I told my daughter –
I bet your mother's never missed your birthday,
how could she?

Mammy's face is cherries.
She is stirring the big pot of mutton soup
singing *I gave my love a cherry*
it had no stone.
I am up to her apron.
I jump onto her feet and grab her legs
like a huge pair of trousers,
she walks round the kitchen lifting me up.

Suddenly I fall off her feet.
And mammy falls to the floor.
She won't stop the song
I gave my love a chicken it had no bone.
I run next door for help.
When me and Uncle Alec come back
Mammy's skin is toffee stuck to the floor.
And her bones are all scattered like toys.

Now when people say 'ah but
it's not like having your own child though is it',
I say of course it is, what else is it?

she's my child, I have told her stories
wept at her losses, laughed at her pleasures,
she is mine.

I was always the first to hear her in the night
all this umbilical knot business is nonsense
– the men can afford deeper sleeps that's all.
I listened to hear her talk,
and when she did I heard my voice under hers
and now some of her mannerisms crack me up

Me and my best pal
don't have Donny Osmond or David Cassidy
on our walls and we don't wear Starsky and Hutch
jumpers either. Round at her house we put on
the old record player and mime to Pearl Bailey
Tired of the life I lead, tired of the blues I breed
and Bessie Smith I can't do without my kitchen man.
Then we practise ballroom dancing giggling,
everyone thinks we're dead old-fashioned.

Chapter 8: Generations from *The Adoption Papers*

The sun went out just like that
almost as if it had never been,
hard to imagine now the way it fell
on treetops, thatched roofs, people's faces.
Suddenly the trees lost their nerves
and the grass passed the wind on
blade to blade, fast as gossip

Years later, the voices still come close
especially in dreams, not distant echoes
loud – a pneumatic drill – deeper and deeper still.

I lived the scandal, wore it casual
as a summer's dress, Jesus sandals.
All but the softest whisper:
"she's lost an awful lot of weight."

Now my secret is the hush of heavy curtains drawn.
I dread strange handwriting
sometimes jump when the phone rings,
she is all of nineteen and legally able.
At night I lie practising my lines
but 'sorry' never seems large enough
nor 'I can't see you, yes, I'll send a photograph.'

I was pulled out with forceps
left a gash down my left cheek
four months inside a glass cot
but
she came faithful from Glasgow to Edinburgh
and peered through the glass
she would not pick another baby

I don't know what diseases
come down my line;
when dentist and doctors ask
the old blood questions about family runnings
I tell them: I have no nose or mouth or eyes
to match, no spitting image or dead cert,
my face watches itself in the glass.

I have my parents who are not of the same tree
and you keep trying to make it matter,
the blood, the tie, the passing down
generations.
We all have our contradictions,
the ones with the mother's nose and father's eyes
have them;
the blood does not bind confusion,

yet I confess to my contradiction
I want to know my blood.

I know my blood.
It is dark ruby red and comes
regular and I use Lillets.
I know my blood when I cut my finger.
I know what my blood looks like.

It is the well, the womb, the fucking seed.
Here, I am far enough away to wonder –
what were their faces like
who were my grandmothers
what were the days like
passed in Scotland
the land I come from
the soil in my blood.

Put it this way:
I know she thinks of me often
when the light shows its face
or the dark skulks behind hills,
she conjures me up or I just appear
when I take the notion, my slippers
are silent and I walk through doors.

She's lying in bed; I wake her up
a pinch on her cheek is enough,
then I make her think of me for hours.
The best thing I can steal is sleep.
I get right under the duvet and murmur
you'll never really know your mother.
I know who she thinks I am – she's made a blunder.

She is faceless
She has no nose
She is five foot eight inches tall
She likes hockey best

She is twenty-six today
She was a waitress
My hair is grey
She wears no particular dress
The skin around my neck is wrinkling
Does she imagine me this way?
Lately I make pictures of her
But I can see the smallness
She is tall and slim
of her hands, Yes
Her hair is loose curls
an opal stone on her middle finger
I reach out to catch her
Does she talk broad Glasgow?
But no matter how fast
Maybe they moved years ago
I run after
She is faceless, she never
weeps. She has neither eyes nor
fine boned cheeks

Once would be enough,
just to listen to her voice
watch the way she moves her hands
when she talks.

Height of Summer

The woman who lay in bed for three days
as if waiting for someone to arrive
had just given birth
to her second baby, a ten-pound boy
(full term, an easy labour),
brain-damaged.
He can breathe but cannot eat.
She was expecting someone else;
she lay there, learning to be
a different kind of mother.

By the dugout on the road I walk
a windmill turns the wind.
Danger. Thin ice, painted on a board
beneath the blades. Today the ice
so thin it's water. Midsummer,
and in the city the daughter of my friend
walks the streets, red-haired and schizophrenic.
There is no comfort, her mother writes,
out of darkness only pain.

The fields of wheat along the road
look thick and lush
but the kernels aren't filling out,
what should be gold stays green.
In this country that yearly battles drought
there's been too much rain.

If my friend were with me
I would tell her of this baby,
the mother who croons his name
so he will know the sound

she calls him by
and answer to it, in whatever dream.

And the father
who goes each night
to the hospital after work
               and sleeps there,
placing his small son on his chest—

                              two hearts beating.

It seems to comfort him,
he says, *and me,*
though he knows in the nursery's
strange light, their love
is a letting go,
                    a holding,
close and brief as breath.

The Abortion

Somebody who should have been born
is gone.

Just as the earth puckered its mouth,
each bud puffing out from its knot,
I changed my shoes, and then drove south.

Up past the Blue Mountains, where
Pennsylvania humps on endlessly,
wearing, like a crayoned cat, its green hair,

its road sunken in like a gray washboard;
where, in truth, the ground cracks evilly,
a dark socket from which the coal has poured,

Somebody who should have been born
is gone.

the grass as bristly and stout as chives,
and me wondering when the ground would break,
and me wondering how anything fragile survives;

up in Pennsylvania, I met a little man,
not Rumpelstiltskin, at all, at all...
he took the fullness that love began.

Returning north, even the sky grew thin
like a high window looking nowhere.
The road was as flat as a sheet of tin.

Somebody who should have been born
is gone.

Yes, woman, such logic will lead
to loss without death. Or say what you meant,
you coward … this baby that I bleed.

RACHEL ROSE

Notes on Arrival and Departure

I could live or not live; it does not matter
to be one stone more, the dark stone,
the pure stone which the river bears away.
—Pablo Neruda, "Oh Earth, Wait for Me"

Because I am a careful woman,
or full of fear, at any rate unwilling to bet
on the constancy of any heart, I will put it
in print. Because
now it's my turn to ask the hard questions, not
why are pumpkins orange? or *why stars?*
but why do I fear death? yours most
but also my own, what would keep me
from you.

When I was wheeled into the delivery room
I told myself no matter what, this cramp
was finite; it had a beginning,
it would have an end. That
comforted me. I am not old or wise enough
to be anyone's mother, I still can't grasp
that there was a beginning before *my* beginning,
that the tale will continue without me.
Still, I am braver than I believed: knowing nothing
I decided to conceive,
and conceived.

As usual, too much is left undone.
In Vancouver, as usual, it rains,
and the pots left soaking in the sink
have reproachfully begun to stink. Then

there are all your little bottles to be reamed with soap
and set to dry on clean towels,
there are all my transparent ambitions for us both.
Nothing has changed since they handed me you,
mesh-capped, greasy and fish-eyed in a swaddle,
nothing has changed in the world since you entered it.

Who said, *None of us are free until we're all free?*
It's not like that at all, though
I guess I'll probably do okay,
live to age, and so will you
already almost two and rushing into a future
of *papier maché*, summer vacations,
the usual teen resentments and then some,
with me as your mother,
arranging our dental appointments, play dates,
separating the whites from the darks,
writing in the spaces in between.

We'll go on, I mean, with our lives,
pass round our merry UNICEF cards.
While other children detonate bombs
on the hard-packed paths
leading from their homes,
we'll learn to make do
with our good luck.

And when I say nothing changed
I mean of course that you changed me utterly,
and though I hoped to avoid the usual things
that fond mothers say, you must know
a few truths: you may search in vain for God,
but don't doubt the love
of your big-assed, big-mouthed
personal creator, the one who gained and lost a third
of her weight for you.

Don't forget

there are ways of living worse
than simply dying, for though I fear death,
I am working on it, getting over it, I mean,
since I must show you how to do this, too,
since the best I can hope for is that you will watch me leave
as I watched you arrive, numb to pain,
with a little fear and great wonder.

When I reclined on the stretcher
the ghosts of mothers whispered
in my drugged ears, all the women
who had never risen from childbed.
The bright new instruments, sterile technique,
bold birth plan—nothing hushed them,
they crowded around the bed,
gripping me with an embrace cool and deadening as epidural,
and I was afraid, *yes*, that I would die,
though in the moment death seemed astonishing most of all.

Just at that point I found peace
though later that night I lost it. Just then,
breathing out, I gave in.
Though vaguely disappointed we hadn't met,
I was not really thinking of you.
You were still inside me, not yet yourself
and I had not yet learned
the first lesson of motherhood:
pretend you are brave
until you are brave.

CLAIRE MILLIKIN

The Next Day

The day after my son was born
I lay on the bed beside him,
late afternoon. Late autumn
sun drew the room
out of itself, into the birches
and the bare lilac branchings,
shadowing things obliquely,
as in photographs of departures
the shadows of hands.

I kept thinking to myself, this
is the first day of his life,
not the day he was born,
but the first real day, the aftermath.

After the three day birth,
he and I lay again alone
on the bed we inherited together.

I imagined I saw, almost, then
the last day of his life
as it would also come, next
century, when I would not be with him.
He was not really sleeping.

We watched each other carefully.
It was a beginning and an ending,

his life exchanged for something,
the way that trees at morning,
in any season, give away
for sun's astringent grains

the blurring of divisions
that night permits, touch
without pressure, a shared pulse.

I barely touched him. Everything
had been broken apart. The drought

that autumn narrowing the wells,
my body unmade for his.

Contributor Notes

Meena Alexander is the author of a number of books including the volumes of poetry *Raw Silk* (TriQuarterly Books, 2004) and *Illiterate Heart* (Northwestern University Press, 2003), winner of a 2002 PEN Open Book Award. Her memoir, *Fault Lines* (Feminist Press, 2003), one of *Publishers Weekly*'s Best Books of 1993, appeared in a new edition in 2003. She is Distinguished Professor of English at Hunter College and the Graduate Center of the City University of New York.

Agha Shahid Ali, a Kashmiri-American, was born in New Delhi and grew up in Kashmir. He is the author of a number of poetry collections including *Rooms are Never Finished* (Norton, 2002). He has received Guggenheim and Ingram-Merrill Fellowships, among others.

Celia Lisset Alvarez holds an MFA in creative writing from the University of Miami. Her poetry has appeared in *The Powhatan Review, Tar Wolf Review,* and the *Iodine Poetry Journal,* and in two collections, *The Stones* (Finishing Line Press, 2006) and *Shapeshifting* (Spire Press, 2006), winner of the 2005 Spire Press Poetry Award. She teaches composition and literature at St. Thomas University in Miami Gardens, Florida, and lives with her husband and their extended family in Miami.

Judith Arcana's first two books, *Our Mothers' Daughters* (Shameless Hussy Press, 1979) and *Every Mother's Son* (Doubleday, 1983), are feminist motherhood classics. Her newest is the poetry collection *What if your mother* (Chicory Blue Press, 2005). Author of the literary biography *Grace Paley's Life Stories* (University of Illinois Press, 1993), she has published poetry and prose in journals and anthologies for more than thirty years. In 2007, her stories and poems may be found in print and online in *5AM, Passager, Bridges, Diner, The Persimmon Tree, Umbrella,* and *Feminist Studies.*

Gabeba Baderoon is a South African poet, and the author of three collections of poetry, *The Dream in the Next Body* (Kwela/Snailpress, 2005), *The Museum* *of Ordinary Life* (DaimlerChrysler, 2005) and *A hundred silences* (Kwela/ Snailpress, 2006). She received the DaimlerChrysler Award for South African Poetry 2005, and *A hundred silences* was short-listed for the 2007 University of Johannesburg Prize.

John Barton has published eight award-winning volumes of poetry and five chapbooks. A new edition of *West of Darkness: Emily Carr, a self-portrait*, his third book of poetry, was republished in a bilingual edition by BuschekBooks in 2006. Co-editor of *Seminal: The Anthology of Canada's Gay Male Poets*, he lives in Victoria, British Columbia, where he edits *The Malahat Review*.

Margo Berdeshevsky lives in Paris. Her book of poetry, *But a Passage in Wilderness*, will be published by Sheep Meadow Press in Fall 2007. She has received three Pushcart nominations, the Robert H. Winner Award from the Poetry Society of America, the *Chelsea* Poetry Award, *Kalliope's* Sue Saniel Elkind Award, places in the Pablo Neruda and the Ann Stanford Awards, and Borders Books/*Honolulu Magazine* Grand Prize for Fiction. Her works have appeared, or are forthcoming, in *The Southern Review, New Letters, Poetry International, Women's Studies Quarterly, Nimrod International, Runes, Chelsea, ACM, Traffic East, Kalliope, Rattapallax, Many Mountains Moving, The Literary Review, Van Gogh's Ear, The Southern California Anthology*, and more.

Nina Bogin was born in New York City in 1952 and grew up on Long Island. She has lived in France since 1976. Her most recent collection of poems is *The Winter Orchards* (Anvil Press, 2001).

Eavan Boland's most recent collections of poems are *Against Love Poetry* (Norton, 2001) and *Domestic Violence* (Norton, 2007). She teaches at Stanford University.

Di Brandt has published a number of collections of poetry including *Now You Care* (Coach House, 2003), *Jerusalem, beloved* (Turnstone, 1995), *mother, not mother* (Mercury, 1992), *Agnes in the sky* (Turnstone, 1990), and *questions i asked my mother* (Turnstone, 1987).

Gwendolyn Brooks is the author of more than twenty books of poetry. She received an American Academy of Arts and Letters award, the Frost Medal, a National Endowment for the Arts award, the Shelley Memorial Award, and fellowships from the Academy of American Poets and the Guggenheim Foundation. She lived in Chicago until her death in 2000.

Nicole Brossard has published more than 30 books since 1965 and has twice won the Governor General's Award for poetry. Many of her books have been translated into English. In 1991, she was awarded le Prix Athanase-David, the highest literary recognition in Quebec. She lives in Montreal.

Nan Byrne is the author of *Uncertain Territory*, a poetry chapbook about mothers and daughters. Her work has appeared in *Seattle Review, New Orleans Review, Potomac Review, Canadian Woman Studies, Critical Matrix, Phoebe, Earth's Daughters, Hurricane Alice, So to Speak, Grove Review, Diner, Red Mountain Review, Other Voices International, Blue Earth*, and elsewhere. She has received grants from the Virginia Center for the Creative Arts and the Vermont Studio Center, and awards for her screenplays. She is currently employed by New Dominion Pictures.

Misha Cahnmann-Taylor has published poems in *APR, Bellevue Literary Review, Quarterly West, Puerto del Sol, Barrow Street, River City, Bridges, Laurel Review*, and *Red Rock Review*, among other journals. She is an Associate Professor of Language and Literacy Education at the University of Georgia. Her research and teaching address bilingualism, bilingual education, arts-based approaches to inquiry, and multicultural education. She received prizes from the Dorothy Sargent Rosenberg Foundation in 2004 and 2005.

Anne Carson, named a MacArthur Fellow in 2000, is the recipient of the 1996 Lannan Award, the 1997 Pushcart Prize, the T.S. Eliot Prize for Poetry, the Griffin Poetry Prize, and the Los Angeles Times Book Prize. Her latest book is *Decreation: Poetry, Essays, Opera* (Knopf, 2005). She currently teaches at the University of Michigan.

Joy Castro's work has appeared in *North American Review, Puerto del Sol, The New York Times Magazine, Quarterly West, Chelsea*, and other magazines, and in anthologies including *Faith and Doubt* and *Without a Net: The Female Experience of Growing Up Working-Class*. Her memoir *The Truth Book* (Arcade, 2005), about being adopted at birth by a family of Jehovah's Witnesses and running away at fourteen, appeared in 2005. She will join the faculty of the University of Nebraska-Lincoln this fall with a joint appointment in English and Ethnic Studies. She also teaches in the low-residency MFA program at Pine Manor College in Boston.

Margaret Christakos has published six collections of poetry and a novel, *Charisma* (Pedlar, 2000), which was a finalist for the Trillium Book Award. Her most recent books are *Sooner* (Coach House, 2005), shortlisted for the Pat Lowther Award, and *Excessive Love Prostheses* (Coach House, 2001), winner of the ReLit Award. She lives with her partner and their three children in Toronto.

Jeanette Clough is the author of *Cantatas* (Tebot Bach Press, 2002) and *Island* (Red Hen Press, 2007). She has received awards from the Ruskin Competition and the Rilke Competition. Her recent poems appear in *Colorado Review, Nimrod, Denver Quarterly, Askew*, and *Pool.*

Wanda Coleman was born in 1946, and is the author of many collections of poetry, including *Bathwater Wine* (Black Sparrow Press, 1998), winner of the 1999 Lenore Marshall Poetry Prize. A former medical secretary, magazine editor, journalist and scriptwriter, she has received fellowships from the National Endowment for the Arts and the Guggenheim Foundation for her poetry.

Anne Compton won the 2005 Governor General's Award for poetry for her collection *Processional* (Fitzhenry & Whiteside, 2005). Her first collection, *Opening the Island* (Fitzhenry & Whiteside, 2002), won the Atlantic Poetry Prize in 2003.

Lorna Crozier's *Inventing the Hawk* won the Governor General's, the Canadian Authors' Association, and the Pat Lowther Awards for poetry in 1992. She has published fourteen books of poetry, the most recent, *Whetstone* (McClelland and Stewart, 2005). The University of Regina awarded her an honorary doctorate in 2004 for her contribution to Canadian literature. Presently, she is a Distinguished Professor at the University of Victoria.

Mahmoud Darwish, a Palestinian from the Galilee, is one of the most important Arabic poets. He has written over thirty books of poetry and prose, and has received numerous international awards, among them the French Chevalier of Arts and Belle Letters, a Lannan award for cultural freedom, and the Prins Claus from Holland. His most recent poetry in English, translated by Fady Joudah, is collected in *The Butterfly's Burden* (Copper Canyon Press, 2006).

Ingrid de Kok has published several volumes of poetry including *Seasonal Fires: New and Selected Poems* (Seven Stories Press, 2006). She lives in South Africa.

Pier Giorgio Di Cicco was born in Arezzo, Italy, and raised in Montreal, Baltimore, and Toronto. In 1984, he became an Augustinian Brother, and was subsequently ordained to the Roman Catholic Priesthood. He returned to the world of literature and education in 2000 with four successive volumes of verse, including *The Dark Time of Angels* (Mansfield Press, 2003), nominated for the Trillium Award in 2004. That year, he was the Emilio Goggio Visiting Professor in Italian Studies at the University of Toronto, and appointed as the City of Toronto's second Poet Laureate.

Christopher Doda is a poet and critic living in Toronto. He is the author of two books of poems, *Among Ruins* (2001) and *Aesthetics Lesson* (2007), both released by the Mansfield Press. He is an editor of *Exile: the Literary Quarterly.*

Rita Dove is Commonwealth Professor of English at the University of Virginia. She is the author of many collections of poetry, including *Mother Love* (Norton, 1995). She was the U.S. Poet Laureate, 1993-1995.

Rishma Dunlop is the author of three books of poetry: *Metropolis* (Mansfield Press, 2005), *Reading Like a Girl* (Moss Press, 2004), and *The Body of My Garden* (Mansfield Press, 2002). She won the Emily Dickinson Prize for Poetry in 2003 and was a finalist for the CBC Literary Awards for Poetry in 1998. She is a professor of English and Creative Writing at York University, Toronto. She is the mother of two daughters, Cara and Rachel.

Beth Ann Fennelly, recipient of a 2003 National Endowment for the Arts Award, has written two books of poetry, *Open House*, which won the 2001 *Kenyon Review* Prize for a First Book and the GLCA New Writers Award, and *Tender Hooks* (W.W. Norton, 2004), as well as a book of essays, *Great With Child* (W.W. Norton, 2006). She has been included in The Best American Poetry Series three times, and is a Pushcart Prize winner. She is an Assistant Professor at the University of Mississippi.

Annie Finch is the author of four volumes of poetry and poetry in translation. Her work has also encompassed libretto and other musical and theater collaborations as well as five innovative anthologies about poetry and two books of poetics. Her recent books include *Calendars* (Tupelo, 2003), shortlisted for the Foreword Poetry Book of the Year Award, a reissue of her early long poem, *The Encyclopedia of Scotland* (Salt Press, 2004), and a book of essays on poetry, *The Body of Poetry: Essays on Women, Form, and the Poetic Self* (University of Michigan Press, 2005). Since 2005 she has served as Director of the Stonecoast graduate creative writing program at the University of Southern Maine.

Ann Fisher-Wirth is the author of two books of poems, *Blue Window* (Archer Books, 2003) and *Five Terraces* (Wind Publications, 2005). She has also published two chapbooks, *The Trinket Poems* (Wind, 2003) and *Walking Wu Wei's Scroll* (Drunken Boat, 2005). The recipient of the Rita Dove Poetry Award and the *Malahat Review* Long Poem Prize, she has been nominated for a Pushcart Prize six times and, in 2006, received a Pushcart Special Mention. Her poems have appeared in *The Georgia Review, The Kenyon Review*, and many other journals and anthologies. She has been a senior Fulbright lecturer at the University of Fribourg, Switzerland, and has held the Fulbright Distinguished Chair in American Studies at Uppsala University, Sweden. She teaches environmental literature, poetry seminars, and workshops at the University of Mississippi.

Carolyn Forché is the recipient of numerous awards including the Yale Series of Younger Poets Award, the Poetry Society of America's Alice Fay di Castagnola Award, and the Lamont Selection of the Academy of American Poets. She has held three fellowships from The National Endowment for the Arts, and in 1992 received a Lannan Foundation Literary Fellowship. Her anthology, *Against Forgetting: Twentieth Century Poetry of Witness*, was published by Norton in 1993, and in 1994, her third book of poetry, *The Angel of History* (HarperCollins), was chosen for *The Los Angeles Times Book Award.* Her most recent collection of poems, *Blue Hour*, was published by HarperCollins in 2003.

Sandra Gilbert's books include *Death's Door: Modern Dying and the Ways We Grieve* (2006) and *Belongings* (2005), both from W.W. Norton. She is the first M.H. Abrams Distinguished Visiting Professor at Cornell University.

Allen Ginsberg was born in Newark, New Jersey, in 1926. After jobs as a laborer, sailor, and market researcher, he published his first volume, *Howl and Other*

Poems, in 1956. "Howl" overcame censorship trials to become one of the most widely read poems of the century. He died in 1997.

Daniela Gioseffi, recipient of the American Book Award, is the author of fourteen books of poetry and prose. Her latest are *Blood Autumn (Autunno di sangue)* (VIA Folios/Bordighera Press, 2006) and *Women on War* (Feminist Press, 2003). She has won two grant awards in poetry from the New York State Council for the Arts and a Lifetime Achievement Award from the Association of Italian American Educators. Her verse has been etched in marble on a wall of PENN Station near verses by Walt Whitman and William Carlos Williams, and she has read her poems throughout the United States and Europe, for National Public Radio and the British Broadcasting Corporation as well as for the Library of Congress Radio Show, *The Poet and the Poem.* In 1993, she won a World Peace Award for her compendium *On Prejudice: A Global Perspective* (Anchor/Doubleday).

Lorri Neilsen Glenn's most recent collection of poetry is *Combustion* (Brick Books, 2007). She was appointed poet laureate for Halifax, Nova Scotia, for 2005-2009.

Susan Glickman's most recent book, *The Violin Lover* (Goose Lane Editions, 2006), has received rave reviews. Her book, *The Picturesque & the Sublime: A Poetics of the Canadian Landscape* (McGill-Queen's University Press, 2003), won both the Gabrielle Roy Prize and the Raymond Klibansky Prize. She has also been a frequent reviewer of contemporary writing in venues like *Books in Canada*, *The Journal of Canadian Poetry*, and *Poetry Canada Review*, and has written essays for *Maisonneuve.*

Louise Glück was born in New York City in 1943 and grew up on Long Island. She is the author of numerous books of poetry, most recently, *Averno* (Farrar, Straus and Giroux, 2006), a finalist for the 2006 National Book Award in Poetry.

Barbara Godard is the recipient of the Gabrielle Roy Prize of the Association for Canadian and Quebec Literatures (1988), the Award of Merit of the Association of Canadian Studies (1995), the Vinay-Darbelnet Prize of the Canadian Association of Translation Studies (2000), and the Teaching Award of the Faculty of Graduate Studies, York University (2002) and of the Northeast Association of Graduate Schools (2002). She is a founding co-editor of the feminist literary theory periodical, *Tessera*.

Marilyn Hacker is the author of eleven books of poems, including *Essays on Departure: New and Selected Poems* (Carcanet, 2006) and *Desesperanto* (W.W. Norton, 2003) as well as seven collections of translations from the French, notably of the work of Vénus Khoury-Ghata and Claire Malroux. She lives in New York and Paris.

Louise Bernice Halfe's first book of poetry, *Bear Bones and Feathers* (Coteau Books, 2004), won the Milton Acorn Award for 1996, and was shortlisted for the Spirit of Saskatchewan Award, the Gerald Lampert Award, and the Pat Lowther First Book Award. Her second book of poetry is entitled *Blue Marrow* (Coteau Books, 2004). Also known as Sky Dancer, she was raised on the Saddle Lake Indian Reserve and attended Blue Quills Residential School. She lives in Saskatchewan.

Suzanne Hancock's first book of poems, *Another Name for Bridge*, was published by Mansfield Press in 2005. One of her poems was nominated for a National Magazine Award in 2006. She recently received an MFA from the University of Michigan in Ann Arbor. She is currently working on a long sequence of poems about bells.

Joy Harjo is an artist of the Mvskoke/Creek Nation. She has published numerous books of acclaimed poetry, including *A Map to the Next World: Poetry and Tales* (Norton, 2000). She is the recipient of the Arrell Gibson Lifetime Achievement Award, the Lifetime Achievement Award from the Native Writers Circle of the Americas, and the William Carlos Williams Award from the Poetry Society of America, among others.

Clarinda Harriss teaches poetry, poetic forms, and editing at Towson University, where she chaired the English Department for a decade. Her most recent collection is *Air Travel* (Half Moon Editions, 2005), and her newest collection, *The Life of Vox*, will come out in 2007. Her awards include first place in the 2005 *Indiana Review* poetry competition and first place in the *Pagitica Magazine* competition the same year. She has worked with prison writers for many years, and some of their work has been brought out by the venerable publishing company which she directs, BrickHouse Books, Inc.

Steven Heighton's poetry has appeared in many magazines and anthologies in Canada and abroad, including *Poetry (Chicago)*, *BRICK*, *The Literary Review*, *Agni*, *Europe*, and *Stand*. His collections include the Lampert Award winner, *Stalin's Carnival* (Quarry Press, 1989), the Governor General's Award finalist, *The Ecstasy of Skeptics* (Anansi, 1994), and *The Address Book* (Anansi, 2004). His most recent book, *Afterlands* (Knopf Canada, 2005), a novel, has appeared in six countries, and was a *New York Times Book Review* Editors' Choice.

Brenda Hillman has published seven collections of poetry, all from Wesleyan University Press, the most recent of which are *Loose Sugar* (1997), *Cascadia* (2001), and *Pieces of Air in the Epic* (2005), which won the 2005 William Carlos Williams Prize for Poetry. She has also edited an edition of Emily Dickinson's poetry for Shambhala Publications, and, with Patricia Dienstfrey, co-edited *The Grand Permission: New Writings on Poetics and Motherhood* (2003). She serves on the faculty of Saint Mary's College in Moraga, California, where she is the Olivia C. Filippi Professor of Poetry.

Susan Holbrook is the author of *misled* (Red Deer Press, 1999) and *Good Egg Bad Seed* (Nomados, 2004). She teaches North American literatures and creative writing at the University of Windsor. Her daughter Elise was born May 20, 2005.

Cornelia Hoogland is the winner of numerous awards, and has been shortlisted for the national CBC Literary Awards. She is the author of several collections including *Cuba Journal* (Black Moss Press, 2003), *You Are Home* (Black Moss Press, 2001), and *Marrying the Animals* (Brick Books, 1995). She is the founder and artistic director of Poetry London, an organization that brings prominent writers into lively discussion with writers and readers in London, Ontario. She teaches at the University of Western Ontario.

Ailish Hopper was educated at Princeton University and received her MFA from Bennington College, where she received the Jane Kenyon Scholarship. Her chapbook, *Bird in the Head*, was selected by Jean Valentine for the 2005 Center for Book Arts Chapbook Competition, and recent poems of hers have appeared in *Poetry*, *Many Mountains Moving*, and *ReVision*. She lives in Baltimore, Maryland, with her husband and son, and teaches at Goucher College.

Ray Hsu is a Ph.D. candidate at the University of Wisconsin-Madison. His first poetry collection, *Anthropy* (Nightwood, 2004), won the League of Canadian Poets' Gerald Lampert Award and was a finalist for the Trillium Book Award for Poetry. He has published poems in *The Walrus, New American Writing,* and *Fence.* Hsu won a Humanities Exposed Evjue Research Award for establishing a creative writing community and ged tutoring program in a prison. He was featured in *Heart of a Poet*, a documentary series on the television network Bravo!

Colette Inez has published nine poetry collections and has won Guggenheim, Rockefeller and two NEA fellowships. She is widely anthologized and teaches in Columbia University's Undergraduate Writing Program. Her latest book, a memoir titled *The Secret of M. Dulong*, has recently been released by The University of Wisconsin Press.

Liesl Jobson, a South African poet and musician, received first prize in the Inglis House Poetry Contest 2003. Her poetry appears in numerous journals online and in print. She won the 2005 People Opposing Women Abuse Poetry Competition and was awarded the 2006 Ernst van Heerden Creative Writing Award for her flash fiction.

Evan Jones was born in Weston, Ontario, and currently lives in Manchester, England. His first collection of poetry, *Nothing Fell Today But Rain* (Fitzhenry and Whiteside, 2003), was short-listed for the Governor-General's Award.

Fady Joudah is a Palestinian-American physician, a field member of Doctors Without Borders. His poems have appeared widely in anthologies and journals. His translation of Mahmoud Darwish's most recent poetry, *The Butterfly's Burden*, is available from Copper Canyon Press, 2006.

Mary Karr is the author of several volumes of poetry and several successful memoirs. Her poems and essays have won Pushcart prizes and have appeared in such magazines as *The New Yorker, The Atlantic*, and *Parnassus*. She is the recipient of a Guggenheim Fellowship for Poetry in 2004.

Jackie Kay was born in 1961 in Edinburgh, and grew up in Glasgow. Her first book of poems, *The Adoption Papers* (Bloodaxe, 1991), was shortlisted for the Mail on Sunday / John Llewellyn Rhys Prize, and won a Scottish Arts Council Book Award. Her television work includes films on, among other things, transracial adoption.

Mimi Khalvati's six Carcanet collections include *Selected Poems* (2000) and *The Chine* (2002). She is the founder of the Poetry School, where she currently teaches, and co-editor with Stephen Knight of *I am twenty people!*, the School's new anthology from Enitharmon Press (2007). She has held fellowships with the Royal Literary Fund at City University and at the International Writing Program in Iowa. In 2006, she received a Cholmondeley Award from the Society of Authors and her new collection, *The Meanest Flower* (Carcanet, 2007), is a Poetry Book Society Recommendation.

Katie Kingston is the author of two chapbooks, *El Rio de las Animas Perdidas en Purgatorio*, winner of the 2006 White Eagle Coffee Store Press Award, and *In My Dreams Neruda*, an editor's choice published by Main Street Rag in 2005. She placed first in the 2007 Ruth Stone Prize in Poetry and is a recipient of the Colorado Council on the Arts Literary Fellowship in Poetry. Her poems have appeared in numerous anthologies and literary journals including *Atlanta Review, Great River Review, Green Mountains Review, Hunger Mountain, Puerto del Sol, Nimrod*, and *Rattle*. She is a graduate of the Vermont College MFA in Writing Program.

Jane Knechtel was born in Toronto in 1962. She has masters degrees from University College, Dublin, in Anglo-Irish Literature, and Lewis and Clark College, in Counseling Psychology. She has worked as a counselor for over seven years, primarily in community mental health centers. Currently, she is raising two boys and studying poetry writing at The Attic, a writing studio in Portland, Oregon. In 2006, she won the Parnell Prize in Poetry and the GSU Review Editor's Choice Award.

Vénus Khoury-Ghata is a Lebanese poet and novelist who has lived in France for thirty years. She is the author of sixteen novels and fourteen collections of poems. Three collections of her poems have appeared in English, translated by Marilyn Hacker: *Here There Was Once a Country* (Oberlin, 2001), *She Says* (Graywolf, 2003), and *Nettles* (Graywolf, 2007).

Laurie Kruk is Associate Professor, English Studies, at Nipissing University, and the mother of two, step-mother of one. She has published *The Voice is the Story: Conversations with Canadian Writers of Short Fiction* (Mosaic Press, 2003) and two collections of poetry, *Theories of the World* (Netherlandic Press, 1992) and *Loving the Alien* (Your Scrivener Press, 2006).

Maxine Kumin was born in Philadelphia in 1925, and has published over fifteen books of poetry. Her awards include the Pulitzer and Ruth Lilly Poetry Prizes and the Harvard Arts and Robert Frost medals. She and her husband live on a farm in New Hampshire.

Lydia Kwa lives and works in Vancouver as a writer and psychologist. She has published one book of poems, *The Colours of Heroines* (Women's Press, 1994) and two novels, *This Place Called Absence* (Turnstone Press, 2000) and *The Walking Boy* (Key Porter Books, 2005).

Sonnet L'Abbé is a Toronto-born writer of French-Canadian and Guyanese descent. She is the author of two collections of poetry, *A Strange Relief* (McClelland and Stewart, 2001) and, most recently, *Killarnoe* (McClelland and Stewart, 2007). Her work has been internationally published and anthologized. In 2000, she won the Bronwen Wallace Memorial Award.

Fiona Tinwei Lam is a Scottish-born Canadian writer of poetry and prose, and a single mother of a young son. Her work has appeared in several Canadian anthologies and major literary magazines. Her book, *Intimate Distances* (Nightwood Editions, 2002), was shortlisted for the City of Vancouver Book Prize.

Patrick Lane has authored more than twenty books of poetry, for which he has received most of Canada's top literary awards, including the Governor General's Award, the Canadian Authors Association Award, and two National Magazine Awards. Today, his poetry appears in all major Canadian anthologies of English literature. He has also been recognized for his gardening skills, and the half-acre he tends has been featured in the Recreating Eden television film series.

Irving Layton was one of Canada's most celebrated poets, and the author of over forty books of poetry. Twice nominated for the Nobel Prize for Literature, he received numerous major awards for his poetry. He died in 2006.

Philip Levine was born in 1928 in Detroit. He is the recipient of many awards for his books of poems including the National Book Award and the Pulitzer Prize.

Diane Lockward is the author of *What Feeds Us* (Wind Publications, 2006), which was awarded the Quentin R. Howard Prize for Poetry. She is also the author of two previous collections, *Eve's Red Dress* (Wind Publications, 2003), and a chapbook, *Against Perfection* (Poets Forum Press, 1998). Her poems have been published in several anthologies, including *Poetry Daily: 366 Poems from the World's Most Popular Poetry Website* (Sourcebooks, 2003) and Garrison Keillor's *Good Poems for Hard Times* (Viking Adult, 2005). Her poems have also appeared in such journals as *The Beloit Poetry Journal, Spoon River Poetry Review, Poetry International, Poet Lore*, and *Prairie Schooner*. A former high school English teacher, Diane now works as a poet-in-the-schools.

Rebecca Luce-Kapler is a poet living just outside Kingston, Ontario. Her poetry collection, *The Gardens Where She Dreams,* was published by Borealis in 2003.

Glenna Luschei is the founder and publisher of the poetry journals *Café Solo* and *Solo* (1969-2006), and is the author of many chapbooks, special editions, and trade books, the latest being *Seedpods* (Presa Press, 2006). She was named Poet Laureate of San Luis Obispo City and County for the year 2000. She has also published an artist book of her translation of Sor Juana Inés de la Cruz's Enigmas (Solo Press, 2006).

Gwendolyn MacEwen was one of Canada's most beloved poets. In 1969, she received the Governor General's Award for her book, *The Shadow-Maker.* She passed away in 1987.

Carol L. MacKay's poems have appeared in a number of literary magazines and anthologies, including *The Fiddlehead, Lichen, CV2, Prairie Journal*, and *Threshold: An Anthology of Contemporary Writing From Alberta* (University of Alberta Press, 1999). Her short collection of poems, *Othala,* was short-listed for the 2004 CBC Literary Awards. She lives in Bawlf, Alberta.

Martha Marinara is currently co-directing the Information Fluency Initiative at the University of Central Florida, where she is an Associate Professor. She received a B.A. in English and an M.A. in Creative Writing from Southern Connecticut State University, and a Ph.D. in Rhetoric from Lehigh University in 1993. She has published two textbooks and numerous articles on writing pedagogy, feminism, and queer theory. She has also published poetry and fiction, and is the author of a novel, *Street Angel* (Fine Tooth Press, 2006).

Daphne Marlatt was born in 1942 in Melbourne, Australia, and immigrated to Canada in 1951. She studied writing and English at the University of British Columbia and comparative literature at Indiana University. She is a poet, novelist, theorist, little-magazine editor, and itinerant university instructor in areas such as creative writing, women's studies, English, and liberal studies. She is the founding co-editor of *Tessera.*

Susan McCaslin is a poet and Instructor of English at Douglas College in New Westminster, British Columbia. She has authored ten volumes of poetry and seven chapbooks, including *A Plot of Light* (Oolichin Press, 2004) and *At the Mercy Seat* (Ronsdale Press, 2003). She is also the editor of the anthologies *A Matter of Spirit: Recovery of the Sacred in Contemporary Canadian Poetry* (Ekstasis Editions, 1998) and *Poetry and Spiritual Practice: Selections from Contemporary Canadian Poets* (The St. Thomas Poetry Series, 2002).

Susan McMaster's ninth book, *Until the Light Bends* (Black Moss Press, 2004), was shortlisted for the Ottawa Book Award and the Lampman Poetry Prize. She is the editor of *Waging Peace: Poetry and Political Action* (Penumbra Press, 2002) and *Siolence: Poets, Violence and Silence* (Quarry Press, 1998). She performs and records with Geode Music & Poetry, SugarBeat, and First Draft. She also founded the national feminist and arts quarterly *Branching Out.*

Samuel Menashe's poetry has appeared in *The New Yorker* and *Poetry.* His latest collection, *New and Selected Poems,* was edited by Christopher Ricks and published by the Library of America in 2005.

Jennifer Merrifield's poetry has appeared, or is forthcoming, in *Natural Bridge, LIT, Columbia,* and *Fourteen Hills.* An MFA candidate at Virginia Commonwealth University, she is the recipient of the 2006 Columbia Poetry Prize.

Vassar Miller published many volumes of poetry, including *If I Had Wheels Or Love: Collected Poems* (Southern Methodist University Press, 1991). She was also the recipient of multiple awards from the Texas Institute of Letters. She passed away in 1998.

Claire Millikin is originally from Georgia, and was raised in Georgia, North Carolina, and overseas. She went north to school, and currently teaches at the

University of Maine-Farmington. She is the mother of Ioannis Markos, who has just turned five years old.

Judith H. Montgomery's poems appear in *The Southern Review, Gulf Coast, Northwest Review,* and elsewhere. She has received prizes from The Bellingham Review, National Writers Union, and *Red Rock Review,* and fellowships from Literary Arts and the Oregon Arts Commission. Her chapbook, *Passion*, received the 2000 Oregon Book Award. Her new collection, *Red Jess* (Wordtech Communications), appeared in Winter 2006. She is the mother of two sons.

Michelle Moore received her MFA in Creative Writing from Vermont College in 2000. Her poems have appeared in *Commonweal, Black Dirt, Rattle, Apalachee Review,* and elsewhere. *Longing for Lightness,* a chapbook of Italian translations, was published by Poetry Miscellany Press in 2002, and *The Deepest Blue*, a chapbook of her poems, was published by Räger Media Publishing in 2007. She currently teaches writing at the University of Akron.

Cherrie Moraga is co-editor of the groundbreaking anthology, *This Bridge Called My Back: Writings by Radical Women of Color* (Persephone, 1981). She has published a number of volumes of poetry.

Catherine Moss grew up in England but has lived in Alberta, Canada since 1963. She is the author of *Swallowing My Mother*, a collection of poems published by Frontenac House in 2001. Her work has appeared in literary magazines in Canada and the United States, and has been aired on CBC Radio.

Yvonne C. Murphy lives in Queens, New York, and teaches as an Associate Professor of Cultural Studies at SUNY Empire State College. She held a Stegner Fellowship in Poetry at Stanford University and received a Ph.D. in Creative Writing from the University of Houston. Yvonne has published poems widely in American and Canadian literary magazines.

Susan Musgrave lives on Vancouver Island and on Haida Gwaii/Queen Charlotte Islands. She teaches in the Optional Residency Creative Writing MFA Programme at the University of British Columbia. Her most recent book is *YOU'RE IN CANADA NOW … A Memoir of Sorts* (Thistledown Press, 2005). She has two daughters, Charlotte and Sophie.

Renee Norman is the author of *True Confessions* (Inanna, 2005), which received the Canadian Jewish Book Award for Poetry in 2006. A second book of poetry, *Backhand Through the Mother*, has just been published (Inanna, 2007). She is a faculty member in the teacher education program at University College of the Fraser Valley where she teaches Language Arts and Fine Arts courses. She lives in Coquitlam, BC, with her daughters and her husband.

Naomi Shihab Nye was born in 1952 to a Palestinian father and an American mother. She is the author of numerous books of poems, including *You and Yours* (BOA Editions, 2005), which received the Isabella Gardner Poetry Award. She has received awards from the Texas Institute of Letters, the Carity Randall Prize, the International Poetry Forum, as well as four Pushcart Prizes. She has been a Lannan Fellow, a Guggenheim Fellow, and a Wittner Bynner Fellow. In 1988 she received The Academy of American Poets' Lavan Award, selected by W. S. Merwin.

Sharon Olds is the recipient of many awards including the inaugural San Francisco Poetry Center Award, the Lamont Poetry Selection in 1983, and the National Book Critics Circle Award. *The Father* (Knopf, 1992) was shortlisted for the T. S. Eliot Prize and was a finalist for the National Book Critics Circle Award. Her recent collections include *The Unswept Room* (Knopf, 2002) and *Strike Sparks: Selected Poems, 1980-2002* (Knopf, 2006).

Eric Ormsby is the author of five collections of poetry, a book of essays, and a number of scholarly studies of Islamic thought. Since 2004, he has written a weekly column on literature for the New York Sun and regularly contributes essays and reviews to *The New Criterion, Books in Canada, The Times Literary Supplement,* and *Parnassus.*

Kathleen Ossip is the author of *The Search Engine* (APR/Copper Canyon Press, 2002), which was selected by Derek Walcott for the APR/Honickman First Book Prize, and of *Cinephrastics*, a chapbook of movie poems (Horse Less Press, 2006). Her poems have appeared in numerous anthologies and journals, including *The Best American Poetry, The Paris Review, The Kenyon Review, The Washington Post,* and *Poetry Review* (London). She teaches at The New School in New York.

Alicia Suskin Ostriker has been twice nominated for a National Book Award, and is the author of eleven volumes of poetry, most recently *No Heaven* (University of Pittsburgh Press, 2005). Her poems have appeared in *The New Yorker, The Paris Review, Antaeus, The Nation, Poetry, American Poetry Review, Kenyon Review, The Atlantic, MS, Tikkun,* and many other journals. Her poetry and essays have been translated into French, German, Italian, Chinese, Japanese, Hebrew, and Arabic. She teaches in the low-residency Poetry MFA program of New England College.

Grace Paley, the first recipient of the Edith Wharton Citation of Merit, was born in the Bronx in 1922. She is the author of several acclaimed collections of fiction and poetry, and received a Guggenheim Fellowship in Fiction in 1961 and the National Institute of Arts and Letters Award for Short Story writing in 1970. In 1980, she was elected to the National Academy of Arts and Letters. She died on August 22, 2007.

Ruth Panofsky, born and raised in Montreal, lives in Toronto where she teaches at Ryerson University. She has published two volumes of poetry: *Lifeline* (Guernica, 2001) and *Laike and Nahum: A Poem in Two Voices* (Inanna, 2007). She is also the author of several scholarly books, most recently *The Force of Vocation: The Literary Career of Adele Wiseman* (University of Manitoba Press, 2006).

Molly Peacock is the author of five volumes of poetry, including *Cornucopia: New & Selected Poems* (Norton, 2002). Recently, she toured with her one-woman show in poems, "The Shimmering Verge," produced by the London, Ontario-based company, Femme Fatale Productions. She is the Poetry Editor of the *Literary Review of Canada* and the author of a memoir, *Paradise, Piece by Piece* (McClelland and Stewart, 1999). Her poems have appeared in *The New Yorker, The Nation, The New Republic, The Paris Review*, as well as *The Best of the Best American Poetry* (Scribner, 1998) and *The Oxford Book of American Poetry* (Oxford University Press, 2006). She is a member of the Graduate Faculty of the Spalding University Brief Residency MFA Program in Creative Writing. A dual citizen of Canada and the United States, she teaches poetry one-to-one, and lives in Toronto with her husband, Professor Michael Groden.

Miranda Pearson was born in England and moved to Canada in 1991. She received an MFA in creative writing from the University of British Columbia, where she was poetry editor for *PRISM* international. She has taught creative writing at Simon Fraser University and the University of British Columbia, and she is the author of two collections of poetry, *Prime* (Beach Holme Publishing, 2001) and *The Aviary* (Oolichan Books, 2006). She lives in Vancouver, British Columbia.

Marilyn Gear Pilling lives in Hamilton, Ontario. She is the author of two collections of short fiction and two books of poetry, including *The Life of the Four Stomachs* (Black Moss Press, 2006). A third collection of poetry, *Cleavage: A Life in Breasts*, will appear in 2007.

Sylvia Plath was born in Boston, Massachusetts. In 1955, she went to Cambridge University on a Fulbright scholarship. She published but one collection of poetry in her lifetime, *The Colossus and Other Poems* (William Heineman, 1960) and a novel, *The Bell Jar* (Faber and Faber, 1963), which appeared shortly before her death in 1963.

Marie Ponsot's books of poems include *True Minds* (City Lights, 1956), *Admit Impediment* (Knopf, 1981), *The Green Dark* (Knopf, 1988), *The Bird Catcher* (Knopf, 1998), and *Springing* (Knopf, 2002). Her awards include the Frost Medal of the Poetry Society, the National Book Critics Circle prize, the Phi Beta Kappa Medal, the Modern Language Association's Shaughnessey medal, a Guggenheim, and an NEA grant.

Cati Porter's poems have appeared in numerous literary journals, including *kaleidowhirl, Literary Mama, MotherVerse, Poetry Midwest*, and *Poetry Southeast*, and the anthologies *The Bedside Guide to No Tell Motel – Second Floor* (No Tell Books, 2007) and *Letters from the World* (Red Hen Press, 2007). Her poem, "Administering My Dog's Cancer Therapy, I Think About My Sons," won first place in the 2006 Gravity and Light poetry contest. She is associate contributing editor for *Babel* and founder and editor of *Poemeleon: A Journal of Poetry*. She lives in Riverside, California, with her husband and two young sons.

Andrea Potos's full-length collection of poems *Yaya's Cloth* is forthcoming by Iris Press. Her poems appear widely in journals and anthologies, including *Poetry East, Prairie Schooner, CALYX Journal, Women's Review of Books, Literary Mama, Mothers & Daughters* (Random House) and *Claiming the Spirit Within* (Beacon Press). She lives in Madison, Wisconsin with her husband and ten-year-old daughter.

Carol Potter has published poems in *Field, The Iowa Review*, and *The Journal*. She is the author of three books of poetry, including *Short History of Pets* (Cleveland State University Poetry Center Press, 2000), which won the Cleveland State University Poetry Center Award in 2001. Her latest book, *Otherwise Obedient,* is due out with Red Hen press in Spring 2007. The mother of two grown daughters, she lives in California.

Minnie Bruce Pratt was born in 1946, in Selma, Alabama. She has published five books of poetry, including *Crime Against Nature* (Firebrand Books, 1990), which explored her relationship to her two sons as a lesbian mother, and was chosen as the Lamont Poetry Selection by the Academy of American Poets. In 1991, *Crime Against Nature* was chosen as a *New York Times* Notable Book of the Year, and given the American Library Association Gay and Lesbian Book Award for Literature. Her most recent book, *The Dirt She Ate: Selected and New Poems,* from the University of Pittsburgh Press, received the 2003 Lambda Literary Book Award for Poetry.

Sina Queyras is the author of the poetry collections *Lemon Hound, Slip*, and *Teethmarks.* Recently she edited *Open Field: Thirty Contemporary Canadian Poets.* She lives in Brooklyn.

Zara Raab's grandparents' grandparents settled on the Lost Coast of California in the 1800s. Wandering through this rainy, remote landscape more than a century later, Zara came to poetry. She has lived in Paris, Ann Arbor, and Washington, D.C., where she worked as a literary journalist and editor for New Republic Books, the National Endowment for the Humanities, and the National Geographic Society. Her poems appear in *Arts & Letters, North American Review, The Carquinez Poetry Review*, and elsewhere.

Claudia Rankine is the author of four volumes of poetry, *Don't Let Me Be Lonely* (Graywolf Press, 2004), PLOT (Grove/Atlantic, 2001), *The End Of The Alphabet* (Grove/Atlantic, 1998), and *Nothing in Nature is Private* (Cleveland State University Poetry Press, 1994). She is also co-editor of *American Poets in the Twenty-First Century: The New Poetics* (Wesleyan University Press, 2007). She teaches at Pomona College.

Adrienne Rich is one of the most celebrated poets in the world. Among her numerous honours, she is the recipient of a Lannan Foundation Lifetime

Achievement Award. Her most recent collection is *The School Among the Ruins: Poems 2000-2004* (Norton, 2004).

Leon Rooke was born in rural North Carolina in 1934. He received the Governor General's Award for Fiction for *Shakespeare's Dog* (Thomas Allen, 2003). He recently published his first collection of poetry, *Hot Poppies* (Porcupine's Quill, 2005).

Rachel Rose is a dual Canadian/American citizen, whose work has appeared in various journals in both countries, including *Poetry, The Malahat Review,* and *The Best American Poetry*, as well as in several anthologies, including *Uncharted Lines: Poems from the Journal of the American Medical Association* (Ten Speed Press, 1998) and *In Fine Form: The Canadian Book of Form Poetry* (Raincoast Books, Polestar, 2005). Her first book, *Giving My Body to Science,* (McGill/Queen's University Press, 1999) was a finalist for The Gerald Lampert Award, The Pat Lowther Award, and the Grand Prix du Livre de Montreal, and won the Quebec Writers' Federation A.M. Klein Award. Her second book, *Notes on Arrival and Departure*, was published by McClelland and Stewart in Spring 2005. Her recent work involves interviewing older people to create biographies, working with emerging writers to draft public poetry from family history, and exploring the intersections between writing and healing.

Laisha Rosnau's poetry and short fiction have been published in literary journals and anthologies in Canada, the United States, and Australia. The author of a novel, *The Sudden Weight of Snow* (McClelland and Stewart, 2002), she published her first collection of poems, *Notes on Leaving* (Nightwood Editions), in 2004. She lives in Vancouver.

Míltos Sachtoúris (1919-2005), a major figure in Greek letters, twice won the National Poetry Award, in 1962 and 1987. More recently, he received the 2003 Grand State Literature Prize for his life's work. He died in March 2005 in Athens.

Robyn Sarah was born in New York City to Canadian parents, and has lived most of her life in Montreal. Her work has appeared on both sides of the border in publications such as *Poetry, The Hudson Review, The Threepenny Review, New England Review, Books in Canada,* and *The New Quarterly*. Her most recent collection of poems is *A Day's Grace: Poems 1997-2002* (The Porcupine's Quill, 2003).

Jane Satterfield's two books of poetry are *Assignation at Vanishing Point* (Elixir Press, 2003) and *Shepherdess with an Automatic* (WWPH, 2000). Her essays on motherhood have received the John Guyon Literary Nonfiction Prize, the Heekin Foundation's Cuchulain Award for Rhetoric in the Essay, and the *Florida Review*'s Editors' Prize for Nonfiction. An associate professor of writing at Loyola College in Maryland and an NEA Poetry Fellow for 2007-2008, she lives in Baltimore with her husband and daughter.

Anne Sexton was born in 1928 and lived all of her life in the Boston area. She published eight volumes of poetry in her lifetime, and received the Pulitzer Prize in 1967. She died in 1974.

Deema K. Shehabi is a Palestinian-American poet. She grew up in the Arab world and arrived in the United States in 1988, where she completed an MS in journalism. In addition to being nominated for a Pushcart Prize, her poetry has appeared in various anthologies and literary journals, including *The Atlanta Review, Crab Orchard, DMQ Review, Drunken Boat, The Kenyon Review, Flyway, Mississippi Review, Valparaiso Poetry Review,* and *The Poetry of Arab Women*. She currently resides in Northern California with her husband and two boys.

Susan Shilliday is the mother of two grown daughters. As a screenwriter, her work includes the screenplay adaptation of Jim Harrison's *Legends of the Fall* as well as many episodes of the Emmy-award winning series *thirtysomething*. Her first published poems appear here.

Martha Silano is the author of two poetry collections, *Blue Positive* (Steel Toe Books, 2006) and the award-winning *What the Truth Tastes Like* (Nightshade Press, 1999). Her poems have appeared in many magazines, including *The Paris Review, Prairie Schooner, Descant*, and *Beloit Poetry Journal*.

Amela Simic is a translator and writer. Her essays and translations of Bosnian poetry have appeared in *Salmagundi, TLS, The Paris Review, Canadian Forum, Meta*, and BBC Radio. She is currently the Executive Director of Playwrights Guild of Canada and lives in Toronto.

Goran Simic was born in Bosnia in 1952 and has lived in Toronto since 1996. He has published eleven books of poetry, drama, and short fiction, including *Immigrant Blues* (Brick Books, 2003). His poetry and drama have been translated into more than ten languages. His poems have also appeared in anthologies of world poetry such as *Banned Poetry* (Index, 1997) and *Scanning the Century* (Penguin, 2002).

Paul Sohar stepped out of his private garden of poetry and started publishing in earnest when he turned his attention to translation. After transplanting seven books into English he finally had his own volume of poetry published, *Homing Poems* (Iniquity Press, 2005) and a musical with his lyrics produced in Scranton, Pennsylvania. He has published in many magazines, including *Chiron, The Kenyon Review, Magma, Poem, Rattle, Runes, Seneca Review,* and elsewhere.

Cathy Stonehouse's work has appeared in a wide range of journals, magazines, and anthologies, including *Grain, The Malahat Review, Room of One's Own, West Coast Line, Beyond the Small Circle: Dropped Threads 3*, and *The Literary Review of Canada*. Between 2001 and 2004, she was the Editor of *Event* magazine, and is currently completing a Young Adult historical novel, provisionally entitled *The Midsummer Fires*, for publication by Annick Press in Fall 2007. The online poetry magazine *Drunken Boat* will feature a chapbook of her work in January 2007, and an anthology of essays by Canadian authors on mothering and writing, co-edited with Fiona Tinwei Lam and Shannon Cowan, provisionally entitled *Beyond Words*, is forthcoming from McGill-Queens University Press in Spring 2008. She lives in Vancouver, and is the mother of a two-year-old daughter, Freya.

Judith Strasser is the author of a memoir, *Black Eye: Escaping a Marriage, Writing a Life* (Terrace Books/University of Wisconsin Press, 2004) and two poetry collections, *The Reason/Unreason Project* (Lewis-Clark Press, 2006), which won the Lewis-Clark Press Expedition Award, and *Sand Island Succession: Poems of the Apostles* (Parallel Press, 2002). Her work has appeared in many literary journals including *Poetry, The Kenyon Review*, and *5AM*. She is the mother of two grown sons.

Yerra Sugarman received the 2005 PEN/Joyce Osterweil Award for Poetry for her first book, *Forms of Gone*, published by the Sheep Meadow Press in

2002. Her second book, *The Bag of Broken Glass*, is forthcoming in January 2008 and will also be published by Sheep Meadow. She is the recipient of a "Discovery"/*The Nation* Poetry Prize, a Chicago Literary Award, the Poetry Society of America's George Bogin Memorial Award, and its Cecil Hemley Memorial Award. Her poems, translations, and critical articles have appeared in *Prairie Schooner, The Nation, ACM, Journal of Feminist Studies in Religion, Nightsun, Lyric, Literary Imagination*, and *Pleiades*, among other publications. She lives in New York City.

Rosemary Sullivan is an acclaimed biographer, poet and editor. She is the author, among other things, of the bestseller, *The Red Shoes: Margaret Atwood Starting Out* (HarperFlamingo Canada, 1998). Her biography of the poet Gwendolyn MacEwen, *Shadow Maker* (HarperPerennialCanada, 2001), won the Governor General's Award for Non-Fiction, the Canadian Authors' Association Literary Award, and the City of Toronto Book Award.

Richard Teleky is the author of *The Paris Years of Rosie Kamin* (Steerforth Press, 1999), which received the Ribalow Prize for the best novel of 1999, *Pack Up the Moon* (Thomas Allen, 2001), *Goodnight, Sweetheart and Other Stories* (Cormorant, 1993), and *Hungarian Rhapsodies: Essays on Ethnicity, Identity and Culture* (University of Washington Press/University of British Columbia Press, 1997). His most recent books include the novel *Winter in Hollywood* (Thomas Allen, 2006) and the poetry collection *The Hermit's Kiss* (Fitzhenry and Whiteside, 2006). He teaches at York University, Toronto.

John Terpstra has published eight books of poetry, the most recent being *Two or Three Guitars: Selected Poems* (Gaspereau Press, 2006). An earlier work, *Disarmament* (2003), was short-listed for the Governor General's award. His poetry has won the CBC Radio Literary Prize, the Bressani Prize, and several Arts Hamilton Literary Awards. He has also published two works of non-fiction, *Falling into Place* (2002) and *The Boys, or Waiting for the Electrician's Daughter* (2005), which was short-listed for both the Charles Taylor Prize for Non-fiction and for the BC Award for Canadian Non-fiction. He lives in Hamilton, where he is self-employed as a cabinet-maker and recently completed a tenure as Writer-in-Residence at McMaster University.

Susan Terris's books of poetry include *Natural Defenses* (Marsh Hawk Press, 2004), *Fire is Favorable to the Dreamer* (Arctos Press, 2003), *Poetic License*

(Adastra Press, 2004), *Curved Space* (La Jolla Poets Press, 1998), and *Eye of the Holocaust* (Arctos Press, 1999). Her poems appear in *The Iowa Review, Field, Calyx, The Journal, Colorado Review, Prairie Schooner, Shenandoah, Denver Quarterly, Southern California Anthology*, and *Ploughshares*. With CB Follett, she is co-editor of an annual anthology, *RUNES, A Review of Poetry*. Her next book, *Contrariwise*, will be published by Time Being Books in 2007. She is the winner of a Pushcart Award for a poem published in 2005 in *Field*.

Russell Thornton was born and grew up in North Vancouver, spent several years dividing his life between North Vancouver and places such as Aberystwyth, Wales, and Thessaloniki, Greece, and now lives in North Vancouver. His recent books are *The Fifth Window* (Thistledown, 2000), *A Tunisian Notebook* (Seraphim, 2002), and *House Built of Rain* (Harbour, 2003), which was a finalist for the Dorothy Livesay Poetry Prize (BC Book Prizes) and for a national ReLit Award. His latest collection is *The Human Shore* (Harbour, 2006).

Eva Tihanyi's fifth poetry collection is *Wresting the Grace of the World* (Black Moss Press, 2005). She teaches English at Niagara College in Welland, Ontario, and is a freelance book reviewer for *The National Post*.

Natasha Trethewey's first collection of poetry, *Domestic Work* (Graywolf Press, 2000), was selected by Rita Dove as the winner of the inaugural Cave Canem Poetry Prize for the best first book by an African American poet and won both the 2001 Mississippi Institute of Arts and Letters Book Prize and the 2001 Lillian Smith Award for Poetry. Her collection *Native Guard* (Houghton Mifflin, 2006) received the Pulitzer Prize for Poetry.

Priscila Uppal is a poet and fiction writer born in Ottawa, Canada, and currently living in Toronto. She has published five collections of poetry, including *How to Draw Blood From a Stone* (1998), *Confessions of a Fertility Expert* (1999), *Pretending to Die* (2001), *Live Coverage* (2003), and *Ontological Necessities* (2006), all with Exile Editions. *Ontological Necessities* was nominated for the Griffin Prize. Her novel *The Divine Economy of Salvation* (2002) was published to critical acclaim by Doubleday Canada and Algonquin Books of Chapel Hill, and translated into Dutch and Greek. Her poetry has been translated into Korean, Croatian, Latvian, and Italian. She has a Ph.D. in English Literature, and is a professor of Humanities and English at York University.

Jean Valentine was born in Chicago, and has lived most of her life in New York City. She won the Yale Younger Poets Award for her first book, *Dream Barker* (Yale University Press) in 1965. Her most recent collection, *Door in the Mountain: New and Collected Poems 1965-2003* (Wesleyan University Press, 2004), is the winner of the 2004 National Book Award for Poetry.

Bronwen Wallace was one of Canada's most important poets, feminist thinkers, essayists, and activists. She won a National Magazine Award, the Pat Lowther Award, and in 1989 was named the Winner of the Commonwealth Writers Prize for the Caribbean and Canada. She passed away in 1989.

Tom Wayman has published more than a dozen collections of poems over the past thirty years. His latest, *My Father's Cup* (Harbour Publishing, 2002), was shortlisted for both the 2003 BC Book Prize and the 2003 Governor-General's Literary Award for poetry. His collection, *High Speed Through Shoaling Water,* is forthcoming in 2007. He has edited several anthologies of poems, most recently *The Dominion of Love: An Anthology of Canadian Love Poems* (Harbour Publishing, 2002). Presently, he teaches English and writing at the University of Calgary. When not away teaching, he is the Squire of Appledore, his estate in the Selkirk Mountains of southeastern British Columbia.

Suellen Wedmore's poetry has been published in *Green Mountains Review, College English, Phoebe*, and many other magazines. Recently she was awarded first place in the *Writer's Digest* rhyming poem contest and first place in the *Byline Magazine* annual literary contest. She was also an international winner in the *Atlanta Review* 2006 poetry contest. After working for twenty-four years as a speech and language therapist, she retired to enter the MFA Program in Poetry at New England College, graduating in 2004. She is Poet Laureate emeritus for the small seaside town of Rockport, Massachusetts.

Elana Wolff's poems have appeared in journals and anthologies in Canada, the U.S. and the U.K. She has published three collections with Guernica, including *Birdheart* (2001), *Mask* (2003), and *You Speak to Me In Trees* (2006), a portion of which was shortlisted for the 2004 CBC Literary Award for Poetry.

C.D. Wright has published numerous books, including *Steal Away: Selected and New Poems* (Copper Canyon Press, 2003), a finalist for the 2003 Griffin Poetry Prize. She is a recipient of fellowships from the Guggenheim Foundation and National Endowment for the Arts, and awards from the Foundation for Contemporary Arts and the Lannan Foundation. In 2004 she was named a MacArthur Fellow. In 2005 she was given the Robert Creeley Award and elected to membership in the American Academy of Arts and Sciences.

Gary Young is a poet and artist whose books include *Braver Deeds* (Gibbs Smith, 1999), winner of the Peregrine Smith Poetry Prize, and *No Other Life* (Creative Arts Book Company, 2002), which won the William Carlos Williams Award of the Poetry Society of America. He has twice received fellowships from the National Endowment for the Arts, and in addition to other awards, he has received a Pushcart Prize and a fellowship from the National Endowment for the Humanities. He edits the *Greenhouse Review Press*, and his print work is represented in many collections including the Museum of Modern Art and the Getty Center for the Arts.

Shana Youngdahl's poems have appeared in *Shenandoah, Margie,* and other magazines. She holds a BA in English from Mills College and an MFA in Poetry from the University of Minnesota, Minneapolis.

Permissions

Meena Alexander: "In Kochi by the Sea" from *Quickly Changing River* (Northwestern University Press, 2008). Copyright © 2008 by Meena Alexander. Reprinted by permission of the publisher. "Rites of Sense" from *Illiterate Heart* (Northwestern University Press, 2002). Copyright © 2002 by Meena Alexander. Reprinted by permission of the publisher.

Agha Shahid Ali: "Lenox Hill" from *Rooms are Never Finished* (Norton, 2002). Copyright © 2002 by Agha Shahid Ali. Reprinted by permission of the publisher.

Celia Lisset Alvarez: "Don't" from *The Stones* (Finishing Line Press, 2006). Copyright © 2006 by Celia Lisset Alvarez. Reprinted by permission of the author.

Judith Arcana: "Felony Booking, Women's Lockup, 11th and State: A Short Literary Epic" and "For all the Mary Catholics" from *What if your mother* (Chicory Blue Press, 2005). Copyright © 2005 by Judith Arcana. Reprinted by permission of the author.

Gabeba Baderoon: "Primal Scene" from *A hundred silences* (Kwela/Snailpress, Cape Town, 2006). Copyright © 2006 by Gabeba Baderoon. Reprinted by permission of the author.

John Barton: "Magnificat" from *Notes Toward a Family Tree* (Quarry Press, 1993). Copyright © 1993 by John Barton. Reprinted by permission of the author.

Margo Berdeshevsky: "Fresque Transposée" and "To An Autumn Mother" from *But A Passage In Wilderness* (The Sheep Meadow Press, 2007). Copyright © 2007 by Margo Berdeshevsky. Reprinted by permission of the author.

Nina Bogin: "Self-Portrait" from *In the North* (Graywolf Press, 1989). Copyright

© 1989 by Nina Bogin. Reprinted by permission of the author.

Eavan Boland: "Legends" and "The Pomegranate," from *In a Time of Violence* by Eavan Boland. Copyright © 1994 by Eavan Boland. Used by permission of W.W. Norton & Company, Inc.

Di Brandt: Excerpt from *Heart* from *Now You Care* (Coach House, 2003). Copyright © 2003 by Di Brandt. Reprinted by permission of the publisher.

Gwendolyn Brooks: "The Mother" from *Selected Poems* (HarperCollins, 2005). Reprinted By Consent of Brooks Permissions.

Nicole Brossard: Excerpt from *Intimate Journal* and "The Garden" (Trans. Barbara Godard) from *Intimate Journal* (Mercury Press, 2004). Copyright © 2004 by Nicole Brossard and Barbara Godard. Reprinted by permission of the author, translator, and publisher.

Nan Byrne: "Motherhood" and "Love Me Tender." Copyright © 2007 by Nan Byrne.

Misha Cahnmann-Taylor: "Animal Moments." Copyright © 2007 by Misha Cahnmann-Taylor.

Anne Carson: "Appendix to Ordinary Time" from *Men in the Off Hours* by Anne Carson, copyright © 2000 by Anne Carson. Used by permission of Alfred A. Knopf, a division of Random House, Inc.

Joy Castro: "How We Are Made." Copyright © 2007 by Joy Castro.

Margaret Christakos: "C1. Staple Sorter," "C2. Obstetrician," and "C3. Minister" from *Excessive Love Prostheses* (Coach House, 2002). Copyright © 2002 by Margaret Christakos. Reprinted by permission of the publisher. "Pumpkins, for Claire." Copyright © 2001 by Margaret Christakos. Reprinted by permission of the author.

Jeanette Clough: "Landsat Image of Mary's Ascension into Heaven" from *Cantatas* (Tebot Bach Press, 2002). Copyright © 2002 by Jeanette Clough. Reprinted by permission of the publisher.

Wanda Coleman: "Dear Mama (2)." Copyright © 1983 by Wanda Coleman. Reprinted from *IMAGOES* (Black Sparrow Press).

Anne Compton: "October Morning." Copyright © 2002 by Anne Compton, Reproduced by permission from the book entitled *Opening the Island*, by Fitzhenry & Whiteside Limited 2006, 195 Allstate Parkway, Markham, ON, L3R 4T8. Reprinted by permission.

Lorna Crozier: "Repetitions For My Mother" from *Inventing the Hawk* by Lorna Crozier © 1992. Published by McClelland & Stewart Ltd. Used with permission of the publisher. "Height of Summer" from *Everything Arrives at the Light* by Lorna Crozier © 1995. Published by McClelland & Stewart Ltd. Used with permission of the publisher.

Mahmoud Darwish: "To My Mother" and "Houriyah's Instruction" (Trans. Fady Joudah). Copyright © 2007 by Mahmoud Darwish and Fady Joudah. Reprinted by permission of the author and translator.

Ingrid de Kok: "Small Passing" and "Revenge of the imagination" from *Seasonal Fires: New and Selected Poems.* Copyright © 2006 by Ingrid de Kok. Reprinted with the permission of the poet and Seven Stories Press, www.sevenstories.com.

Pier Giorgio Di Cicco: "Permutations" was originally published in *Post-Sixties Nocturne.* Copyright © 1985 by Pier Giorgio Di Cicco. Reprinted by permission of Goose Lane Editions.

Christopher Doda: "Stillbirth Machine I" and "Stillbirth Machine II" from *Among Ruins* (Mansfield Press, 2001). Copyright © 2001 by Christopher Doda. Reprinted by permission of the publisher.

Rita Dove: "Mother Love," from *Mother Love* by Rita Dove. Copyright © 1995 by Rita Dove. Used by permission of W.W. Norton & Company, Inc.

Rishma Dunlop: " Dearest Rachel" first published in a slightly different version titled "Postscript" in *Reading Like a Girl* (Black Moss Press, 2004). Copyright © by Rishma Dunlop. Reprinted with permission of the author and publisher. "Film Noir" from *Metropolis* (Mansfield Press, 2005). Copyright © by Rishma Dunlop. Reprinted with permission by the author and publisher.

Beth Ann Fennelly: "Latching On, Falling Off," from *Tender Hooks: Poems by Beth Ann Fennelly*. Copyright © 2004 by Beth Ann Fennelly. Used by permission of W.W. Norton & Company, Inc.

Annie Finch: "Over Dark Arches" and "The Coming of Mirrors" from *Calendars* by Annie Finch, published by Tupelo Press. Copyright © 2003 by Annie Finch. All rights reserved. Reproduced by permission of Tupelo Press. "Gulf War and Child: A Curse" from *Eve* (Story Line Press, 1997). Copyright © 1997 by Annie Finch. Reprinted by permission of the author.

Ann Fisher-Wirth: "Devotions," "In Crescent," and "Moth" from *Five Terraces* (Wind Publications, 2005). Copyright © 2005 by Ann Fisher-Wirth. Reprinted by permission of the publisher.

Carolyn Forché: Page 3 from *The Angel of History* by Carolyn Forché. Copyright © 1994 by Carolyn Forché. Reprinted by permission of HarperCollins.

Sandra Gilbert: "Chocolate" from *Belongings*. Copyright © 2005 by Sandra Gilbert. Used by permission of W.W. Norton & Company, Inc.

Allen Ginsberg: L. 1-13 from "Kaddish" from *Collected Poems 1947-1980* by Allen Ginsberg. Copyright © 1959 by Allen Ginsberg. Reprinted by permission of HarperCollins Publishers.

Daniela Gioseffi: "Some Slippery Afternoon" from *Blood Autumn* (VIA Folios/Bordighera Press, 2006). Copyright © 2006 by Daniela Gioseffi. Reprinted by permission of the author.

Lorri Neilsen Glenn: "Combustion" from *Combustion* (Brick Books, 2007). Copyright © 2007 by Lorri Neilsen Glenn. Reprinted by permission of the author. "Lucy: A love story about daughters" from *Silver Line* (Rubicon Press, 2007). Copyright © 2007 by Lorri Neilsen Glenn. Reprinted by permission of the author.

Susan Glickman: "Between God and Evil" from *Running in Prospect Cemetery* (Signal Editions/Véhicule Press, 2004). Copyright © 2004 by Susan Glickman. Reprinted by permission of the author and the publisher. "The Reproof." Copyright © 2007 by Susan Glickman.

Louise Glück: "The Wound" from *The First Four Books of Poems by Louise Glück*. Copyright 1968, 1971, 1972, 1973, 1974, 1975, 1976, 1977, 1978, 1979, 1980, 1985, 1995 by Louise Glück. "Brown Circle" from *Ararat* by Louise Glück. Copyright © 1990 by Louise Glück. Reprinted by permission of HarperCollins Publishers.

Marilyn Hacker: "1973" and "Towards Autumn" from *Selected Poems* (Norton, 1994). Copyright © 1994 by Marilyn Hacker. Reprinted by permission of the publisher.

Louise Bernice Halfe: Excerpt from *Blue Marrow* by Louise Bernice Halfe, published by Coteau Books, Regina. Used by permission of the Publisher.

Suzanne Hancock: "The Tree" from *Another Name for Bridge* (Mansfield Press, 2005). Copyright © 2005 by Suzanne Hancock. Reprinted by permission of the publisher.

Joy Harjo: "A Map to the Next World," from *A Map to the Next World: Poems and Tales* by Joy Harjo. Copyright © 2000 by Joy Harjo. Used by permission of W.W. Norton & Company, Inc.

Clarinda Harriss: "Blood Mother" from *The Bone Tree* (NPS, 1971). Copyright © 1971 by Clarinda Harriss. Reprinted by permission of the author. "Chopped Liver" from *Air Travel* (Half Moon Editions, 2005). Copyright © 2005 by Clarinda Harriss. Reprinted by permission of the author.

Steven Heighton: "2001, An Elegy" from *The Address Book* (Anansi, 2004). Copyright © 2004 by Steven Heighton. Reprinted by permission of the publisher.

Brenda Hillman: "Two Rivers" by Brenda Hillman from *Loose Sugar* (Wesleyan University Press, 1997). © 1997 by Brenda Hillman and reprinted by permission of Wesleyan University Press. "Shared Custody" by Brenda Hillman from *The Grand Permission: New Writings on Poetics and Motherhood*, eds. Patricia Dienstfrey and Brenda Hillman (Wesleyan University Press, 2003). © 2003 by Brenda Hillman and reprinted by permission of Wesleyan University Press.

Susan Holbrook: Excerpt from "Nursery." Copyright © 2007 by Susan Holbrook.

Cornelia Hoogland: "Especially O, Especially *Darling*" first appeared in *Journal of the Association for Research on Mothering*. Copyright © 2002 by Cornelia Hoogland. Reprinted by permission of the author.

Ailish Hopper: "Proximity of Milk and *Mine*." Copyright © 2007 by Ailish Hopper.

Ray Hsu: "Traitor" appeared in *New American Writing* and *existere*. Copyright © 2007 by Ray Hsu.

Colette Inez: "Thinking of My Parisian Mother's Discretion (Only Her Confessor Knows) in Not Telling Her Sister or Hardly Anyone About My Birth" from *Clemency* (Carnegie Mellon University Press, 1998). Copyright © 1998 by Colette Inez. Reprinted by permission of the author.

Liesl Jobson: "At the Home of a Colleague from the Child Protection Unit" first appeared in *The Mississippi Review*. Copyright © 2004 by Liesl Jobson. Reprinted by permission of the author.

Evan Jones: "Antigone." Copyright © 2007 by Evan Jones.

Fady Joudah: "Mother Hair" and "Cloud Watching." Copyright © 2007 by Fady Joudah.

Mary Karr: "Sad Rite" and "Soft Mask" by Mary Karr, from *The Devil's Tour*, copyright © 1993 by Mary Karr. Reprinted by permission of New Directions Publishing Corp.

Jackie Kay: Excerpts from *The Adoption Papers* (Bloodaxe Books, 1991). Copyright © 1991 by Jackie Kay. Reprinted by permission of the publisher.

Mimi Khalvati: "Motherhood" and "Ghazal: My Son" from *The Meanest Flower* (Carcanet Press Limited, 2007). Copyright © 2007 by Mimi Khalvati. Reprinted by permission of the publisher.

Katie Kingston: "Listen to her Face" from *El Río de las Animas Perdidas en Purgatorio* (White Eagle Coffee Store Press, 2006). Copyright © 2006 by Katie Kingston. Reprinted by permission of the author.

Jane Knechtel: "Grief" first appeared in *Reed: A Journal of Poetry and Prose.* Copyright © 2007 by Jane Knechtel. Reprinted by permission of the author.

Vénus Khoury-Ghata: One poem from "Early Childhood" from *Here There Was Once a Country*, translated from the French by Marilyn Hacker, Oberlin College Press, © 2001. Reprinted by permission of Oberlin College Press.

Laurie Kruk: "the children of her men" from *Loving the Alien* (Your Scrivener Press, 2006). Copyright © 2006 by Laurie Kruk. Reprinted by permission of the publisher.

Maxine Kumin: "The Chain." Copyright © 1985 by Maxine Kumin, "Sunbathing On a Rooftop in Berkeley," from *Selected Poems: 1960-1990* by Maxine Kumin. Copyright © 1996 by Maxine Kumin. Used by permission of W.W. Norton & Company, Inc.

Lydia Kwa: "VIEW." Copyright © 2007 by Lydia Kwa.

Sonnet L'Abbé: "The Third Breast" from *Killarnoe* by Sonnet L'Abbé © 2007. Published by McClelland & Stewart Ltd. Used with permission of the publisher.

Fiona Tinwei Lam: "Father's Day" from *Intimate Distances* (Nightwood Editions, 2002). Copyright © 2002 by Fiona Tinwei Lam. Reprinted by permission of the publisher.

Patrick Lane: "Lilies" and "My Father's Watch" from *Go Leaving Strange* (Harbour Publishing, 2004). Copyright © 2004 by Patrick Lane. Reprinted by permission of the publisher.

Irving Layton: "Keine Lazarovitch: 1870-1959" from *Selected Poems: A Wild Peculiar Joy* by Irving Layton © 1982, 2004. Published by McClelland & Stewart Ltd. Used with permission of the publisher and the author's estate.

Philip Levine: "My Mother with Purse the Summer They Murdered the Spanish Poet," from *The Simple Truth* by Philip Levine, copyright © 1994 by Philip Levine. Used by permission of Alfred A. Knopf, a division of Random House, Inc. "The Mercy," from *The Mercy: Poems* by Philip Levine, copyright

© 1999 by Philip Levine. Used by permission of Alfred A. Knopf, a division of Random House, Inc.

Diane Lockward: "First Cold" and "Her Daughter's Feet" from *Eve's Red Dress* (Wind Publications, 2003). Copyright © 2003 by Diane Lockward. Reprinted by permission of Wind Publications.

Rebecca Luce-Kapler: "my mother's hands" first appeared in *Queen's Alumni Review*. Copyright © 2005 by Rebecca Luce-Kapler. Reprinted by permission of the author.

Glenna Luschei: "Trailer." Copyright © 2007 by Glenna Luschei.

Gwendolyn MacEwen: "Morning Laughter" from *The Rising Fire* (Contact Press, 1963). Copyright © Carol Wilson. Permission granted by the author's family.

Carol L. MacKay: "Burning Day Behind 'Country Books'" and "Shawl." Copyright © 2007 by Carol L. MacKay.

Martha Marinara: "Reflection in a Well House, Tuscumbia, Alabama, 1887." Copyright © 2007 by Martha Marinara.

Daphne Marlatt: Excerpt from *Seven Glass Bowls* (Nomados 2003). Copyright © 2003 by Daphne Marlatt. Reprinted by permission of the author.

Susan McCaslin: "Anorexia." Copyright © 2007 by Susan McCaslin.

Susan McMaster: "Birthday Tales" from *Dark Galaxies* (Ouroboros, 1986). Copyright © 1986 by Susan McMaster. Reprinted by permission of the author.

Samuel Menashe: "Triptych" from *New and Selected Poems* (The Library of America, 2005). Copyright © 2005 by Samuel Menashe. Reprinted by permission of the author.

Jennifer Merrifield: "American Proper" first appeared in *Phoebe: A Journal of Literary Arts*. Copyright © 2007 by Jennifer Merrifield. Reprinted by permission of the author.

Vassar Miller: "Whitewash of Houston" from *If I Had Wheels or Love: Collected Poems of Vassar Miller* (Southern Methodist University Press, 1991). Copyright © 1991 by Vassar Miller. Reprinted by permission of the publisher.

Claire Millikin: "Weaning" and "The Next Day." Copyright © 2007 by Claire Millikin.

Judith H. Montgomery: "Correspondence: to a Never-Girl" first appeared in *Sow's Ear Poetry Review*. Copyright © 2007 by Judith H. Montgomery. Reprinted by permission of the author. "Listen." Copyright © 2007 by Judith H. Montgomery.

Michelle Moore: "Grace" and "Whitman by Candlelight" from *The Deepest Blue* (Rager Media, 2007). Copyright © 2007 by Michelle Moore. Reprinted by permission of the publisher.

Cherrie Moraga: "For the Color of My Mother" from *Loving in the War Years* (South End Press, 1983). Copyright © 1983 by Cherrie Moraga. Reprinted by permission of the publisher and the author.

Catherine Moss: "Bomb" from *Swallowing My Mother* (Frontenac House, 2001). Copyright © 2007 by Catherine Moss. Reprinted by permission of the author.

Yvonne C. Murphy: "Girls Jumping On Beds." Copyright © 2007 by Yvonne C. Murphy.

Susan Musgrave: "The Laughter in the Kitchen" from *Things That Keep and Do Not Change* (McClelland & Stewart, 1999). Copyright © 1999 by Susan Musgrave. Reprinted by permission of the author.

Renee Norman: "Hannah's Child" first appeared in *Journal of the Association for Research on Mothering*. Copyright © 2001 by Renee Norman. Reprinted by permission of the author.

Naomi Shihab Nye: "For the First Time He Says." Copyright © 2007 by Naomi Shihab Nye.

Sharon Olds: "The Latest Injury," from *The Gold Cell* by Sharon Olds, copyright

© 1987 by Sharon Olds. Used by permission of Alfred A. Knopf, a division of Random House, Inc.

Eric Ormsby: "Fragrances" and "My Mother in Old Age" from *Time's Covenant: Selected Poems* (Biblioasis, 2007). Copyright © 2007 by Eric Ormsby. Reprinted by permission of the publisher.

Kathleen Ossip: "Nursling" from *The Search Engine* (American Poetry Review/ Copper Canyon Press, 2002). Copyright © 2002 by Kathleen Ossip. Reprinted by permission of the author.

Alicia Suskin Ostriker: "Baby Carriages," "The Birth of Venus," and "Wooden Virgin with Child," from *No Heaven*, by Alicia Suskin Ostriker, © 2005. Reprinted by permission of the University of Pittsburgh Press.

Grace Paley: "On Mother's Day" from *New and Collected Poems* (Tilbury House, Publishers, 1992). Copyright © 1992 by Grace Paley. Reprinted by permission of the author.

Ruth Panofsky: "Laike's Loss" from *Laike and Nahum: A Poem in Two Voices* (Inanna, 2007). Copyright © 2007 by Ruth Panofsky. Reprinted by permission of the author and the publisher.

Molly Peacock: "The Fare," from *Cornucopia: New and Selected Poems by Molly Peacock*. Copyright © 2002 by Molly Peacock. Used by permission of W.W. Norton & Company, Inc.

Miranda Pearson: "Dinner with Friends on a Midsummer's Evening" and "Falling in Love" from *Prime* (Beach Holme Publishing, 1992). Copyright © 1992 by Miranda Pearson. Reprinted by permission of the publisher.

Marilyn Gear Pilling: "Twelve" and "Fourteen" from *The Life of the Four Stomachs* (Black Moss Press, 2006). Copyright © 2006 by Marilyn Gear Pilling. Reprinted by permission of the publisher.

Sylvia Plath: "The Disquieting Muses," from *The Colossus and Other Poems by Sylvia Plath*, copyright © 1957, 1958 ,1959 ,1960, 1961, 1962 by Sylvia Plath. Used by permission of Alfred A. Knopf, a division of Random House, Inc.

Marie Ponsot: "LATE," from *Admit Impediment* by Marie Ponsot, copyright © 1981 by Marie Ponsot. Used by permission of Alfred A. Knopf, a division of Random House, Inc.

Cati Porter: "Administering My Dog's Cancer Therapy, I Think About My Sons." Copyright © 2007 by Cati Porter.

Andrea Potos: "Mother/Reader." Copyright © 2007 by Andrea Potos.

Carol Potter: "Cartographer of the Most Serene Republic" first appeared in *The Journal.* Copyright © 2005 by Carol Potter. Reprinted by permission of the author.

Minnie Bruce Pratt: "Poem for My Sons," "Declared Not Fit," and "Down the Little Cahaba" from *The Dirt She Ate: Selected and New Poems,* by Minnie Bruce Pratt, © 2003. Reprinted by permission of the University of Pittsburgh Press. "The Child Taken from the Mother" and "At the Vietnam Memorial" from *Crime Against Nature* (Firebrand Books, 1990). Copyright © 1990 by Minnie Bruce Pratt. Reprinted by permission of the author.

Sina Queyras: Excerpt from "On the Scent" from *Lemon Hound* (Coach House, 2006) Copyright © 2006 by Sina Queyras. Reprinted by permission of the publisher.

Zara Raab: "The Flight into Egypt." Copyright © 2007 by Zara Raab.

Claudia Rankine: "The Birth" and "Birthright" from *Nothing in Nature is Private* (The Cleveland Poetry Center at Cleveland State University, 1994). Copyright © 1994 by Claudia Rankine. Reprinted by permission of the publisher.

Adrienne Rich: "Night-Pieces: For a Child." Copyright © 2002 by Adrienne Rich. Copyright © 1966 by W.W. Norton & Company, Inc, from *The Fact of a Doorframe: Selected Poems 1950-2001* by Adrienne Rich. Used by permission of the author and W.W. Norton & Company, Inc.

Leon Rooke: "Bonnie Dressed to Kill (Sam)" and "What I Learned from Dr. Phil About Becoming an Effective Lover." Copyright © 2007 by Leon Rooke.

Rachel Rose: "Wandering Womb" and "Notes on Arrival and Departure" from *Notes on Arrival and Departure* by Rachel Rose © 2005. Published by McClelland & Stewart Ltd. Used with permission of the publisher.

Laisha Rosnau: "Beg and Choose" from *Notes on Leaving* (Nightwood Editions, 2004). Copyright © 2004 by Laisha Rosnau. Reprinted by permission of the publisher.

Míltos Sachtoúris: "Mother" (Trans. Evan Jones). Copyright © 2007 by Míltos Sachtoúris and Evan Jones. Reprinted by permission of Kedros Books of Athens and translator.

Robyn Sarah: "To a Daughter in Her Twentieth Year" reprinted from *A Day's Grace: Poems 1997-2002* by Robyn Sarah by permission of the Porcupine's Quill. Copyright © Robyn Sarah, 2003.

Jane Satterfield: "Hope" from *Assignation at Vanishing Point* (Elixir Press, 2003). Copyright © 2003 by Jane Satterfield. Reprinted by permission of the publisher.

Anne Sexton: "The Abortion" from *All My Pretty Ones* by Anne Sexton. Copyright © 1962 by Anne Sexton, renewed 1990 by Linda G. Sexton. Reprinted by permission of Houghton Mifflin Company. All rights reserved. "Unknown Girl in the Maternity Ward" from *To Bedlam and Part Way Back*. Copyright © 1960 by Anne Sexton, renewed 1988 by Linda G. Sexton. Reprinted by permission of Houghton Mifflin Company. All rights reserved. "Pain for a Daughter" from *Live or Die* by Anne Sexton. Copyright © 1966 by Anne Sexton, renewed 1994 by Linda G. Sexton. Reprinted by permission of Houghton Mifflin Company. All rights reserved.

Deema K. Shehabi: "Of Harvest and Flight" first appeared in *Crab Orchard Review* and *Valparaiso Poetry Review*. Copyright © 2004 by Deema K. Shehabi. "Curves in the Dark" won third place in *Baltimore Review*'s national poetry contest. Copyright © 2007 by Deema K. Shehabi.

Susan Shilliday: "My Daughter is Twenty-two" and "The Tui, Beloved of Crossword Constructors." Copyright © 2007 by Susan Shilliday.

Martha Silano: "Harborview" and "I Can't Write" from *Blue Positive* (Steel Toe Books, 2006). Copyright © 2006 by Martha Silano. Reprinted by permission of the publisher.

Goran Simic: "The Wall of Horror" (Trans. Amela Simic) from *From Sarajevo with Sorrow* (Biblioasis, 2005). Copyright © 2005 by Goran Simic and Amela Simic. Reprinted by permission of the publisher.

Paul Sohar: "At the Spa with Mother." Copyright © 2007 by Paul Sohar.

Cathy Stonehouse: "Collision" and "in memory of Gracie: still shaken by the stillness of your name." Copyright © 2007 by Cathy Stonehouse.

Judith Strasser: "9 AM, Room 214, Holiday Inn Express." Copyright © 2007 by Judith Strasser.

Yerra Sugarman: "6. a woman is a drawer — a keeper of threads — " is excerpted from a poetic sequence titled, "My Bag of Broken Glass, 1939-1978," which first appeared in the journal, *ACM: Another Chicago Magazine*. "My Bag of Broken Glass, 1939-1978" will also appear in the book, *The Bag of Broken Glass*, which will be published by the Sheep Meadow Press in January 2008. Reprinted by permission of the author.

Rosemary Sullivan: "Letter to My Daughter" and "Sisters of the Holy Name" from *The Bone Ladder: New and Selected* (Black Moss Press, 2000). Copyright © 2000 by Rosemary Sullivan. Reprinted by permission of the publisher.

Richard Teleky: "Legacy" and "Mother's Garden" © copyright by Richard Teleky, Reproduced by permission from the book entitled *The Hermit's Kiss,* Fitzhenry & Whiteside Limited 2006, 195 Allstate Parkway, Markham, ON, L3R 4T8. Reprinted by permission.

John Terpstra: "Restoration" from *Disarmament,* copyright © John Terpstra, 2003, reprinted by permission of Gaspereau Press, Printers and Publishers.

Susan Terris: "Josephs, In a Time of No Peace." Copyright © 2007 by Susan Terris.

Russell Thornton: "A Woman and Child" from *The Human Shore* (Harbour, 2006). Copyright © 2006 by Russell Thornton. Reprinted by permission of the publisher.

Eva Tihanyi: "Mother Fear" from *Wresting the Grace of the World* (Black Moss Press, 2005). Copyright © 2005 by Eva Tihanyi. Reprinted by permission of the publisher.

Natasha Trethewey: "My Mother Dreams Another Country," from *Native Guard: Poems by Natasha Trethewey.* Copyright © 2006 by Natasha Tretheway. Reprinted by permission of Houghton Mifflin Company. All rights reserved.

Priscila Uppal: "Motorcycle Accidents and Other Things That Remind Me of Mother" from *Ontological Necessities* (Exile Editions, 2006). Copyright © 2006 by Priscila Uppal. Reprinted by permission of the author. "My Mother is One Crazy Bitch." Copyright © 2007 by Priscila Uppal.

Jean Valentine: "My Mother's Body, My Professor, My Bower" by Jean Valentine from *Door in the Mountain: New and Collected Poems, 1965-2003* (Wesleyan University Press, 2004). © 2004 by Jean Valentine and reprinted by permission of Wesleyan University Press.

Bronwen Wallace: "The Woman in This Poem" by Bronwen Wallace is reprinted from *Signs of the Former Tenant* by permission of Oberon Press.

Tom Wayman: "Anti-Mother Ballad." Copyright © 2007 by Tom Wayman. Reprinted by permission of the author.

Suellen Wedmore: "Son." Copyright © 2007 by Suellen Wedmore.

Elana Wolff: "Cutters" from *You Speak to Me in Trees* (Guernica, 2006). Copyright © 2006 by Elana Wolff. Reprinted by permission of the publisher.

C.D. Wright: "King's Daughters, Home for Unwed Mothers, 1948" from *Steal Away: Selected and New Poems.* Copyright © 1991, 2003 by C.D. Wright. Reprinted with the permission of Copper Canyon Press, www.coppercanyonpress.org.

Rishma Dunlop is the author of three books of poetry: *Metropolis, Reading Like a Girl*, and *The Body of My Garden*. She is coeditor (with Priscila Uppal) of *Red Silk: An Anthology of South Asian Canadian Women Poets*. Her radio drama, "The Raj Kumari's Lullaby," was commissioned and produced by CBC Radio. Her essays, poetry, reviews, and lectures have been published internationally in literary and scholarly journals. She is a professor in the Department of English at York University, Toronto, and Coordinator of the Creative Writing Program.